INDIAN LOGIC AND ATOMISM

INDIAN LOGIC AND ATOMISM

An Exposition of the
Nyaya and Vaicesika Systems

by

ARTHUR BERRIEDALE KEITH

GYAN

Published by

Gyan Publishing House
5, Ansari Road
Daryaganj, New Delhi-110002
Phone: 011-47034999, 9811692060
E-mail: books@gyanbooks.com

Distribution Network
gyanbooks.com
India, USA, Canada, UK, Australia, France

ISBN : 978-81-212-9976-3 (PB)
First Published, 1921

2nd Impression 2021

Printed at: Gyan Press, Delhi.

Indian Logic and Atomism
Author: Arthur Berriedale Keith

INDIAN LOGIC AND ATOMISM

AN EXPOSITION OF THE NYĀYA AND VAIÇEṢIKA SYSTEMS

BY

ARTHUR BERRIEDALE KEITH

D.C.L., D.LITT.

OF THE INNER TEMPLE, BARRISTER-AT-LAW; REGIUS PROFESSOR OF SANSKRIT AND COMPARATIVE PHILOLOGY AT THE UNIVERSITY OF EDINBURGH; AUTHOR OF 'THE SĀṀKHYA SYSTEM', ETC.

OXFORD

AT THE CLARENDON PRESS

1921

PREFACE

WHILE the philosophy of the Vedānta is well known in Europe, the Nyāya and Vaiçeṣika, the Indian systems of logic and realism, have attracted hardly a tithe of the interest due to them as able and earnest efforts to solve the problems of knowledge and being on the basis of reasoned argument. The systems are indeed orthodox, and admit the authority of the sacred scriptures, but they attack the problems of existence with human means, and scripture serves for all practical purposes but to lend sanctity to results which are achieved not only without its aid, but often in very dubious harmony with its tenets.

The neglect of these schools in Europe is abundantly explained by the nature of the original sources. The contempt of Indian science for the uninitiated has resulted in modes of expression unequalled for obscurity and difficulty; the original text-books, the Sūtras, present endless enigmas, which have not, one feels assured, yet been solved, and which in most cases will never yield their secrets. The works of the Nuddea school of Bengal in their details frequently defy explanation, and in translation are more obscure if possible than their originals. Hence, even historians of Indian philosophy like Professors F. Max Müller and P. Deussen have contented themselves with sketches which ignore entirely the serious and valuable thought of the schools. The result is gravely embarrassing for any serious study of Indian philosophy as a whole, and for this reason I have deemed it desirable to attempt to set out the fundamental doctrines of the systems with due regard to their history and their relations to Buddhist philosophy. The difficulty of the task is such that no absolutely certain results can be achieved; the Sūtras are still presented in India in the light of centuries of development, and often with patent disregard of the meaning of the text, even by competent philosophic students, and the originals of many Buddhist works are lost, and we are compelled to rely on Thibetan versions. But it is clearly an indispensable preliminary to further progress that some effort should be made to formulate the results attainable with the information now at our disposal.

Considerations of space have rendered it necessary to omit all mere philological discussion and all treatment of points of minor philosophic interest. On the same ground no effort has been made to trace the vicissitudes of either system in China or Japan, or to deal with either Buddhist or Jain logic save where they come into immediate contact with the doctrines of the Nyāya and Vaiçeṣika.

I have given references to the original authorities for any statement of importance, but I desire to express a more general debt to the works of Y. V. Athalye, S. C. Vidyābhūṣaṇa, H. Jacobi, Gaṅgānātha Jhā, Th. de Stcherbatskoi, and L. Suali. To my wife I am indebted for advice and criticism.

A. BERRIEDALE KEITH.

September, 1919.

CONTENTS

PART I. THE LITERATURE OF THE NYĀYA AND VAIÇEṢIKA

PART II. THE SYSTEM OF THE NYĀYA-VAIÇEṢIKA

A. *EPISTEMOLOGY*

ABBREVIATIONS

AGWG. Abhandlungen der königl. Gesellschaft der Wissenschaften zu Göttingen.

BI. Bibliotheca Indica, Calcutta.

BP. Bhāṣāparicceheda, ed. and trs. E. Röer, BI., 1850.

BS. Brahma Sūtra of Bādarāyaṇa, ed. BI.

BSS. Bombay Sanskrit Series.

Colebrooke. *Miscellaneous Essays*, ed. E. B. Cowell, London, 1873.

Deussen, P. *Allgem. Gesch. Allgemeine Geschichte der Philosophie*, I. i–iii, Leipzig, 1906–8.

Garbe, R., *Sāṁkhya. Die Sāṁkhya-Philosophie*, Leipzig, 1894 (2nd ed., 1917).

GSAI. Giornale della Società Asiatica Italiana.

JAOS. Journal of the American Oriental Society.

JASB. Journal of the Asiatic Society of Bengal, new series.

JBRAS. Journal of the Bombay Branch of the Royal Asiatic Society.

JRAS. Journal of the Royal Asiatic Society.

KKK. Khaṇḍanakhaṇḍakhādya, trs. Gaṅgānātha Jhā (reprint from Indian Thought).

Kir. Kiraṇāvalī of Udayana, ed. with Praçastapāda, Benares, 1885 and 1897.

Kus. Kusumāñjali of Udayana, ed. and trs. E. B. Cowell, BI., 1864.

MBh. Mahābhārata.

MS. Mīmāṅsā Sūtra of Jaimini, ed. BI.

Müller, F. Max, *Six Systems. The Six Systems of Indian Philosophy*, London, 1899.

NA. Nyāyāvatāra of Siddhasena Divākara, ed. and trs. S. C. Vidyābhūṣaṇa, Calcutta, 1909.

NB. Nyāyabindu of Dharmakīrti, ed. P. Peterson, BI. 1890.

NBT. Nyāyabinduṭīkā of Dharmottara, ed. u. s.

NBh. Nyāyabhāṣya of Vātsyāyana, ed. Benares, 1896.

NGWG. Nachrichten der königl. Gesellschaft der Wissenschaften zu Göttingen.

NK. Nyāyakandalī of Çrīdhara, ed. Benares, 1895.

NKoça. Nyāyakoça by Bhīmācārya Jhaḷkīkar, BSS. xlix, ed. 2, 1893.

NL. Nyāya Philosophy, Sādholal Lectures, by Gaṅgānātha Jhā (in Indian Thought).

NM. Nyāyamañjarī of Jayanta, ed. Benares, 1895.

NS. Nyāya Sūtra, ed. and trs. S. C. Vidyābhūṣaṇa, SBH. viii, 1909.

NSM. Nyāyasiddhāntamañjarī of Jānakīnātha (in The Pandit, new series).

NSāra. Nyāyasāra of Bhāsarvajña, ed. S. C. Vidyābhūṣaṇa, BI. 1910.

NV. Nyāyavārttika of Uddyotakara, ed. BI. 1887–1904.

NVT. Nyāyavārttikatātparyaṭīkā of Vācaspati Miçra, ed. Benares, 1898.

NVTP. Nyāyavārttikatātparyapariçuddhi of Udayana, ed. BI.
Oltramare, P. *L'histoire des idées théosophiques dans l'Inde*, vol. i, Paris, 1907.
PBh. The Bhāṣya of Praçastapāda, ed. Benares, 1895.
PMS. Parīkṣāmukhasūtra of Māṇikya Nandin, ed. BI.
PMV. Parīkṣāmukhasūtralaghuvṛtti of Anantavīrya, ed. BI.
PP. Prakaraṇapañcikā of Çālikānātha, ed. Chowkhambā Sanskrit Series, 1903-4.
PSPM. The Prābhākara School of Pūrva Mīmāṁsā, by Gaṅgānātha Jhā, Allahabad, 1911.
ÇD. Çāstradīpikā of Pārthasārathi Miçra, ed. The Pandit.
ÇV. Çlokavārttika of Kumārila, trs. Gaṅgānātha Jhā, BI.
SAB. Sitzungsberichte der königl. preussischen Akademie der Wissenschaften zu Berlin.
Sugiura, Sadajiro, *Hindu Log.* *Hindu Logic as preserved in China and Japan*, Philadelphia, 1900.
SBE. Sacred Books of the East, Oxford.
SBH. Sacred Books of the Hindus, Allahabad.
SBNT. Six Buddhist Nyāya Tracts in Sanskrit, ed. Haraprasād Shāstri, BI. 1910.
SDS. Sarvadarçanasaṁgraha of Mādhava, ed. Ānandāçrama Sanskrit Series, no. 51.
ṢDS. Ṣaḍdarçanasamuccaya of Haribhadra, ed. BI.
ṢDST. Ṣaḍdarçanasamuccayaṭīkā of Guṇabhadra, ed. BI.
SM. Siddhāntamuktāvalī, ed. with BP.
SP. Saptapadārthī of Çivāditya, ed. V. S. Ghate, Bombay, 1909.
SS. Sāṁkhya Sūtra, ed. BI.
SSS. Sarvasiddhāntasaṁgraha, attributed to Çaṅkara, Madras, 1909.
Suali, L., *Intr.* *Introduzione allo studio della filosofia indiana*, Pavia, 1913.
TA. Tarkāmṛta of Jagadīça, ed. Calcutta, 1880.
TAS. Tattvārthādhigama Sūtra of Umāsvāti, ed. BI; trs. H. Jacobi, ZDMG. lx.
TB. Tarkabhāṣā of Keçava Miçra, ed. S. M. Paranjape, Poona, 1894.
TC. Tattvacintāmaṇi of Gaṅgeça, ed. BI.
TK. Tarkakaumudī of Laugākṣi Bhāskara, ed. M. N. Dvivedi, BSS xxxii, 1886.
TR. Tārkikarakṣā of Varada, ed. Benares, 1903.
TS. Tarkasaṁgraha of Annam Bhaṭṭa, ed. Y. V. Athalye, BSS. lv, 1897 (preface by M. R. Bodas).
TSD Tarkasaṁgrahadīpikā, ed. u. s.
VOJ. Vienna Oriental Journal.
VS. Vaiçeṣika Sūtra, ed. BI.; trs. SBH. vi, 1911.
VSU. Vaiçeṣikasūtropaskāra of Çaṅkara Miçra, ed. BI.
VSV. Vaiçeṣikasūtravṛtti of Jayanārāyaṇa, ed. BI.
Vidyābhūṣaṇa S. C., *Med. Log.* *History of the Mediaeval School of Indian Logic*, Calcutta, 1909.
YS. Yoga Sūtra of Patañjali, ed. BSS. xlvi, 1892.
ZDMG. Zeitschrift der Deutschen Morgenländischen Gesellschaft.

PART I

THE LITERATURE OF THE NYĀYA AND VAIÇEṢIKA

CHAPTER I

THE ORIGIN AND DEVELOPMENT OF THE SYSTEMS

1. *The Antecedents of Logic and the Atomic Theory.*

INDIA, incurious even of her varied and chequered political history, has neglected even more signally the history of her philosophical achievements. Even in the period when discussions between the schools resulted in the production of sketches of the several systems, such as those of Haribhadra and Mādhava, the expositions given attempt no historical treatment of the various systems, but treat them merely from the point of view of their relation to the favourite system of the author, whether Jain or Vedānta. The earliest works of the Nyāya and Vaiçeṣika present us with definitely formed schools, which presuppose much previous discussion and growth, but it is only occasionally that a later commentator like Vātsyāyana assures us definitely that another school—doubtless an older one—gave the syllogism ten in place of the traditional five members,[1] or mentions so much divergence of opinion, as in the case of the forms

[1] On NS. i. 1. 32.

of inference,[1] as to induce the belief that the variation of view did not merely arise after the production of the Sūtra. We are reduced, therefore, to seek outside the schools in the Brahmanical, Buddhist, and Jain literature for hints of the origin of the logic and atomic theory of the Nyāya and the Vaiçeṣika.

On one point there can be no dispute; the Brāhmaṇas and the Upaniṣads do not present us with anything which can be said to foreshadow these doctrines. The public controversy of the Upaniṣads may, however, be noted as a feature which favoured the growth of logic and sophistry, and, apart from the great weight allowed to the Veda in general and the Upaniṣads in particular in the arguments of the two schools, it may be pointed out that the doctrine of the place taken in perception by mind is foreshadowed in the Upaniṣads,[2] whence also is derived in a revised form the Nyāya doctrine of sleep.[3] In even the Dharma Sūtras, which are the latest stratum of the true Vedic writings, neither system finds mention, and this is the more important in that Nyāya there occurs in its general sense of argument or conclusion, and also in Āpastamba,[4] in the specific sense of the principles of the Pūrva Mīmāṅsā school. In it we have the result of reasoning addressed to the determination of the conflicting declarations of Vedic texts regarding the order and mode of performance, the purpose and results of the sacrifice, while many of the important sacrifices included in their course discussions by the priests on sacred topics (*brahmodya*).[5] As astronomy, geometry, philology, and other sciences arose in close connexion with the sacrificial ritual, so we are entitled to regard the Nyāya as a development of a tendency which is seen in operation first in

[1] NS. i. 1. 5. [2] Pt. II, ch. ii, § 1. [3] Pt. II, ch. i, § 3.
[4] ii. 4. 8. 13; 6. 14. 13; Bühler, SBE. II.[2] xxviii.
[5] Bloomfield, *Religion of the Veda*, pp. 216 ff.

the Mīmāṅsā school.[1] But in the hands of the Paṇḍits[2] who took it up, logic was applied to a wider range of interests than the sacrifice, and developed for its own sake. Thus most easily is explained the fact that Nyāya which remains to the end a characteristic term of the Mīmāṅsā is the specific appellation of the Nyāya school, while the Buddhists retain it in the larger sense of inference.

In the earlier grammatical literature Pāṇini, Kātyāyana, and Patañjali know the meaning of Nyāya as conclusion, but show no trace of recognizing a Nyāya system.[3] The great epic, however, gives us positive evidence of such a system; apart from other references,[4] the sage Nārada is described as skilled in Nyāya, able to distinguish unity and plurality, conjunction and inherence, priority and posteriority, deciding matters by means of proof, and a judge of the merits and demerits of a five-membered proposition.[5] The mention of inherence shows plainly that the Vaiçeṣika is also recognized, though its name does not occur, and sophistry is denounced in several passages. But the mention of Nyāya here and in the Purāṇas[6] is useless for purposes of dating; none of the references need be earlier than the appearance of the schools, though the omission of Kaṇāda's name is worth noting. The Smṛti of Yājñavalkya also, which mentions Nyāya with Mīmāṅsā as a science,[7] is not earlier than the third century A.D.

More interest attaches to the term Ānvīkṣikī as a name

[1] Bodas, TS., pp. 27–9. 'Inference' occurs in TĀ. i. 2.

[2] Jacobi, SAB. 1911, p. 732.

[3] Goldstücker (*Pāṇini*, p. 157) holds otherwise of the two last, but without plausibility.

[4] Hopkins, *Great Epic of India*, pp. 97 ff.; SBH. VIII. xv. ff.

[5] ii. 5. 3–5.

[6] MBh. i. 70. 42; xii. 210. 22; *Matsya P.*, iii. 2, &c.

[7] i. 3.

of a science which appears in the *Gautama Dharma Sūtra* [1] beside the Vedic science (*trayī*) as a just subject of study for a king, while he is enjoined to use reasoning (*tarka*) in arriving at conclusions in law (*nyāya*). By means of it Vyāsa claims to have arranged the Upaniṣads as recorded in the *Mahābhārata*.[2] In the *Rāmāyaṇa* [3] Ānvīkṣikī is censured as leading men not to follow the prescriptions of the Dharmaçāstras. Manu, who excommunicates [4] men who disregard the Vedas and Dharma Sūtras on the strength of reasoning by logic (*hetuçāstra*), admits [5] as legitimate for a king Ānvīkṣikī Ātmavidyā, 'the science of the self based on investigation', and Vātsyāyana claims in his *Nyāyabhāṣya* [6] that this is precisely the character of the Nyāyaçāstra, that, while a doctrine of the self like the Upaniṣads, it relies on reasoning, defined as the investigation of that which perception and authority have already conveyed. Against this may be set the fact that in the *Kauṭilīya Arthaçāstra* [7] Ānvīkṣikī is declared to include only the Sāṁkhya, the Yoga, and the Cārvāka system, under its name of Lokāyata. It has been deduced hence that at 300 B.C. the traditional date of the *Arthaçāstra* the Nyāya and Vaiçeṣika were not known as such; the conclusion is, in view of the facts set out above, doubtless correct but not because of this piece of evidence, which necessitates the assumption [8] of an interpolation in the *Gautama Dharma Çāstra*, for the Arthaçāstra is probably a work of several centuries after the Christian era.[9] The evidence, such as it is, rather leads to the view that Ānvīkṣikī was first applied to secular ends, such as those of justice, which

[1] xi. [2] Quoted by Viçvanātha, NSV. i. 1. 1.
[3] ii. 100. 36. [4] ii. 11. [5] vii. 43. [6] p. 3.
[7] p. 7; Jacobi, SAB. 1911, pp. 733 ff.
[8] SAB. 1911, p. 740.
[9] Keith, JRAS. 1915, pp. 130–7; Jolly, ZDMG. lxviii. 355–9.

would account for its sharp opposition to the Vedic science, and that at an early period it was applied also to sacred things, and fusing with the Nyāya developed from the Mīmāṅsā produced the Nyāya as a logical school. This may account for the extent to which logic seems to have disengaged itself from the Mīmāṅsā.

A final hint of the date of the schools is suggested by the fact that Caraka in his medical Saṁhitā [1] gives a sketch of some of the Nyāya principles, not without variation in detail, and of the Vaiçeṣika categories, in such a way as to indicate that he regarded the systems as supplementing each other. Unhappily, however, not only is Caraka's date uncertain, but his work has suffered refashioning, and the authenticity of the text cannot be admitted. Nor can any stress be laid on the variations from the Nyāya school; [2] an unscientific exposition of this kind need reflect nothing more than the lack of knowledge of its author, and sheds no light on the early history of the school.

The literature of Buddhism gives little aid; the Buddhist doctrine of perception in its developed form has affinity with the Nyāya, but no derivation suggests itself; either follows a line of thought already foreshadowed in the Upaniṣads.[3] The old Pāli texts[4] ignore the names Nyāya or Vaiçeṣika: in the *Brahmajālasutta* we hear in lieu of them only of *takkī*, 'sophist' and *vīmaṅsī* 'casuist' and in the *Udāna* *takkikas* appear as in the epic and Purāṇas. The silence is of importance, still more so the fact that in the *Kathāvatthuppakaraṇa*, which does not claim to a greater antiquity than Açoka's alleged Council about 255 B.C., we find no reference to either school, and nothing more significant than the use of the terms *patiññā*,

[1] iii. 8. 24 ff.; i. 1. 43 ff.

[2] SAB. 1911, p. 736, n. 1.

[3] Rhys Davids, *Buddh. Psych.*, pp. 68 ff.

[4] Vidyābhūṣaṇa, *Med. Log.*, pp. 61 ff.

'proposition', *upanaya*, 'application of a reason', and *niggaha*, 'humiliation', which later in Gautama's logic are technical terms, but which at this period have their more general sense. It is in keeping with this that the Nyāya, under the name Nīti and the Vaiçeṣika, first appear in the *Milindapañha*, but unhappily the date of that text is wholly uncertain, as in its present form the work represents an elaborated version of a simpler original, and references of an incidental kind such as this could easily be added.[1] Of more precision is the Buddhist tradition[2] which asserts that Vaiçeṣika adherents were alive at the time of the Buddhist Council of Kaniṣka, which may be placed at the end of the first century A.D. But here again we have no assurance of the value of this tradition, for all regarding Kaniṣka's Council, if it were held, is fabulous and confused.

The Jains texts yield a little more. Their tradition,[3] preserved in a late text the *Āvaçyaka*, in a possibly interpolated passage, and in late prose versions, attributes the Vaiçeṣika system to a Jain schismatic 544 years after Vardhamāna, Rohagutta, of the Chaūlū family, whence the system is styled Chaluga. The summary of principles given is clearly Vaiçeṣika, of the Kaṇāda type, nine substances, seventeen qualities, five forms of motion, particularity, and inherence with, however, three forms of generality somewhat obscurely phrased. Here again, however, the date of the *Āvaçyaka*, not to mention this passage, is unknown, but doubtless late, and not the slightest faith can be put in the claim that the Vaiçeṣika was an offshoot of Jainism, nor is any useful purpose served by endeavouring to find in Chaluga a corruption of

[1] Cf. Winternitz, *Gesch. d. Ind. Litt.*, II. i. 139 ff.

[2] *Journ. Buddh. Text Soc.* i. 1 ff.; Ui, *V. P.*, pp. 38 ff.

[3] Weber, *Ind. Stud.*, xvi. 351; Leumann, xvii. 116–21; SBE. XLV. xxxv ff.; Ui, pp. 35 ff., 66 ff.

Aulūkya. What is of importance is the question whether in the Jaina system there is evidence of anything which could give rise to the Nyāya or Vaiçeṣika systems. The Jain system [1], in its view of knowledge, takes the peculiar view that direct knowledge (*pratyakṣa*) is that which the soul acquires without external aid, such as the senses; it takes the form of direct knowledge of things beyond our perception (*avadhi*), of the minds of others (*manaḥ-paryāya*), and complete knowledge (*kevala*). Under indirect knowledge (*parokṣa*) is included direct sense perception (*mati*) and that which is obtained by reasoning (*çruti*). In the *Sthānāñga Sūtra* we find mention made of the usual four means of proof, perception, inference, comparison, and verbal testimony, and there are given certain classes of inference, but in view of the uncertain date of this text it is idle to claim priority for the Jain logic, nor, as it appears in such authors as Umāsvāti [2] and Siddhasena Divākara,[3] is there anything to suggest that logic was the original possession of the Jains. The more characteristic doctrine of knowledge [4] of that school is summed up in the doctrines of indefiniteness (*syād-vāda*) and aspects (*naya*). To the Jains everything is indefinite and changing in point of quality, permanent only in respect of substance, and thus to make any true statement about it demands a qualification: of anything we can say, 'In a sense it is, or is not, or is and is not, or is inexpressible, or is or is not and is inexpressible, or both is and is not and is inexpressible.' Similarly the Nayas are modes of regarding reality from different points of view. In all this, which is of dubious date and still more dubious value, it would be vain to find a model for the Nyāya.

[1] Vidyābhūṣaṇa, *Med. Log.*, pp. 3 ff.

[2] *Tattvārthādhigama Sūtra*, before sixth century A. D.; ZDMG. lx. 288 ff.

[3] *Nyāyāvatāra*, c. 533 A. D.

[4] H. L. Jhaveri, *First Principles of Jain Philosophy*, pp. 34 ff.

The case is different with the atomic theory, for in this case we do find a definite similarity between the atoms of the Vaiçeṣika and those of the Jain. In the Jain conception,[1] however, the atom has taste, colour, smell, two kinds of touch, and is a cause of sound though soundless, and thus differs from the Vaiçeṣika atom, which has no connexion with sound, and has one, two, three, or four of the ordinary qualities according as it is air, fire, water, or earth. The Jain atoms are thus qualitatively alike, the Vaiçeṣika not. In both cases the atom is thus a relatively complex conception, as remarked by Çaṅkara in his refutation of the atomic theory,[2] and it is by no means easy to say that the Vaiçeṣika conception must have been, or even probably was, derived from the Jain; the fact that the Jain school retained the theory without any substantial development is merely one of many proofs of the metaphysical barrenness of the school. Nor is it difficult apart from Jain influence to believe in the development of the doctrine in the school from the natural aim to find something abiding in the flux of phenomena, which Buddhists asserted, while the Aupaniṣada doctrine offered a permanent abiding reality in the absolute but only at the cost of denying the reality of the finite multitude. There was room, therefore, for a solution which would attain a reality not transcendental as in the case of the Upaniṣads, but lying at the basis of the real, though momentary or temporary, phenomena of the world. That this was the line of reasoning which led to the acceptance of the atomic theory appears from the earnestness with which the *Nyāya Sūtra* attacks the Buddhist doctrine that there was no substance behind the qualities, no whole beside the parts. The

[1] J. L. Jaini, *Outlines of Jainism*, p. 90; SBE. xlv. 198, 209, 210.

[2] On BS. ii. 2. 15.

acceptance of such views led to the disappearance of all solidity in existence, and the atomic theory makes good this lack by affording a real basis for the substance we see. When it is investigated, it does not reduce itself as claimed by the Buddhists to its constituents or qualities, but is ultimately a congeries of atoms which are real, but in themselves imperceptible.[1]

There remains, however, the possibility of Greek influence on India in the case of this doctrine. It must be admitted that it appears in India at a late date; certainly no proof of it exists until India had been in contact with the Greek kingdom of Bactria and the Greek influences which came in with the occupation of territory on the north-west by princes of Greek culture. In Greece the doctrine was not merely one of a small school; the adoption of it by the Epicureans raised it into a widespread belief, and it would be irrational to deny that it might easily have been conveyed to India, just as Greek astronomy and astrology unquestionably were. The nature of such borrowings is often misunderstood; the mere adoption without alteration of an opinion would be wholly un-Indian; though we know that Greek astronomy was borrowed, we find it was recast in an entirely un-Greek fashion,[2] and so changed and developed were Greek Mathematics that the borrowing has often been ignored.[3] It is no argument against borrowing then that the Greek doctrine that the secondary qualities were not inherent in the atoms was not accepted, and that the motion of the atoms was

[1] On the general appearance of Jain doctrines as influenced by Vaiçeṣika views cf. Bhandarkar, *Report for 1883–4*, pp. 101 ff.. A primitive view recognizing the self as well as the five elements appears in the *Sūtrakṛdaṅga* (SBE. XLV. xxiv), but this is very far from the Vaiçeṣika. The age of Buddhist atomism (Ui, pp. 26 ff.) is very dubious.

[2] Thibaut, *Pañcasiddhāntikā*, pp. ciii ff.

[3] Kaye, *Indian Mathematics*, pp. 8 ff.

ascribed, as early as Praçastapāda at least, to a creator. On the other hand, the most peculiar part of the Indian doctrine, which finds that the smallest thing possessing magnitude must be made up of three double atoms, and which has, therefore, been claimed [1] as disproving Greek origin, is no original part of the system. The problem of origin, therefore, must remain open; for borrowing the chief evidence, apart from the obvious similarity of the doctrines in their conception of the unit atom and its imperceptibility, is the sudden appearance of the dogma in Indian thought at a period when Greek art had profoundly influenced the art of India, and India had long been in contact with the western world, in which the doctrine had passed into a common and popular, as opposed to an esoteric, doctrine.

Of logical doctrine in its early stages there is no reason whatever to suspect a Greek origin: the syllogism of Gautama and Kaṇāda alike is obviously of natural growth, but of stunted development. It is with Dignāga only that the full doctrine of invariable concomitance as the basis of inference in lieu of reasoning by analogy appears, and it is not unreasonable to hazard the suggestion that in this case again Greek influence may have been at work. But the possibility of a natural development is not excluded; only it must be remembered that, perhaps two centuries before Dignāga, Āryadeva, one of the great figures of Mahāyāna Buddhism, uses terms displaying knowledge of Greek astrology, and that by A. D. 400, the probable date of Dignāga, spiritual intercourse between east and west was obviously easy. Nor is it without interest to note that some evidence has been adduced of Aristotelian influence on the dramatic theory of India as preserved in the *Bharata Çāstra.*[2]

[1] Max Müller, *Six Systems*, p. 584.

[2] M. Lindenau, *Festschrift E. Windisch*, pp. 38–42. On Greek influence on Indian thought cf. also S. Lévi, *Mahāyānasūtrālaṁkāra*, ii. 17, 18.

2. *The Nyāya and Vaiçeṣika Sūtras.*

The earliest exposition of the tenets of either school is contained in five books of aphorisms on the Nyāya, and ten books on the Vaiçeṣika, handed down under the names of Akṣapāda Gautama, or Gotama,[1] and Kaṇāda respectively. In either case the aphorisms are largely unintelligible without a commentary, and it must be assumed that they represent the summing up in definite form of doctrines long discussed in the schools, and that they were meant to do no more than serve as mnemonics, on which to string a full exposition given in the oral method traditional in India. Doubtless the desire of secrecy told in favour of this style, while another result was the absence of definite order, which was a minor consideration for those who were not compelled to master the system from a mere written text.

Of the two systems (*darçanas*) the Nyāya is the less badly arranged. Book I defines the sixteen categories of the system; Book II deals with doubt, the four means of proof, and their validity, and proves that there are no other valid means of demonstration; Book III discusses the self, the body, the senses and their objects, cognition and mind; Book IV disposes of volition, fault, transmigration, the good and evil fruits of human action, pain and final liberation; then it passes to the theory of error and of the whole and its parts; Book V deals with unreal objections (*jāti*), and occasions for rebuke of an opponent (*nigraha-sthāna*). The contents of the *Vaiçeṣika Sūtra* are much less intelligibly arranged. Book I discusses the five categories—substance, quality, motion, generality and particularity; Book II deals with the

[1] The form varies, but Gautama is the older.

substances, earth, water, fire, air, ether, space, and time; Book III treats of the objects of sense, and establishes the existence of the self and the mind, dealing also with the theory of inference; Book IV contains the atomic theory, and discusses the visibility of quality and the nature of body; Book V deals with motion; Book VI with the merit of receiving gifts and the duties of the four stages of life; Book VII mixes up quality, the atomic theory, the self, and inherence; Books VIII and IX are mainly concerned with perception and inference; and Book X deals with causality, among other topics.

Of the personalities of Gautama and Kaṇāda we know absolutely nothing. The personal name of the former Akṣapāda has the appearance [1] of being a nickname such as early India seems to have loved, 'one whose eyes are directed at his feet', but it is variously interpreted [2] and embellished with idle legends. Kaṇāda,[3] alias Kaṇabhuj or Kaṇabhukṣa, denotes 'atom (of grain) eater', and would naturally be interpreted as a nickname due to his theory; Çrīdhara,[4] however, reports it as due to his habit of living on grains fallen on the road like a pigeon. To Praçastapāda [5] we owe the knowledge that his gentile name was Kāçyapa, and that Çiva revealed in owl (*ulūka*) shape the system to him as a reward for austerity, whence the name Aulūkya which the *Nyāya-vārttika* [6] already applies to it. The worthless Purāṇa tradition proceeds to invent Akṣapāda, Kaṇāda and Ulūka as sons of Vyāsa, while ingenuity, ancient and modern, has invented equally worthless identifications with the Gautama of the *Gautama Dharma Çāstra* and

[1] Garbe, *Beiträge z. ind. Kulturgesch.*, p. 38.

[2] SBH. VIII. v, vi; NL., pp. 8–10.

[3] That Kaṇāda = crow-eater = owl (SBE. XLV. xxxviii) is an idle fiction.

[4] NK., p. 2.

[5] pp. 200, 329.

[6] p. 168; Kumārila, *Tantravārttika*, i. 1. 4; cf. Açvaghoṣa (Ui, p. 41).

other members of that great clan, based on nothing more secure than the identity of the family name. In truth we are left entirely to internal evidence and the history of the texts to discover their date.

The first point which may be treated as certain is that both texts were known to Vātsyāyana, who, as will be seen, lived before Dignāga, probably in the second half of the fourth century A.D. He commented on the *Nyāya Sūtra*, and used the Vaiçeṣika categories, he quotes aphorisms found in Kaṇāda's Sūtra,[1] and appears to have recognized it as in some degree a kindred school. This fact renders specially difficult the second question which presents itself, that of the priority of one or other of the two texts. It must be recognized at once that there is no possibility of treating the two systems as having grown up apart without mutual influence. In favour of the priority of Gautama's work some evidence can be adduced; the *Vaiçeṣika Sūtra* marks in treating of inference a definite attempt to enumerate the real relations which afford the ground of, and justify, the inference, while no attempt of this sort is made in Gautama; again, while the Vaiçeṣika doctrine of fallacies is different from, and simpler than, Gautama's, Kaṇāda uses without explanation the term *anaikāntika*,[2] 'indeterminate', as the description of a fallacy, while Gautama has it in a definition. Much more doubtful is a third piece of evidence; Gautama[3] in proving the self refers to mental phenomena alone as signs of its existence, while the Vaiçeṣika mentions also the physical signs of expiration, inspiration, winking, the vital processes, the movement of mind and the activities of the other sense

[1] iii. 1. 16 in Comm. on NS. ii. 2. 34; iv. 1. 6. in Comm. on iii. 1. 33.
[2] iii. 1. 17; NS. i. 2. 46.
[3] i. 1 10; VS. iii. 2. 4. Nāgārjuna, Deva, and Harivarman (Ui, pp. 43 ff.) know a Vaiçeṣika.

organs. The last case seems rather to indicate that the Vaiçeṣika is the older, standing as it does on a less philosophical standpoint. This conclusion [1] is supported by the fact that Gautama deals carefully with other points which have less effective treatment in the Vaiçeṣika, such as the eternity of sound, the nature of the self, the process of inference and fallacies generally, and the reference to a *pratitantra-siddhānta* must be understood—though curiously enough in his comment on this passage Vātsyāyana illustrates the relation by the Sāṁkhya and Yoga—as an allusion to the Vaiçeṣika, which Vātsyāyana elsewhere accepts in this relation. Gautama [2] refers also to the question of the action of a creator (*īçvara*), though he leaves the main question unsolved. It is difficult, therefore, to evade the impression that Kaṇāda is the older of the two, and that the failure of the Nyāya to accept his classification of the grounds of inference was not due to its being a later product, but to its being a part of the Vaiçeṣika system which the Nyāya rejected. The great improvement in the order of the *Nyāya Sūtra* is also symptomatic of a later date for the redaction of that system.

Further support for this view, as well as some vague indication of the period of redaction of the Nyāya, may be derived from the patent fact of the polemic carried on in the school against Buddhist doctrines. The most important point in this regard is whether the Buddhist views attacked are those of the nihilist Mādhyamika school or the idealist Yogācāra school, the former of which is connected with the name of Nāgārjuna, who has been assigned to the third century A.D., as his contemporary Āryadeva mentions the days of the week, an

[1] The term category (*padārtha*) is used in a much more natural sense in the Vaiçeṣika; Deussen, *Allgem. Gesch.*, I. iii. 361, 362.

[2] iv. 1. 19-21.

innovation probably of that period, while the latter seems to have been developed in the middle of the fourth century by Asaṅga and Vasubandhu.[1] Gautama[2] clearly refers to the view of Nāgārjuna and Āryadeva that the effect before production is neither existent, non-existent, or both; to the doctrine of the former that all things have no real existence, possessing merely an illusory interdependence; to the assertion that a substance has no reality independent of its qualities nor the whole apart from its parts; to the denial of the doctrine of atoms,[3] and to the belief that means of proof and their objects are no more than a dream or a mirage, as well as to less distinctive Buddhist doctrines as the momentary character of existence, and the defilements (*kleça*). It is a much more doubtful theory that one passage of the Sūtra is directed against the Yogācāra doctrine which accepted ideas alone as real, for the contents on the whole better fit the Mādhyamikas, and the most striking evidence[4] in favour of the other view, the parallelism between the wording of one aphorism and a passage in the *Laṅkāvatāra Sūtra*, is not convincing, because the Sūtra in its present form is not earlier than the sixth century A.D., as it prophesies the Hun rule of that period,[5] and because the doctrine enunciated there can be interpreted equally well as a Mādhyamika principle, namely that on investigation of any object no substance is found outside its parts or qualities.[6]

[1] Jacobi, JAOS. xxxi. 1 ff.; Keith, JRAS. 1914, pp. 1090 ff.

[2] Cf. iv. 1. 48 with *Mādhyamika Sūtra*, vii. 20; *Vṛtti*, p. 16; iv. 1. 40, *Sūtra*, xv. 6; iv. 1. 34, 35, *Vṛtti*, pp. 64-71.

[3] iv. 2. 18-24; 31, 32 (*Mādh. Sūtra*, vii. 34; *Vṛtti*, p. 109); iii. 2. 11; iv. 1. 64. That Nāgārjuna knew NS. (Ui, p. 85) is unlikely.

[4] SBH. viii. 133; NS. iv. 2. 26.

[5] Winternitz, *Gesch. d. ind. Litt.*, II. i. 243.

[6] In this sense it appears in SDS., p. 12 (erroneously as *Alaṁkārāvatāra*); KKK. i. 40.

We reach, therefore, the conclusion that the *Nyāya Sūtra* does not combat the Yogācāra view despite Vācaspati Miçra's opinion to the contrary, but the upper limit of date remains uncertain, for we cannot assert that the Mādhyamika principles were first developed by Nāgārjuna; the famous poet Açvaghoṣa was also a philosopher, and seems clearly to have believed in nihilism.[1] On the other hand, Nāgārjuna's works evidently were of much influence on the development of Indian philosophy, and his dialectic as sophistic was too much in harmony with the taste of Gautama not to attract his attention. It is, therefore, not improbable that we may assert that the *Nyāya Sūtra* falls in the period after the appearance of Nāgārjuna and before that of Asaṅga, and that the *Vaiçeṣika Sūtra* was probably somewhat earlier. Of the mutual relation of the systems as such prior to redaction we of course thus learn nothing; the obvious view is that there arose a school of dialectic on the one hand and an atomic theory on the other, and that at an early period the two showed tendencies to fuse, the realism of the one blending well with the positive spirit of logical inquiry.

The precise relations of the two Sūtras to those of the other schools permits of no definite answer, save in the case of the *Yoga* and *Sāṁkhya Sūtras*, the former of which is probably of the fifth century A. D., while the latter is a recent compilation.[2] In the case of the *Brahma* and *Mīmāṅsā Sūtras* redaction at a time of reciprocal influence is patent; Bādarāyaṇa[3] refutes the atomic theory; Kaṇāda[4] declares that the soul is not proved by scripture alone, that the body is not compounded of three or five elements, and his use of *avidyā*,

[1] JRAS. 1914, pp. 747, 748.
[2] Keith, *Sāṁkhya System*, pp. 91 ff.
[3] ii. 2. 11 ff.
[4] iii. 2. 9; iv. 2. 2, 3; Bodas, TS., p. 19.

'ignorance', and *pratyagātman*, 'individual self' is reminiscent of the *Brahma Sūtra*. Gautama is familiar with the terminology of the *Brahma Sūtra*,[1] and also with that of the *Mīmāṅsā*, which is probably not later than the *Brahma Sūtra*. But to claim that the *Nyāya* or *Vaiçeṣika* was redacted later than the other two Sūtras is wholly impracticable. It is more interesting to note that an early exponent of the Mīmāṅsā seems to have been familiar with the Nyāya terminology.[2] But his date is wholly uncertain; though the fact is important as a sign that the Nyāya early influenced very powerfully the Mīmāṅsā, and received stimulus from it in return.

3. *Praçastapāda, Vātsyāyana, and Uddyotakara.*

The Bhāṣya[3] of Praçastapāda is undoubtedly the most important work of the Vaiçeṣika school. It is no commentary in the strictest sense of the term; the aphorisms of Kaṇāda are not cited *in extenso* or by catchword as normal in commentaries; the order of the Sūtra is not followed, and careful research reveals at least forty aphorisms which have no place in the Bhāṣya apart from the additions which it makes to the doctrine. The arrangement of the material is that which is adopted

[1] Cf. NS. iii. 2. 14-16 with BS. ii. 1. 24; for Mīmāṅsā see NS. ii. 1. 61-7.

[2] Cf. *Çābarabhāṣya*, p. 10; the Vṛttikāra is usually identified with Upavarṣa, but see JAOS. xxxi. 17, where Bodhāyana is suggested; Keith, JRAS. 1916, p. 370. Arguments in favour of Gautama's date as the fourth century B.C. on the score of Upavarṣa being a contemporary of a Nanda need not seriously be refuted. Speculations (e.g. *Bhandarkar Comm. Vol.*, pp. 161 ff.; Deussen, *Allgem. Gesch.*, I. iii. 388) as to an original Nyāya Sūtra consisting of Book I, or less, lead to no definite result, but the suggestion that Vātsyāyana is responsible for remodelling the Sūtra is wholly unsupported by evidence.

[3] ed. Vindhyeçvarī Prasāda Dvivedin, Benares, 1895, with Çrīdhara's comm.; in part only with Udayana's comm., Benares, 1885–97.

throughout the period of syncretism; after a statement of the categories and an exposition of their points of agreement and disagreement, the six categories are discussed in detail, the topics under each being treated in order of enumeration. Thus the doctrine of knowledge appears under the treatment of cognition as a quality of the self. Among the important developments of Praçastapāda may be noted his recognition in place of the seventeen qualities of Kaṇāda of twenty-four; his development of the doctrines of generality and particularity and inherence, which assume new shapes in his hands; the occurrence of a complete theory of creation in which the Supreme Lord appears as creator; and the elaboration of logical doctrine, which is particularly evident in the case of the doctrine of fallacies in which either Praçastapāda or a predecessor went so far as to alter the text of the Sūtra. Whether in other regards the Sūtra was refashioned [1] in his time must remain uncertain.

Praçastapāda's date is unknown, but he is clearly referred to both in connexion with the atomic theory and logical doctrine by Uddyotakara,[2] who is of the seventh century A.D., and it is probable that Çaṅkara had his work before him in writing his attack on the atomic theory in the *Çārīrakabhāṣya*, though he practically ignores his doctrine of creation. Udayana [3] and others treat the Bhāṣya as if it were a part of the same treatise as the Sūtra, so that omissions in the latter may properly be made good from the former, which shows that by his time Praçastapāda was held to be of venerable age. The upper limit of date is suggested by Praça-

[1] Bodas, TS., pp. 30 ff.; Faddegon, *Vaiç. System*, pp. 22 ff.

[2] Jacobi, ERE. i. 201; NGWG. 1901, p. 484. Kumārila plainly uses him, e.g. ÇV., pp. 201, 398 ff. Cf. PBh., p. 200; NV., p. 122.

[3] See Vindhyeçvarī Prasāda's ed. (1885), pp. 14 ff.

stapāda's indebtedness to Dignāga, a Buddhist logician whose most probable date is about 400 A.D., and it would accord well enough with all probability, if Praçastapāda were referred to the fifth century. Between him and Çañkara appears to have intervened a *Rāvaṇabhāṣya*,[1] if we can trust an assertion of the commentator Çrīcaraṇa on Çañkara's Bhāṣya, but of this work, which may have been a comment on Kaṇāda or on Praçastapāda, we know no more than that in his comment on the *Kiraṇāvalīprakāça* Padmanābha asserts that it was used in Udayana's *Kiraṇāvalī*.

Of Vātsyāyana we know, if possible, less than of Praçastapāda. His commentary, *Nyāyabhāṣya*,[2] on the *Nyāya Sūtra* is not, like the Bhāṣya of Praçastapāda, an epoch-making text: it is based closely upon the Sūtra itself, upon which it marks no decided advance. It is clear that Vātsyāyana knew the categories of the Vaiçeṣika, of which, indeed, he makes use, showing already the tendency of the systems to syncretism. But his logical doctrine is still meagre: inference is a mysterious thing, really argument from analogy, while Praçastapāda has a fully developed theory of invariable concomitance as the basis of inference. It is inconceivable that conservatism[3] would have induced any writer to ignore the new advance made by Praçastapāda, and this normal conclusion receives ample confirmation from the fact that Vātsyāyana was severely handled by the Buddhist logician Dignāga, who in all probability was the source

[1] Ibid., p. 12 n. That Praçastapāda had predecessors is obvious, and it is from one of these doubtless that Dignāga borrows the passages, cited in *Muséon*, v. 170, 171, from his *Pramāṇasamuccaya*.

[2] ed. Benares, 1896; BI. 1864–5; Windisch, *Ueber das Nyāyabhāṣya*, Leipzig, 1888; trs. Gañgānātha Jhā, *Indian Thought*, iv–. There are clear traces of an earlier commentary; see trs. ii. 45 n. There is no evidence of any corruption of his text.

[3] Jacobi, NGWG. 1901, p. 482.

of Praçastapāda's doctrine. It is reasonably safe, therefore, to assign Vātsyāyana to a period before A.D. 400. Of his personality we know nothing save that his name was Pakṣilasvāmin.

The attacks of Dignāga were replied to by Uddyotakara, 'the illustrator', whose family name was Bhāradvāja, but whose personal name we do not know. He himself is silent as to the name of the author against whom his polemic is directed, but the omission is supplied by his commentator Vācaspati Miçra, and his statement is amply confirmed by what we know of the literary history of India. His date can be determined within fairly close limits;[1] he cites a *Vādavidhi* and *Vādavidhānaṭīkā* which can with certainty be identified with the *Vādanyāya* and *Vādanyāyaṭīkā* of the Buddhist logicians Dharmakīrti (about A.D. 630) and Vinītadeva respectively, and in turn is referred to in fairly clear terms by Dharmakīrti in his *Nyāyabindu*, in which a system of logic based on Dignāga is set out. The date thus suggested is confirmed by the fact that Subandhu in his *Vāsavadattā* refers to his establishment of the Nyāya, evidently against the Buddhist doctrines, and Subandhu's work doubtless fell in the seventh century. A reference to Çrughna in his *Nyāyavārttika*[2] even lends colour to the view that he lived at Thānesar and possibly enjoyed the patronage of the great Harṣa (608–48), though tradition places his birthplace at Padmāvatī, now Narwar in Malwa, which a century later was certainly celebrated as a school of logic.[3]

[1] Vidyābhūṣaṇa, JRAS. 1914, pp. 601-6; Keith, pp. 1102, 1103; *contra*, Gaṅgānātha Jhā, NS. i. 441, n.

[2] ed. BI., Calcutta, 1904; trs. Gaṅgānātha Jhā, *op. cit.*

[3] About A.D. 600 was written Candra's *Daçapadārthaçāstra*, a Vaiçeṣika treatise, based on Praçastapāda, preserved only in a Chinese version of A.D. 648, and without influence on the school in India (ed. v. trans. H. Ui).

CHAPTER II

THE SYNCRETISM OF THE SCHOOLS

1. *Vācaspati Miçra, Bhāsarvajña, Udayana and Çrīdhara.*

For practically two centuries after Uddyotakara there is no trace of the literature of the Nyāya until, about the middle of the ninth century, there appears the *Nyāyavārttikatātparyaṭīkā*[1] of Vācaspati Miçra, a commentary on Uddyotakara's treatise, the *Nyayasūcīnibandha*, an index to the Sūtra of Gautama, and the *Nyāyasūtroddhāra*, a brief treatise similar in character. Vācaspati was a man of remarkable versatility, for he composed commentaries of the first order on Sāṁkhya, Yoga, Vedānta, and Mīmāṅsā texts. He lived under a king Nṛga, and was a Brahman of Mithilā; his *Nyāyasūcīnibandha* was composed in the year 898, as he tells us himself. The only doubt, therefore, can be as to the era to which this year refers. It would be necessary to refer it to the Çaka epoch and equate it with A.D. 976, if we were compelled to accept the tradition that the *Rājavārttika* to which he alludes in his *Sāṁkhyatattvakaumudī* was a work of, or dedicated to, Bhoja of Dhārā (1018–60), though even then difficulties would arise. But the tradition of this authorship is extremely uncertain, and it is certain that the author of the *Apohasiddhi*, a Buddhist logical tract, freely uses Vāca-

[1] ed. Gaṅgādhara Çāstrī Tailaṅga, Benares, 1898.

spati, while ignoring Udayana, of whom we have the date A.D. 984. The year 898 may therefore reasonably be referred to the Vikrama era and be equated with A.D. 841, in which case we must assume that Vācaspati wrote his commentary on Çañkara's Bhāṣya on the *Vedānta Sūtra* some years later, as Çañkara probably flourished in the first quarter of the ninth century.[1]

Possibly in the earlier part of the tenth century may be placed Bhāsarvajña, whose *Nyāyasāra* [2] is a brief compendium of the Nyāya in two chapters. It shows, however, while generally agreeing with Gautama and his commentators, independence of view and Buddhist influence. Thus the old division of sixteen categories which the Buddhists rejected, confining themselves to the topics of the means of proof and knowledge alone, is set aside for a division of the whole subject into consideration of perception, inference, and verbal testimony as means of proof, though the greater part of Gautama's logical and dialectical categories are dealt with in conjunction with the question of inference. More important is the rejection of comparison as a separate means of proof; it is probable that here Vaiçeṣika influence is visible, since the school rejected it *in toto*,[3] and Udayana, who defends it, makes it clear that its part in knowledge is reduced to ascertainment of the direct signification of words without regard to the realities signified. Again Bhāsarvajña shows a marked Çaiva influence; he

[1] See Woods, *Yoga Sūtra*, pp. xxi–xxiii; Keith, JRAS. 1908, pp. 523 ff.

[2] ed. BI., Calcutta, 1910, with Jayasiṅha Sūri's *Nyāyatātparyadīpikā* (fourteenth century). Cf. Hall, *Bibliog. Index*, p. 26.

[3] SSS. v. 33 recognizes a Vaiçeṣika school with three means of proof, and so also a Nyāya (vi. 5). Unhappily the attribution of this text to Çañkara is not certain, indeed probably wrong. The 21-fold division of pain (pp. 34, 35) seems to be borrowed by SP. § 64, but cf. NV. p. 2; TB., p. 91; the work is freely used in TR. and Kir., p. 43, cites a Bhūṣaṇa who may be the Bhūṣaṇakāra freely cited in TR.

goes so far as to style the system he expounds a Çaiva system, and promises the earnest student who practises concentration the vision of the god himself. His work, therefore, may be assigned with some plausibility to Kashmir, where Çaiva belief was always strong. The precise date is possibly indicated if we can believe that the *Nyāyabhūṣaṇa*, to which the Buddhist writer Ratnakīrti,[1] in the tenth century, refers, is the commentary of that name on the *Nyāyasāra*, but the evidence is disputed. The work is, however, the subject of a commentary, probably written in A.D. 1252; it is cited by Mādhava and it appears established as an authority in Guṇaratna's commentary on the *Ṣaḍdarçanasamuccaya*[2] of Haribhadra, and is, therefore, not later than the twelfth century. But it stands somewhat apart from the main stream of Nyāya, and it is certainly improbable that it could have been composed after Gañgeça's work.

Of far greater importance both for the Nyāya and the Vaiçeṣika is Udayana, whose date, after many vicissitudes of opinion, is definitely fixed at A.D 984 by his own statement in the *Lakṣaṇāvalī*.[3] He wrote a commentary on Praçastapāda's Bhāṣya, the *Kiraṇāvalī*, and one on Vācaspati Miçra's commentary on Uddyotakara, the *Nyāyavārttikatātparyapariçuddhi*;[4] much more famous is his *Kusumāñjali*,[5] which is the classic exposition of the proof of the existence of God, conducted from the point of view of the Nyāya system but accepting so far as in accordance with that system the view of the Vaiçeṣika. The same theme is sustained in a polemic

[1] SBNT., p. 11; the editor (p. 3) denies the reference.

[2] p. 94.

[3] Keith, JRAS. 1908, pp. 523 ff.; Suali, *Intr.*, pp. 61, 62. Part of the *Kiraṇāvalī* and the *Lakṣaṇāvalī* are included in the Benares ed. of Praçastapāda, 1885-97. A *Lakṣaṇāmālā* (*not* the *Lakṣaṇāvalī*) is cited in TR., p. 179.

[4] ed. BI., Calcutta, 1911-.

[5] ed. BI., Calcutta, 1864.

against the atheism of the Buddhists and the Jains in the *Ātmatattvaviveka*[1] or *Bauddhadhikkāra*, and to Udayana doubtless belongs the credit of making theism a principal tenet of the school, though we have no reason to suppose him the inventor of the doctrine. On the first three of these works we have, among others, commentaries by Vardhamāna, son of the great logician Gaṅgeça, and all his treatises and minor works were busily commented on in the Nuddea school. In him the tendency of the two schools to merge is strongly marked, but he does not attempt a formal synthesis and cannot be deemed strictly a syncretist author.

There is much in common between him and Çrīdhara, who wrote, as he tells us, in A.D. 991 his commentary, *Nyāyakandalī*,[2] on Praçastapāda's Bhāṣya, and who appears to cite with disapproval an opinion of Udayana.[3] Both recognize non-existence as a category by itself as opposed to the positive categories, both accept the existence of God, and both support it by arguments which have not a little in common. Yet a third commentator on Praçastapāda may be ascribed to this period, if we trust the record of Rājaçekhara[4] that Vyomaçiva's *Vyomavatī* came first in the order of comments, followed by the *Nyāyakandalī*, the *Kiraṇāvalī* and the *Līlāvatī* of Çrīvatsācārya. It must be admitted that the order of the *Nyāyakandalī* and *Kiraṇāvalī* seems wrongly stated, but that Vyomaçiva preceded Udayana is stated by Vardhamāna.[5] It is much more doubtful if he is to be identified with Çivāditya, author of the syncretist *Saptapadārthī*, especially as he recognized three means of proof as against Çivāditya's two.

[1] ed. BI. [2] ed. Benares, 1895.

[3] Candrakānta, *Kusumāñjali*, p. 19.

[4] Peterson, *Report for 1884–6*, p. 272; cf. Guṇaratna, GSAI. xx. 64, where no order is given, and the name is *Vyomamati*.

[5] Kir., p. 114, n. 3.

Of doubtful date is Jayanta Bhaṭṭa, author of an exposition of the Sūtra, the *Nyāyamañjarī*[1], and *Nyāyakalikā*, whom Gañgeça mentions as one of the old Nyāya school; like Bhāsarvajña he appears to have been a native of Kashmir. He cites Vācaspati and is cited by Deva Sūri (A.D. 1088–1169).

2. *Gañgeça and the Nuddea School.*

Probably within two centuries from Udayana and Çivāditya there flourished the famous Gañgeça or Gañgeçvara, the author of the *Tattvacintāmaṇi*,[2] in which the logic of the Nyāya attains its final shape. A native, according to tradition, of Eastern Bengal, he must have lived after Udayana, whose proof of the existence of God has plainly influenced his treatment of the inference of God, and after Çivāditya and Harṣa, whom he cites. On the other hand one of his commentators, Jayadeva, is the author of a work, the *Pratyakṣāloka*, of which a manuscript[3] bears the apparent date of Lakṣmaṇasena epoch 159 or probably A.D. 1278. Jayadeva is also the author of the *Prasannarāghava*, a drama of no great merit, and it is improbable that his date is later than A.D. 1200, so that, as Jayadeva studied under an uncle of his, Harimiçra, it is not improbable that Gañgeça may be referred, without great risk of error, to A.D. 1150–1200. His treatise follows the model, hitherto only seen in Bhāsarvajña, of an independent treatise on the Nyāya, in which the dialectical portion which forms the main part of the

[1] ed. Benares, 1895. See Keith, *Karma-Mīmāṅsā*, pp. 15, 16.

[2] ed. BI., Calcutta, 1808–1900; cf. *I. O. Catal.*, pp. 611–38.

[3] Mitra, *Notices*, v. 299, 300; Candrakānta, *Kusumāñjali*, pp. 22 ff.; Vindhyeçvarī Prasāda, TR., pp. 21–4, whose dating is probably wrong, resting on the assumption that Bhagīratha Ṭhakkura (alive in A.D. 1556) was a direct pupil of Jayadeva, which is not necessarily the case. His drama is before A.D. 1363.

Sūtra is made to yield the place of honour to the systematic treatment in four books of the four means of proof, under inference being included a special treatise on the inference of God. Thus the doctrine of the theory of knowledge is presented in a definitive form freed from intermixture with the miscellany of contents of the Sūtra, and placed in a position to confront the attacks of the Buddhists and the Jains. So well done also is the task that it proved the last work of outstanding merit in the school; those who followed abandoned the study of the Sūtra and the commentaries to devote themselves to the minute discussion of the points which were early raised as to the interpretation of the views of Gañgeça and the correctness of his opinions.

The tradition of the *Tattvacintāmaṇi* was carried on by Vardhamāna,[1] the son of Gañgeça, whom tradition ascribes to Mithilā, and who wrote a commentary on his father's work as well as dissertations on other topics and comments on Udayana's three main treatises. Not much later, presumably, was Harimiçra, whose nephew Jayadeva's *Āloka* is a comment on the *Tattvacintāmaṇi*. A pupil of Jayadeva was Rucidatta, the author of the *Kusumāñjaliprakāçamakaranda*, a commentary on Vardhamāna's comment on the *Kusumāñjali*, and other works.[2]

There follows then a clear break in the tradition,[3] which legend seeks to fill up by assigning Jayadeva as

[1] Lists of the works of the members of the school are given in Aufrecht's *Catalogus Catalogorum*, i–iii. His comm., *Nyāyaprakāçanibandha*, on Udayana's *Nyāyavārttikatātparyapariçuddhi* freely gives his father's views as opposed to Udayana's. He also wrote an independent comm. on the Sūtra, *Indian Thought*, vii. 297, 298.

[2] The assumption to him of a commentary on a work of Raghudeva (*Catalogus*, i. 528) is an error, if Jayadeva's date is as taken above.

[3] Candrakānta, *Kusumāñjali*, pp. 24 ff.; Vindhyeçvarī Prasāda, PBh. (1885), pp. 30 ff.; Bodas, TS., pp. 44 ff.; Suali, *Intr.*, pp. 81–4; Keith,

a contemporary of Vāsudeva Sarvabhauma, author of the *Tattvacintāmaṇivyākhyā*, an exposition of Gañgeça, who may be regarded as the first of the Nuddea (Navadvīpa) school of lower Bengal. Vāsudeva had four famous pupils, Caitanya, the Vaiṣṇava saint and reformer, Kṛṣṇānanda, a great authority on Tantric rites, Raghunandana, the renowned lawyer, and Raghunātha, the greatest logician after Gañgeça. The commentary of the last on the *Tattvacintāmaṇi* covers the first two books only, thus dealing with the really philosophical parts of the system. In addition to the *Dīdhiti* Raghunātha was author of *Padārthakhaṇḍana*,[1] or criticism of the Vaiçeṣika tenets and other works. He had as pupil Mathurānātha, a commentator of prodigious fertility both on his master's work and on the *Tattvacintāmaṇi* itself. Tradition makes him a teacher of Raghudeva, and if so he was a contemporary of Harirāma Tarkālaṁkāra, who was certainly the preceptor both of Raghudeva and of Gadādhara: to all three authors the school was indebted for many works, based on Gañgeça and Raghunātha, exhibiting a vast mass of perverted ingenuity worthy of the most flourishing days of mediaeval scholasticism. As Caitanya's dates are known, we can safely assign the period of Vāsudeva's influence to the beginning of the sixteenth century, and with this accords the fact that Mathurānātha is held to have been a contemporary of Jagadīça, author of a commentary on the *Dīdhiti*, who certainly lived about A. D. 1600. On this work of Jagadīça a comment was composed by Çañkara Miçra who was a pupil of Raghu-

Bodleian Catal. App., pp. 73, 74. Vindhyeçvarī Prasāda (*Khaṇḍanoddhāra*, pp. 4, 5) asserts that a MS. of the *Khaṇḍanakhaṇḍakhādyaṭīkā* of Çañkara Miçra is dated *saṁvat* 1529 (= A. D. 1472). This contradicts the references in *Catalogus*, i. 625, to commentaries by him on Jagadīça and Gadādhara and pupilship of Raghudeva, and is open to doubt.

[1] ed. as *Padārthatattvanirūpaṇa*, *The Pandit*, xxiv, xxv.

deva, but who is much more famous as the author of the *Upaskāra*, a complete commentary on the *Vaiçeṣika Sūtra*,[1] the first as yet available, for Praçastapāda's Bhāṣya is a restatement rather than commentary. The work is, however, far removed from the original, which it interprets often in a manner obviously impossible of acceptance.

The reversion to the Sūtra as a source of guidance seen in Çañkara Miçra, who asserts his independence in his work, has a curious contemporary parallel in the action of Viçvanātha, author of the syncretist work, the *Bhāṣāpariccheda*, in writing a formal commentary to the Sūtra of Gautama.[2] The mass of comment had, at last, it seems, wearied the authors, and induced them to return to more original sources of knowledge.

3. *The Syncretist School.*

The fullest development of the tendency to syncretism in the schools is seen in the work of Çivāditya, who must be reckoned the earliest of the authorities of the joint school, though it may safely be assumed that he was not the first thus to amalgamate the systems in exposition. The *Saptapadārthī*[3] is based on the Vaiçeṣika system in its arrangement and treatment; following the order indicated in the fourth aphorism of Kaṇāda's Sūtra, he enumerates the categories, and their subdivisions, explains the purpose of the enumeration and

[1] ed. BI., Calcutta, 1861, with a Vivṛti by Jayanārāyaṇa; a recent commentary is that of Candrakānta, Calcutta, 1887. An edition by Gañgādhara (1868) purports to be based on a *Bhāradvājavṛtti*, but is clearly unauthentic; Faddegon, pp. 34–40.

[2] Another commentary, *Bhāṣyacandra* on Vātsyāyana and the Sūtra, has been found; *Indian Thought*, vii. 379. It is by Raghūttama.

[3] ed. Rāmaçāstrī Tailañga, Benares, 1893; V. S. Ghate, Bombay, 1909; trans. A. Winter, ZDMG. liii.

the nature of supreme felicity which constitutes the end, and then gives in detail the exposition of the matter set out in the enumeration. On the other hand, he introduces the substance of the Nyāya logic which is included under the quality cognition, though he does not expressly set out the Nyāya categories. His date is uncertain; he is known to Gañgeça,[1] and, unlike Udayana who treats non-existence as a category opposed in a sense to the six of existence, he makes it a seventh category. This points to a date after Udayana. On the other hand, if, as suggested by the colophon of one manuscript—not a strong piece of evidence, he is identical with Vyomaçiva, author of a comment on Praçastapāda he is probably anterior to Udayana, who in one place cites a view of a teacher, whom Vardhamāna identifies with Vyomaçiva, and Rājaçekhara mentions Vyomaçiva's commentary as prior to Çrīdhara's and Udayana's. But identification with Vyomaçiva rests on too slight a basis for serious argument. He wrote also the *Lakṣaṇamālā*. On the *Saptapadārthī* there are many commentaries, of which may be mentioned those of Jinavardhana Sūri (c. A.D. 1415), Mādhava Sarasvatī (before A. D. 1523), and Çeṣānanta (before A. D. 1608).

Nor less uncertain is the date of Keçava Miçra, author of the *Tarkabhāṣā*.[2] His work follows the order of the Nyāya school, but he shows the full influence of the Vaiçeṣika, enumerates its categories, and is influenced by its doctrine of causation and perception. Moreover, his logic is on the same plane as that of Gañgeça, and he cites Udayana. On the other hand, his commentator Cinna Bhaṭṭa wrote under Harihara, brother of Bukka I of Vijayanagara, in the first half of the fourteenth century,

[1] TC. i. 830; NSM., p. 9; above, p. 32.

[2] ed. S. M. Paranjape, Poona, 1894 (2nd ed., 1909); trans. Gañgānātha Jhā, *Indian Thought*, ii.

and therefore Keçava must fall not later than A. D. 1300, possibly earlier. Of commentaries there are those of Govardhana, whose brother wrote in A. D. 1578, Gaurīkānta, and Mādhavadeva (before A. D. 1681).

More recent, doubtless, is the *Tarkakaumudī*[1] of Laugākṣi Bhāskara, which is a clear and elegant exposition of the syncretist school, following the Bhāṣya of Praçastapāda. The author was son of Mudgala, and grandson of the poet Rudra, and the only hints we have of his place and time are the facts that he refers to Benares and to a philosopher, Çūlapāṇi Miçra, who conceivably may be identified with Çañkara Miçra, the commentator on the *Vaiçeṣika Sūtra*. The similarity of his style and manner of treatment to that of Annam Bhaṭṭa and Jagadīça render it reasonable to suppose that he was of approximately the same period. He wrote also on the Vaiçeṣika and on Mīmāṅsā.

Jagadīça is of more certain period; a pupil of his was alive in A. D. 1649, and he was pupil of Bhavānanda, father of Vidyānivāsa, and grandfather of Viçvanātha who was alive in 1634, so that Jagadīça must have lived about 1600. He was one of the most industrious of the Nuddea school, and his *Tarkāmṛta*[2] is marked by an innovation in arrangement: while he mentions cognition as a quality of the self under the category of quality, he reserves its treatment at large for the end of his treatise, thus restoring the topic to a position more in keeping with its true importance. Viçvanātha was a younger contemporary; his commentary on the *Nyāya Sūtra* was composed in A. D. 1634. His syncretist treatise is the *Bhāṣāpariccheda*,[3] in which in 168

[1] ed. M. N. Dvivedi, Bombay, 1886; trans. E. Hultzsch, ZDMG. lxi. 763–802.

[2] ed. Calcutta, 1880; trans. L. Suali, Pavia, 1908.

[3] ed. and trans. E. Röer, Calcutta, 1850; G. Shāstri Bākre, Bombay, 1903. For date see Haraprasād Shāstri, JASB. 1910, pp. 311 ff.

memorial verses of the most prosaic kind he summarizes the topics of the system; the arrangement is an exposition of the categories and their subdivisions followed by an account of their analogies and differences, and then an elaborate description of substance and quality. Cognition is treated of as a quality of substance, but also by way of supplement in a later part of the text. The verses are explained in the author's own commentary, the *Siddhāntamuktāvalī*. Both works are distinguished by the comparative clearness of their exposition, which is based on Raghunātha Çiromaṇi, and have formed the subject of many comments.

Last but not least is Annam Bhaṭṭa, whose name, like that of his father Tirumala, indicates his connexion with the Telugu country. His date is uncertain; he seems to have used Raghunātha's *Dīdhiti*, and tradition attributes to him knowledge of Gadādhara, whence his date may fairly be placed not before A.D. 1600. He wrote also on grammar, on Vedānta, of which his father was a teacher, and on Mīmāṅsā. His syncretist work is the short *Tarkasaṁgraha*,[1] which in eighty-one paragraphs sums up the system in the same order as the work of Laugākṣi Bhāskara. More important is his own commentary, the *Tarkasaṁgrahadīpikā*, which discusses the definitions given in the text, amplifies the statement, and occasionally corrects it, a sign that it was composed after the issue of the text. Important commentaries are Govardhana's *Nyāyabodhinī*, whose author was apparently different from the commentator on the *Tarkabhāṣā*, Kṛṣṇa Dhūrjaṭi's *Siddhāntacandrodaya*, the *Nīlakaṇṭhī* of Nīlakaṇṭha, who died A.D. 1840, and his son *Lakṣmīnṛsiṁha's* super-commentary, *Bhāskarodayā*.[2]

[1] ed. Y. V. Athalye, Bombay, 1897; trans. E. Hultzsch, AGWG., phil.-hist. Klasse, ix. 5, Berlin, 1907.

[2] ed. Bombay, 1903.

Of greater extent and importance is the polemical treatise *Tārkikarakṣā*[1] of Varada Ācārya, consisting of memorial verses with a prose commentary (*Sārasaṅgraha*) in three books, in which the order of the Nyāya is followed. The date is after Vācaspati, Udayana, Jayanta, and Bhūsaṇakāra, presumably the commentator on the *Nyāyasāra*, but before Mādhava who uses the work in the *Sarvadarçanasaṁgraha*. Nor is there any reference to Harṣa (A.D. twelfth century), whose *Khaṇḍanakhaṇḍakhādya*[2] is an elaborate refutation from the point of view of sceptical Vedantism of the Nyāya system, in the course of which much useful information of its details is given. A comparatively early date is also suggested by the fact that the commentator Jñānapūrṇa gives as his teacher Viṣṇusvāmin who may be the predecessor of Nimbāditya, and if so falls in the eleventh century A.D. There is also a comment by Mallinātha (fourteenth century).

Of uncertain but not early date is the *Nyāyasiddhāntamañjarī*[3] of Jānakīnātha Bhaṭṭācārya Cūḍāmaṇi, which in four chapters deals with the means of proof of the Nyāya system, and has been commented on freely, among others by Laugākṣi Bhāskara and Yādava. Other treatises both general and on particular points are numerous, but do not reveal original thought.

From Gāngeça and Jayanta onwards reference is frequently made in the texts to ancient and modern schools.[4] The precise signification of these terms is often in doubt; in some cases the distinction is between

[1] ed. Benares, 1903; for date see A. Venis, pp. iii, iv; a MS. of the commentary is dated *saṁvat* 1457.

[2] ed. *The Pandit*; trans. Gaṅgānātha Jhā, *Indian Thought*, i-vii; cf. Keith, JRAS. 1916, pp. 377-81.

[3] ed. with Yādava's commentary in *The Pandit*.

[4] Bodas, TS., p. 49; NL., pp. 19, 20.

the Vaiçeṣika and the Nyāya views, in others between such authorities as Vātsyāyana and Praçastapāda in contrast with the Nuddea school, or even merely between those of Gañgeça and of Raghunātha Çiromaṇi and his followers. Uddyotakara already refers to many diverse views held in the school itself, and Jayanta alludes to many opposing views of which traces here and there occur in the later literature, as in the *Sarvasiddhānta-saṁgraha*.

PART II

THE SYSTEM OF THE NYĀYA-VAIÇEṢIKA

EPISTEMOLOGY

CHAPTER I

KNOWLEDGE AND ERROR

1. *The Nature and Forms of Knowledge.*

COGNITION (*buddhi*) in the Nyāya-Vaiçeṣika is essentially a property of the self, being described as a quality: it differs, therefore, from either the act of understanding, or the instrument, as which it ranks in the Sāṁkhya school. The function of instrument falls on mind, which also performs the function of perceiving cognition, though it itself is imperceptible. Cognition receives in the early texts no serious definition: Gautama[1] gives it as synonymous with knowledge (*jñāna*) and apprehension (*upalabdhi*), while Praçastapāda[2] merely adds another synonym, comprehension (*pratyaya*). Çivāditya's[3] contribution is the definition as 'a light which abides in the self'.

A nearer approach to reality is made by Keçava Miçra,[4] who gives among other alternatives the suggestion that cognition is what makes things understood. Annam

[1] i. 1. 15.
[2] p. 171; VSU. viii. 1. 1.
[3] § 93.
[4] p. 89; TR., p. 125; see Lakṣ. p. 11.

Bhaṭṭa[1] describes cognition as the special cause of the utterance of words intended to communicate ideas, suggesting the view that cognition is a quality of the self, through which the latter has at once the idea to express and the word to give it utterance. This definition, however, fails to include the case of indeterminate perception, which is equivalent to bare sensation, and cannot be expressed in language. More complete and fundamental is the other definition given by the same author, which makes cognition the knowledge which forms the content of the consciousness expressed in the phrase 'I have this consciousness'. The essence of this aspect of cognition is the recognition of the reference to self, which is implicit in ordinary consciousness. From the contact of the external thing and the organ of sense, mediated by mind, the self has the cognition 'This is a jar'. This cognition of a jar (*ghaṭa-jñāna*) is, therefore, a property of the self, a fact expressed in the judgement 'I am possessed of the knowledge of a jar' or more simply 'I know a jar'. Cognition thus conceived is styled *anuvyavasāya*,[2] because it is consequent upon mere consciousness of an object, a point in which the Nyāya-Vaiçeṣika departs from both the Sāṁkhya[3] and the Vedānta,[4] who do not recognize that the simple consciousness is thus the content of a further consciousness involving reference to the self, and give to a single consciousness the duty both of cognition of an object and of cognition. In the Sāṁkhya view all is mechanical process without consciousness, until enlightenment takes place through the soul, which at the same time is

[1] § 34.

[2] NVTP., pp. 48, 113–17, 178; TC. i. 784 ff. On the implication of self-consciousness in knowledge cf. W. Sorley, *Moral Values*, pp. 202–7.

[3] Cf. SS. v. 51, Garbe's note; Vijñānabhikṣu, i. 147.

[4] KKK. i. 25 ff., 58, 250, 253; ii. 115.

revealed.[1] In the Vedānta doctrine there is nothing ultimately save knowledge which reveals itself, and this also is the position of the Vijñānavāda, or Idealist, school of Buddhism, though it differs fundamentally from the Vedānta in denying the existence of a single intelligent abiding principle, and admits only a series of impressions, which in some way or other must be conceived as giving self consciousness. To this view the logicians are entirely opposed; they insist on the distinction of the self which knows, the cognition, and the object cognized, and refuse to permit consciousness to play all three parts. Thus they differ from the Sautrāntika and Vaibhāṣika schools of Buddhists, which accept external reality, either as inferred or directly apprehended, but unite in one the agent and the cognition itself, and agree with the Prābhākara school of Mīmāṅsā, which, however, does not accept the principle that mental perception gives knowledge of the self as cognizing, but assigns this function to the form of inference classed as presumption, the existence of a cognizing self being essential to explain the fact of cognition.[2] The position of Kumārila is less clear, but he seems to have more closely approximated to the Nyāya view, while admitting the Vedāntic doctrine of the self as consisting of pure consciousness.[3]

Knowledge, therefore, is primarily directed to something not the knower himself, who is only apprehended either directly by mental perception as cognizing, feeling, or willing, or, as the Vaiçeṣika holds, inferred as the substrate of these mental acts which it admits, unlike

[1] Keith, *Sāṅkhya System*, p 95.

[2] PSPM., pp. 25 ff.; cf. SSS. vii. 7, 8. Cognition is self cognized but as such, not as object; Keith, *Karma-Mīmāṅsā*, pp. 20–22, 68–71.

[3] PSPM., pp. 27 ff.; cf. Keith, JRAS. 1916, pp. 374; ÇV., pp. 383–408.

Prabhākara, to be the objects of mental perception.[1] Knowledge, whether true (*yathārtha*)[2] or false (*ayathārtha*), *pramā* or *apramā* in the Vaiçeṣika terminology, is a representation of reality. In each judgement there is an object of knowledge (*viçeṣya*), which possesses in reality certain attributes (*viçeṣaṇa*); this attribute is represented in the judgement by a characteristic (*prakāra*) which, if the judgement is to be true, must correspond to the attribute as it really exists. The judgement 'This is a flower' asserts that a portion of reality presented to us has certain attributes which are summed up in the characteristic of being a flower. 'This flower is blue' does not differ[3] in any essential from such a judgement, both being equally analytic and synthetic; in both reality presented is accorded a characteristic, which ought to correspond to the real attributes of the object. Correct apprehension may, therefore, briefly be described[4] as that which attributes to an object with a certain attribute the corresponding[5] characteristic (*tadvati tatprakāraka*), while false apprehension is one which ascribes a characteristic to a thing which has not the corresponding attribute (*tadabhāvavati tatprakārakaṁ jñānam*).[6]

This is a perfectly definite if difficult theory of judgement, and it is defended with energy against opposing views. To Prabhākara consciousness, not involving memory, alone gives true knowledge;[7] in the view of

[1] Below, ch. ix, § 1.

[2] NBh., p. 2; SP. § 140; TB., p. 89; NVTP., p. 168.

[3] As suggested by Suali, *Intr.*, p. 278.

[4] NSāra, p. 1; Kus. iv. 1; TA., p. 12; TR., pp. 8-11; TS. § 35; NSM., pp. 5 ff.

[5] How correspondence exists is unanswered, realism ignoring here the problem; cf. Pringle-Pattison, *The Idea of God*, pp. 110-30.

[6] TC. i. 401 ff.; PBh., p. 177.

[7] PSPM., pp. 19-21, 28, 29; PP., p. 42; Kus. iv. 1 ff.; TR, pp. 19-39; NVTP., pp. 151, 152; SS. v. 53; *Bhandarkar Comm. Volume*, pp. 167-70.

Kumarila [1] a means of proof is that which determines as such a thing not previously experienced. To these views the Nyāya has the obvious objection that in any judgement which is articulate there must be recognition which involves memory, but the Mīmāṅsā answer is that cognition essentially consists in the production of a quality of cognizedness (*jñātatā*) in the object which then becomes the object of perception as e.g. 'This jar is known', and that this quality is generated on each occasion. To this the Nyāya reply is that cognition has no special form, but is rather a potency which receives in each case its special character from the attribute abiding in the object. Cognition must not be regarded as transforming what it cognizes; to be cognized is no quality of the object but a relation *sui generis* (*svarūpa-saṁbandha*) existing between the object and cognition. The Mīmāṅsā doctrine of the grounds of validity of ideas is also criticized. The most advanced form of the doctrines is that of Prabhākara, who maintains flatly the truth of every cognition as such, as is indicated by the fact that the water we actually see and the water seen in a mirage produce similar tendencies to action on the part of the percipient. All direct apprehension is valid, indirect apprehension due to memory introduces invalidity. When a piece of shell is mistaken for silver the process is due to memory which, through properties common to the shell and silver, produces recollection of silver, not differentiated as it should be with the mark of its past character. So also memory accounts for the apparent seeing in dreams of non-existing things. In other cases, where there is apparent error, it does not lie in the cognition. The man whose vision is defective sees two moons, the images not being fused in one as usual; the man who sees the white

[1] PSPM., pp. 21–5, 29–31; ÇV., pp. 28 ff.; ÇD., pp. 15, 35; TR., pp. 39–54; SDS., pp. 106, 107; BP. 135.

conch as yellow fuses the perception of the conch with the yellowness of the bile which prevents his eyes seeing true. Kumārila is equally clear that the cognition is really true; what is in any case corrected is not the cognition but what is cognized, giving the doctrine of the self evidence (*svataḥ-prāmāṇya*) of cognitions subject to external invalidation. The two forms of such invalidation are discovery by other means of the real character of the object, and discovery of defects in the instruments of cognition, such as bile in the eyes. Though the older Nyāya[1] tradition is not so emphatic on the subject as the later, it is claimed by both that the self evidence of cognitions is unsustainable.[2] The truth of a cognition must be established by an inference, ultimately by an appeal to facts. If every cognition carried with it its validity, it would be impossible for us to feel, as we unquestionably do, doubt. In point of fact the real process is that on the judgement 'This is a horse' there arises the further judgement 'I see a horse', and its validity is proved by actually handling the object. Similarly a cognition of water is held valid only because we have been accustomed to verify it by drinking the water, and come to hold its truth without verification in each case, but subject always to such verification. The true nature of false cognition, therefore, does not lie in any confusion of what is perceived and what is remembered; through some defects of the organs of perception we apprehend something incorrectly, and then *ab extra* correct, not our cognition, which was as accurate as its mode of production permitted, but the result of the cognition; the silver which we believed we saw is replaced by the shell we really had

[1] NM., p. 174.

[2] TC. i. 198 ff.; NM., *l. c.*, TA., p. 16; TB., pp. 55 ff.; TK., p. 18; TSD. § 68; BP. 136; NV., pp. 3, 4; NVT., pp. 3, 4; NVTP., pp. 47–61, 98–102.

before us. Error thus lies not as in the Mīmāṅsā view in non-apprehension (*a-khyāti*)),[1] whether of the thing or of difference between what is seen and what is remembered, but in misapprehension (*anyathā-khyāti*).[2] The divergence of view between the two schools as to the self evidence of cognition was of the greater interest to either, as the Mīmāṅsā view allowed its supporters to maintain the self-evident truth of the uncreated Veda, while the Nyāya maintained that the authority of the Veda must rest on its production by an omniscient creator.

The Nyāya refuted also the Sautrāntika Buddhist view which, following Dharmakīrti,[3] regards a means of proof as that which determines an object. This, it is argued, cannot be sense, for the eye gives us diverse colours, but must be the form (*ākāra*) of the object which, cognized, affects cognition with its specific character and thus determines the object. Similarity with the object is thus declared to be the means of proof, since by reason of it apprehension of anything takes place.[4] This view also is rejected; the form can be nothing but the idea, and the idea can neither produce, nor make known, nor determine itself; it cannot act on itself to create itself; it cannot make itself known in view of its very nature; nor can it give rise to a judgement 'I know this as black' based on itself as 'This is black', for in a cognition which is self illuminating, like that assumed by the Sautrāntika, these two sides are inseparably connected. At best the idea could only be deemed a means of proof by virtue of its pointing to the external reality whence

[1] NL., pp. 61-3; NVT., pp. 55 ff.; NVTP., pp. 417 ff.; KKK. i. 244; NSM., comm., pp. 69 ff.

[2] TC. i. 430 ff.; NM., pp. 180-3; KKK. i. 141, 145.

[3] NB., p. 103, is reproduced NVTP., pp. 152, 153; cf. JRAS. 1910, p. 135, n. 4; *Madh. Vṛtti*, p. 71.

[4] NVT., p. 15; NVTP, pp. 152-4, 177-80.

it is derived, and the use of language forbids us to regard as a proof a thing which does not produce, even if like the supposed form it determines in this sense, true knowledge. It is obvious, also, that in the Sautrāntika view the Nyāya criterion of truth, conformity with external reality, disappears, and nothing is left but ideas, whence the mere existence of an outer reality is inferred as an explanation of their existence, but not of their specific forms.[1]

Still less does the Nyāya accord with the purely idealist theory of Buddhism, which regards ideas as the sole reality, and finds that there is identity between cognizer, cognition, and its object; externality thus is due to an error which causes what is really part of an internal series of cognitions to be regarded as something external (*ātma-khyāti*).[2] The Nyāya naturally objects strongly to a theory which deprives the external world of all reality; they insist, moreover, that, if all is but idea, it would be impossible to have such judgements as 'This is blue', since the judgement would necessarily take the form 'I am blue', which is absurd. It is not denied that there may be confusion of what is external and what is merely internal in individual cases, but that is simply a special instance of the general doctrine of error as misapprehension accepted by the Nyāya. Still more objectionable, if possible, is the nihilist doctrine of the Mādhyamikas, according to which all apprehension is of the non-existence (*asat-khyāti*),[3] and is itself non-existence, a view based on the allegation of the incompatibility of all notions.

On the other hand the Buddhist schools have strong arguments to urge against the Nyāya doctrine of know-

[1] Below, ch. ii, § 1; ch. iii, § 2.
[2] NVT., p. 54; NVTP., pp. 409-12; VPS. i. 85 ff.
[3] NVT., p. 58; NVTP., pp. 412, 413; KKK. i. 141; ii. 189, 240.

ledge.[1] Perception plainly rests largely on recognition, which alone makes it articulate, but is recognition valid? Sense is sense, and impression impression; how can they fuse to produce a whole or give testimony to the continued existence of a substance in time? Assuming that there is a fusion, what is perceived can only be either a pure case of remembrance, if it refers to the past, or imagination if it refers to the future, or of present apprehension, for, as the previous cognition is past, it cannot be possible to apprehend a thing as qualified by a previous cognition. To this argumentation the Nyāya reply is simple: the sense organ as affected by the impression is ample to produce the result; when in eating fruits we come to our hundredth we recognize it as such by reason of those we have consumed already; the past is gone, but the relation with the past is real. Recognition gives us knowledge of present objects as qualified by the past or, if we prefer, as qualified by previous cognitions of themselves.

In the *Nyāya Sūtra*[2] itself a determined effort is made to meet the Buddhist argument that correct knowledge was impossible of attainment by reason of the impossibility of any of the three possible time relations (*traikālya*) between means of proof and its object. Thus, if perception precedes colour, it cannot be, as held by the Sūtra, due to the contact of sense organ and object; if it follows on colour, then you cannot say that perception as means of proof establishes colour; if simultaneous, then we would have at one moment two cognitions, which is impossible on the Nyāya view, and similar arguments can be applied to the other means of proof. The reply given is that, if there are no means of proof, you cannot prove that fact. The difficulty of time is

[1] NM., pp. 448 ff.; TC. i. 839 ff.; cf. VPS. i. 177–81. KKK. i. 166 ff. demolishes all the proofs of Nyāya; NSM., p. 12.

[2] ii. 1, 8–19. Cf. NSāra, pp. 20, 21; Nāgārjuna, in Ui, p. 85.

not real; there are in fact diverse relations, thus a drum precedes its sound, illumination succeeds the sun, and smoke and fire are contemporaneous, and so with means of proof and what is proved. An object of proof is weighed as it were in the balance of means of proof, and so with the means itself. If it is objected that, as each means of proof has to be established by another means, then the object will need a series of means of proof, and not one only, or, if means of proof establish themselves then why not the object of proof? the reply is that means of proof are established like the illumination of a lamp, an expression which suggests that to Gautama perception and other means of proof proved themselves.

Another difficulty as to knowledge presents itself from the Nyāya view of its transitory character,[1] which is proved by the fact that recollection is only possible because knowledge does not last, but is a constant series of cognitions. If so, how can things be known distinctly, for there is no clear perception of colour in the lightning flash? The example, it is replied, does illustrate the truth of the Nyāya proposition; we have only a hasty vision of the lightning and so an imperfect perception, but a clear perception is attainable when there is continuity of momentary impressions as in the case of the rays of a lamp which themselves are transitory, but of which by the continuity of the experience we obtain clear knowledge. The answer is ingenious, for the Nyāya doctrine of the transient character of cognition had obviously dangerous affinities to the Buddhist doctrine of the momentary character of cognitions and their falsity.

On the other hand, the Nyāya[2] equally rejects the

[1] iii. 2. 45–9. Cf. the difficulty as to the possibility of *anuvyavasāya* discussed TC. i. 804 ff.; below, ch. vii, § 5.

[2] iii. 2. 1–10; cf. Kumārila, ÇV., pp. 382–408; SS. i. 145; NBh., NV., NVT., i. 1. 15.

conception of knowledge as a permanent abiding thing like the intellect (*buddhi*) of the Sāṁkhya. The recognition of objects does not mean the permanency of intellect, which on the Sāṁkhya theory is not conscious, but of a conscious subject. It is impossible to admit the view that the intellect is abiding, and that appearance of difference arises in it as colours appear in a crystal, through the reflection of objects on it by the senses. For this assertion of the unreality of the modes of consciousness there is no evidence whatever, the idea being merely an invention of the Sāṁkhya to meet a difficulty of its own creating. If knowledge as a mode of the intellect is not different from it, it follows that knowledge would be permanent which it is not, and that we could receive various kinds of knowledge simultaneously which is not true, while when recognition ceased, as it in fact does, we would cease to have intellect. The facts of successive apprehension and inability to attend to one thing when observing another are inexplicable on the Sāṁkhya view, for a permanent intellect could not connect itself successively with different senses in order to receive impressions, as it would possess, unlike the mind in the Nyāya view, no power of motion.

The Vedānta [2] doctrine of a single consciousness is equally open to objection as it does not permit of any reasonable explanation of our cognition. In its theory of error moreover (*anirvacanīya-khyāti*) it has to postulate three forms of existence, the absolutely real, the empirical which is illusory, and the apparent which is still more illusory, nescience operating through the internal organ to produce the false cognition. On the other hand, the Vedānta doctrine has the merit of insisting on the distinction between cognizer and cognition, it admits an empirical if illusory external reality, and it

[1] VPS. i. 35 ff.; KKK. ii. 145; *Advaitasiddhi*, trans., pp. 31 ff.

permits of the apprehension by the internal organ of the self as modified by that organ and empirically existent, thus in some degree aiding the Nyāya contention. The Jain[1] view again recognizes the distinction of cognizer, cognition, and cognized, but tends to accept the Mīmāṅsā view of the self evidence of cognitions. It is possible, as we have seen, that this was Gautama's own view, for his commentators[2] are driven to argue that the *regressus ad infinitum* of the proof of perception, &c., by other means of proof is evaded by the fact when being proved a means of proof ceases to be such and becomes an object of proof. The more fruitful conception of truth as a system was evidently impossible for them as rigid realists. Knowledge for them is rendered possible by the reality of generality and particularity whose simultaneous presence in perception[3] lies at the root of all judgement and inference.

2. *The Forms of Knowledge and Proof.*

Cognition is variously divided in the texts of the schools. Praçastapāda[4] adopts as the *principium divisionis* the distinction between true knowledge and false knowledge: the former is subdivided into four categories: (1) perception, subdivided as omniscient, which is possessed only by a divine intelligence, and non-omniscient, which is appropriate to man, and manifests itself as indeterminate or determinate; (2) inferred knowledge; (3) remembrance; and (4) the insight of seers (*ārṣa*), which is a peculiar form of perception possessed by these adepts alone. In the accepted doctrine of the syncretist school,[5] which follows the Nyāya tradition, cognition is

[1] Siddhasena, NA. 5 with commentary.
[2] NBh., NV., NVT., ii. 1. 19; TC., i. 278 ff.
[3] Criticized in *Advaitasiddhi*, trans., pp. 93 ff.
[4] pp. 172 ff.
[5] Cf. NS. i. 1. 3 ff.

divided into the two great heads of apprehension (*anubhava*) and remembrance (*smṛti*). The former is then divided into (1) perception (*pratyakṣa*); (2) inferred knowledge (*anumiti*); (3) analogical judgement (*upamiti*); and (4) verbal knowledge (*çābda*). The latter has no distinct species, though the question is raised, and decided in the negative, of the inclusion in it of recognition (*pratyabhijñā*). Of perception there are two distinct kinds, that of God which is omniscient and eternal, and that of man which is transient, and which may either be true or false. The other kinds of knowledge are proper to man as opposed to God, and admit therefore of truth and falsity. In the case of perception there is recognized also for man an essential difference between indeterminate and determinate perception in the former of which man comes into direct contact with the world of reality without him. This division of forms of knowledge covers the whole field: axioms in so far as they receive any recognition in the system fall under transcendental perception, which is a special form of determinate perception, and belief is included under verbal knowledge.

The four kinds of apprehension are ascribed to four kinds of means of proof (*pramāṇa*) by Annam Bhaṭṭa, as by Gañgeça, making explicit a relationship which does not so explicitly appear in Gautama. The term *pramāṇa*, however, is not without ambiguity. By Vātsyāyana[1] it is defined merely as an instrument of knowledge, 'that by which the knowing subject knows the object'. The ambiguity left by this definition, which is applicable in a purely psychological sense, is cleared up in the definition of Çivāditya,[2] which ascribes to a *pramāṇa* association with true knowledge (*pramā*),

[1] NBh., p. 1. [2] SP., § 144; TC. i. 401 ff.

a view which brings out at once the fact that a *pramāṇa* produces knowledge, and that, if it is to deserve its name, that knowledge must be true, i. e. in accord with reality. Annam Bhaṭṭa[1] and Keçava Miçra[2] recognize that the logical implication is as necessary as the psychological, and Mādhava[3] gives a fuller definition which emphasizes this and other features necessary in a true *pramāṇa*. Means of proof, in this view is that which is always accompanied by true knowledge, and at the same time is not disjoined from the appropriate organs or from the seat of consciousness, i. e. the soul. The expression 'accompanied' (*vyāpta*), which here takes the place of cause (*karaṇa*) in describing the relation of *pramāṇa* to *pramā*, is used to convey the fact that the means of proof does not merely produce knowledge but assures its correctness, while the addition to the definition makes it clear that means of proof is different from the self, the mind, or the organs of sense, though all these have their parts to play in mental activity. The true sense of *pramāṇa* thus appears not as a mere instrument of proof, but the mode in which the instrument is used, the process by which the knowledge appropriate to each means of proof is arrived at. The definition of Mādhava has in his view the further recommendation that it includes implicitly the doctrine of the Nyāya[4] that God is the fountainhead of all true knowledge, since God is the seat of all knowledge, and is ever conjoined with it.

As all truth depends on agreement of knowledge and reality, each of the modes of proof must conform to this test in the mode appropriate to it. In the technical phraseology of the Nyāya this doctrine takes the form that each cognition is true in virtue of a quality (*guṇa*),

[1] TS. § 34. Cf. NSāra, p. 1; TR., p. 8. [2] pp. 8, 9.
[3] SDS., p. 92.
[4] NS. ii. 1. 69; Kus. iv. 5, 6; TR., pp. 11, 12, 58; NVTP., p. 2.

which it possesses, and is false in virtue of a defect (*doṣa*); or more simply a cognition is true or false as it fulfils or fails to fulfil some requisite. Thus a perception is true if the object really possesses the attributes which correspond to the notion expressed in the judgement of perception; an inference if the process of inferring is busied about a subject which really possesses the qualities which in the conclusion are inferred of it; a comparison if the similarity is rightly apprehended as existing; and verbal knowledge if the compatibility of the words heard is known. These conditions are defeated by such conditions as in the case of vision bile in the eye or excessive distance, or in the case of inference by logical errors of any kind.

There is, however, a serious divergence of view between the Nyāya and the Vaiçeṣika regarding the number of means of proof. The syncretist school, with the exception of Çivāditya, follow the Nyāya[1] and accept four; perception which inconveniently enough bears the same name as the resulting knowledge, though *sākṣātkāra* is occasionally used for the latter; inference (*anumāna* as distinct from *anumiti*), comparison (*upamāna* as opposed to *upamiti*); and word or verbal testimony (*çabda* as opposed to *çābda*). From the normal Nyāya list there is, however, a departure in the case of Bhāsarvajña by whom comparison is included under word, the means of proof thus being reduced to three, while the Vaiçeṣika refuses to accept the separate validity of comparison and word which they reduce to inference. The Buddhists likewise accept in a sense perception and inference as proofs, while the Jains in one school divided means of proof into direct and indirect and included perception under the first, inference and

[1] TC. i. 508; iv. 2. 860-6; TR., pp. 55, 56. Some Vaiçeṣikas allowed verbal testimony; SSS. v. 38; Vyomaçiva, GSAI. xx. 68.

word under the second.[1] The same three were adopted by the Sāṁkhya,[2] the Yoga,[3] and in part by the Vedānta, though in the strict sense revealed truth alone exists for the Vedānta. The Mīmāṅsā and the normal Vedānta view accept, in addition to the four of the Nyāya, intuition or presumption (*arthāpatti*), and, save Prabhākara, also non-perception (*anupalabdhi*). The latter in the Nyāya view in only an accessory condition of the direct perception of non-existence,[4] while the former is reduced to a form of inference.[5] The number was raised to eight by the Paurāṇikas who included tradition (*aitihya*) and equivalence or inclusion (*saṁbhava*) among the means of proof: the former the Nyāya naturally reduced to word, while the latter falls under inference.[6] A ninth, gesture (*ceṣṭā*) added by the Tāntrikas falls under word, and elimination (*pariçeṣa*), which some Mīmāṅsā authorities made a separate proof, is plainly part of inference. On the other hand, the Cārvāka school reduced to perception alone, understood in the narrowest sense, the means of proof, a doctrine which they had to establish, unhappily for themselves by inference, while like the materialism which it accompanied it was entirely opposed to the whole system of the Nyāya.[7]

Remembrance as a rule lies outside the field of the

[1] Vidyābhūṣaṇa, *Med. Log.*, pp. 10 ff., 86 ff. ; NL., pp. 108, 109.

[2] Keith, *Sāṁkhya System*, p. 72.

[3] Deussen, *Vedānta*, ch. v ; NL., pp. 117, 118 ; P. Tuxen, *Yoga*, pp. 106 ff.

[4] *abhāva* is given in NS. ii. 2. 7-12 as included in inference ; cf. Kus. iii. 20 and commentary ; PSPM., pp. 72, 73 ; contra ÇV., pp. 245 ff. NBh., NV. and NVT. do not differ from NS., but see NV., p. 33.

[5] NS. ii. 2. 1-6 ; PB., p. 223.

[6] NS. ii. 2. 2 ; cf. for all these VSU. ix. 2. 5 ; NSāra, pp. 30, 32-4 ; TR., pp. 96-118; SS. i. 88 ; PBh., pp. 225, 230 ; in one version *saṁbhava* is probability, *Padārtharatnamālā*, pp. 19, 20.

[7] SDS., ch. i ; contra, NM., pp. 36, 64.

operation of the means of proof; Laugākṣi Bhāskara[1] alone frames his definition of means of proof so as to cover remembrance.[2] The reason for the omission is clear: remembrance itself has no independent value, being based on previous experience, and the normal opinion is satisfied with referring its character as true or false to the original whence it is derived. There is the obvious difficulty, moreover, that a remembrance may be hard to verify as compared with the original impression, if time has elapsed or the subject of the experience has gone to another place. It is obvious, however, that the mere reference for their truth or falsity of remembrances to the sources whence they were derived is not completely satisfactory: if the original impression were correct there may be forgetfulness in whole or part, but the nature and condition of such errors are not the subject of investigation. Remembrance is traced to an impression (*saṁskāra, bhāvanā*), produced by experience, which must be regarded as in some manner a mental operation (*vyāpāra*), which functions until it results in remembrance when an idea is recalled by an apprehension which awakens it (*udbodhaka*) by relations of various kinds.[3]

As the product of an abiding impression alone,[4] remembrance differs from recognition (*pratyabhijñā*), which is also in part due to an impression but has as its immediate cause the presence to perception of some object of previous experience, recognition thus being due to sense accompanied by an impression produced by a previous apprehension.[5] Or from another point of view the cause

[1] p. 7; contrast Kus. iv. 1, and cf. TR., pp. 19 ff.; NVTP., pp. 445, &c.

[2] NK., p. 257, already recalls the position of PBh., pp. 172, 186.

[3] NS. iii. 2. 43, 44; VS. ix. 2. 6; PBh., p. 256; below, ch. ix, § 1.

[4] TS., § 34.

[5] TB., p. 109; cf. NBh., pp. 177, 178; NV., pp. 68 ff.; NSāra, pp. 37,

of recognition is the knowledge of the identity of the new and old experiences rather than an intermediate process of remembrance, or, as Çivāditya has it, recognition is the perception of an object qualified by the idea of being past. The importance of the part played by memory, however, is not denied, and in the developed doctrine of determinate perception some recognition is given to the part played by memory in our actual concrete perceptions.

Apart from its character as knowledge, cognition is of vital importance from the standpoint of the interests of man. Taking the traditional fourfold division[1] we have that which is to be avoided (*heya*), that is pain and its sources, ignorance, desire, merit, and demerit; that which destroys pain (*hāna*), the knowledge of truth; that which brings this about, the science; and the final end, the removal of pain; and of these the knowledge of truth, or the instruments which produce that knowledge, ranks highest. Knowledge, we must remember, is not for its own sake alone; Çivāditya[2] recognizes an essential feature of the system when he classifies it, at first sight irrationally, according to its nature as mere recognition, acceptance as attractive (*upādāna*), rejection as painful (*hāna*), or treatment as indifferent (*upekṣā*).

3. *The Nature and Forms of Error.*

The essence of false knowledge (*aprama*) or error results immediately from the conception of true knowledge: it consists in having the knowledge of an object as possessed of attributes, which are not in accord with the real nature of the thing, and it is manifold in kind.

266, 267; NM., pp. 458 ff.; TC. i. 839 ff.; TK., p. 6; SP., § 167; CV., pp. 473, 474; PSPM., pp. 19, 20; YS. i. 11; Raghunātha, PTN., pp. 58, 59; *Padārtharatnamālā*, p. 10.

[1] NV., p. 4.

[2] SP., § 87.

The mode of division of error, however, is much less matter of agreement than that of knowledge, though the principles on which a division can be attempted are simple enough, and generally recognized. Thus false knowledge may be deliberately held and believed in: man may have a certainty which is yet untrue, and his position constitutes error proper (*bhrama*). Or he may merely be lacking in certainty, in which case his condition is that of doubt (*saṁçaya*). Or again his ignorance may be real and involuntary arising from causes which he is unable to control, or he may deliberately for his own purposes make a false assumption with a view to a *reductio ad absurdum* (*tarka*). Or again there is the peculiar form of error seen in dreams.

In the classification of Praçastapāda[1] the division is fourfold, possibly not uninfluenced by a desire to make the subdivisions of error correspond in number with those of true knowledge, which in his system are also somewhat artificially reckoned as four. They are doubt, error, indeterminateness, and dream. This division, which is in essence found in Kaṇāda,[2] is retained as it stands by Jagadīça[3]; but the other members of the school endeavour to effect a reconciliation between the view of Praçastapāda and that of Gautama[4] with whom doubt and *reductio ad absurdum* form two distinct categories. The most interesting of the attempts to follow Praçastapāda is that of Çivāditya[5] who reduces the subdivisions to two, but manages to find a place in them for the others. His classification assumes the two classes of doubt and error: in the former he includes conjecture (*ūha*) and indeterminateness,[6] as well as *reductio ad absurdum*; in the second he includes dreams. Annam

[1] pp. 172 ff. [2] ix. 2. 10 ff. [3] p. 12.
[4] i. 1. 23, 30. [5] SP., § 32; cf. CV., p. 29.
[6] So NSāra, pp. 1, 2.

Bhaṭṭa[1] adopts a triple classification into doubt, error, and *reductio ad absurdum*, a view also taken by Keçava Miçra.[2] Laugākṣi Bhāskara,[3] on the other hand, contents himself with the bare categories of doubt and error, without subdivisions, while Viçvanātha[4] treats doubt and error as the classes of false knowledge, but gives a separate place by itself to the topic of *reductio ad absurdum*. The efforts to rearrange the views of the two schools to form a harmony thus show different aspects. On the one hand the Nyāya category *reductio ad absurdum* loses its place as of equal rank with doubt, while on another view it appears as a third class alongside doubt and error, thus according it a higher rank than the Vaiçeṣika was prepared to give.

Doubt is essentially knowledge which has for its characteristic the absence or presence of contrary attributes in the same object, as defined by Viçvanātha,[5] or more simply, in the words of Annam Bhaṭṭa[6] is the knowledge of contrary properties in one and the same object. Doubt, therefore, has three characteristics: there must be knowledge of several qualities; they must be irreconcilable (*viruddha*) with one another; and they must be apprehended in one and the same object. The question of what is meant by irreconcilable is obviously difficult, but must be resolved, according to the principles of the system, by experience which alone affords us knowledge of what attributes may consistently be attributed to one and the same object at the same time. More precisely still the nature of doubt is defined by Laugākṣi Bhāskara[7] as knowledge consisting in an alternative between various contradictory attributes in regard to one and the same object (*ekasmin dharmiṇi*

1 TS., § 64.
2 TB., pp. 39 ff.
3 TK., pp. 6, 7.
4 BP. 127 ff.
5 BP. 130.
6 TS., § 64.
7 TK., p. 7.

viruddhanānākoṭikaṁ jñānam). This last definition makes it clear how doubt differs from indeterminate perception which is in reality mere sensation, and which therefore lies far behind the stage at which doubt can possibly arise. On the other hand, doubt in the precise sense of the word differs from conjecture, which Çivāditya[1] classes under it: in the former case, if, for instance, we see at a distance an indeterminate object which we conclude must either be a man or a pole, that is doubt: if we advance to the stage at which we decide tentatively and without assurance in favour of it being a man, conjecture is reached. Indeterminateness, which Çivāditya makes another subdivision of doubt, is exemplified by the uncertainty which one may have regarding the precise species of a tree: it is therefore a modified and limited form of doubt.

The various causes which can give rise to doubt are variously given by Mādhava,[2] Viçvanātha, and Keçava Miçra. The most obvious, and the stock case, is that where the object is seen to possess attributes which are generic in character, and therefore may belong to several different things, as in the usual example of the object which with outstretched arms or branches seen at a distance may be taken for a tree trunk or a motionless ascetic. The alternatives here, it is pointed out, are really four: the thing may be a man, or a tree trunk, or some-

[1] SP., § 164; NSāra, pp. 1. 2.

[2] SDS., pp. 92, 93. Cf. NS. i. 1. 23, where perception and non-perception make up five; so NSāra, *l. c.*; the number is reduced to three in TR., pp. 165-8, refuting NSāra, and explaining NS. Cf. also NS. ii. 1. 1-7 for a proof of the reality of doubt. NB. accepts five classes, NV. and NVT. three; NM., pp. 556-62, five; cp. PSPM., p. 32; KKK. ii. 187-96. Deussen (*Allgem. Gesch.* I. iii. 377) suggests that originally it referred to two opposing views only. PBh., pp. 174 ff. divides doubt as internal and external; criticized by Raghunātha, PTN., pp. 67-91.

thing which is not a man yet not a tree, or something which is not a tree, yet not a man. Or two opinions may be before the subject which he has no means to decide between. Or the object may have qualities too ill defined to secure its recognition. Or on another interpretation even if the object has a specific quality as the earth has odour, yet one who knows that the quality of odour is quite different from the quality of being eternal or the reverse, but does not know the position of the earth in this regard, may doubt whether or not the earth is eternal or not.

While doubt shares falsity in virtue of the fact that it is the knowledge of an object, but only in an indeterminate manner, error is absolutely false, as it consists of certainty of the opposite of the truth, the object presenting itself with attributes which are repugnant to those which it possesses in reality. Thus error is simply equivalent to false knowledge, consisting as it does in perceiving an object differently from what it actually is. Doubt, if the doubter decide in favour of the wrong alternative, becomes error, but that is only when certainty, though in the wrong sense, has replaced the former doubt. Again, error to be such must, properly speaking, be involuntary, due to physical or external causes, apart from the will of him who commits the error. Such are the errors which occur in the case of perception through debilities of the organs or circumstances such as excessive distance or too diminutive size which preclude the due functioning of the means of perception.[1]

From error of this type which is involuntary differs entirely the form of error which consists in the *reductio ad absurdum*, and which plays a great part in logic,

[1] Cf. VS. ix. 2. 10; BP. 131.

being dignified by Gautama with the rank of a category.[1] The error involved, of course, is the false assumption which forms the basis of the reasoning, and which essentially differs from real error by reason of its deliberate assumption for the purpose of proving some proposition, or of confirming a proof arrived at in some other way. From doubt it differs essentially also: in doubt there must be several alternatives available: the *reductio ad absurdum* is intended to show that something must exist in some determined mode, or else some absurd result will be obtained.

The utility and force of the process may be seen at its best in the stock example, which seeks to prove the truth of the conclusion that the mountain is fiery, because it has smoke.[2] Where this inference is set out, when the propounder of the theory has enunciated the proposition and the reason, he proceeds to give the general proposition, 'Wherever there is smoke, then there is fire'. At this point, however, he may find that his antagonist will not admit the truth of this proposition, and denies the universal concomitance of smoke with fire. He then resorts to a *reductio ad absurdum.* He asks his adversary whether the mountain is fiery or not: if the reply is in the affirmative, obviously he need not proceed further as his conclusion is proved. If in the negative, he proceeds to the proposition, 'If the mountain is not fiery, then it cannot be smoky.' If the adversary will not admit this, then he is challenged to produce an instance in which smoke is found in the absence of fire: this he cannot do, and therefore must admit the truth of the proposition, 'Where there is no

[1] i. 1. 40; NBh., pp. 65-7; NV., pp. 161-5.

[2] Jacobi, NGWG. 1901, pp. 464, n. 2, 469, n. 1; see TC. ii. 219-42; TR., pp. 185-204; NVT., pp. 41, 42; NVTP., pp. 325-38; KKK. ii. 206-45.

fire, there is no smoke'. From this it follows that, as there is no fire on the mountain, there can be no smoke, a conclusion which manifestly contradicts the truth, and drives the adversary to admit his error in opposing the original demonstration. In the technical jargon [1] of the schools the procedure of *reductio ad absurdum* appears as the admission of the concomitant (*vyāpaka*), i.e. in the supposed case the non-existence of smoke, as a consequence of having admitted that of which it is the concomitant (*vyāpya*), i.e. the non-existence of fire. The propriety of classing *reductio ad absurdum* as error lies technically in the conclusion which is reached by the process, and which is palpably false. The account given by Gautama is simpler: *reductio ad absurdum* appears as an investigation regarding an object, whose nature is unknown, carried on for the purpose of ascertaining that nature, and based on the fact that there must be some cause involved. As Vātsyāyana [2] explains the process, the knowing subject confronted by an object recognizes that it may possess one or other of two contradictory attributes, and finally reaches a conclusion based on causality, a view which represents the process as it presents itself to one who is seeking to find for himself the truth, while the later texts give the process as used in controversy in order to convict an opponent of error.

The older Nyāya—not Gautama or his exponents—admits eleven divisions of the general class *tarka*: of these the modern school admit only five, the last of which *pramāṇabādhitārthaprasaṅga* is *reductio ad absurdum* as just described: the other four are properly forms of logical error; they are reasoning in a circle (*cakra*); *regressus ad infinitum* (*anavasthā*); dilemma (*anyonyāçraya*); and *ignoratio elenchi* (*ātmāçraya*).

[1] TS., § 64. [2] In NS. i. 1. 40.

These and other logical errors, whether due to sophistry or incapacity for correct argument, have no real affinity with the process of *reductio ad absurdum*, which in effect is a valuable means of proof.

The dream state appears with Praçastapāda as the fourth form of false knowledge, and Keçava Miçra[1] makes the matter more precise by explaining that in the waking state memory may be true or false, but that the dream is always false, because we erroneously substitute the idea 'this' for 'that'. In remembrance in fact we recall an object as past: I remember that flower which I saw yesterday. In the dream state, which is really memory, I fall into the delusion that I actually see this flower, which in reality I merely remember before my eyes.[2]

The exact process of the dream is indicated by Praçastapāda[3] and Çañkara Miçra developing Kaṇāda's[4] doctrine that dream arises, like remembrance, from a previous impression and a special contact between mind and the self. Dream knowledge is the apprehension which arises when the senses have ceased to be active and the mind is quiescent. It is of three kinds: it may be due to the vividness of the impression received in the waking state previous to slumber; it may arise from a disorder of the humours, wind, bile, and phlegm; it may be caused as in the Vedānta view by merit or demerit arousing pleasing or terrifying visions, quaint details of which the texts give, including among the ill-omened the spectacle of one's own marriage. From dream knowledge is distinguished that which inheres in or lies near to sleep or dream (*svapnāntika*).[5] Praça-

[1] TB., p. 89.

[2] Cf. Kumārila, ÇV., p. 173; VPS. i. 97: ÇD., p. 39; PSPM., pp. 31, 32.

[3] pp. 183, 184.

[4] ix. 2. 7.

[5] ix. 2. 8; Chatterji, *Hindu Realism*, p. 161.

stapāda tells us that this is the cognition which springs up in a dream in the form of the recollection of something actually experienced in the dream state. Thus the visions of a dream are accorded power to leave impressions, though themselves nothing save impressions of experience, a suggestion which might have evoked the idea that the dream was really the expression of a personality other than that dominant in waking life, had not any form of panpsychism been abhorrent to the school. Other interpretations of the phrase were also current; in one view it denotes a prophetic dream, in another that dream experience which is felt as actual perception owing to its vivid character.

The dream state is possible only in that form of sleep (*nidrā*) in which contact of mind and self is possible, though contact between mind and the other sense organs has ceased,[1] a condition which Yogins can artificially produce. In deep sleep (*suṣupti*) all contact of mind and self ceases, and the self, as in Prabhākara's view, ceases to have consciousness, for which mediation by mind is requisite, while on the Vedānta view shared by Kumārila it regains its condition of pure consciousness, in which of course no dream is possible.[2] The physical possibility of this severance of mind and self rests on the atomic size of the latter and on the view that in deep sleep mind retires to the *purītat*, apparently conceived as a fleshy bag near the heart, in which in some unexplained way it is severed from the all pervading self.[3] This grotesque speculation of the school is due as in the Sāṁkhya and Vedānta which have an analogous doctrine, to the influence of the *Bṛhadāraṇyaka Upaniṣad* which tells us of the departure of something—the soul according to the Vedānta—into the *purītat* in sound sleep.

[1] SP., § 165; PBh., p. 258. [2] NS. iv. i. 63; PSPM., pp. 78, 79.

[3] Athalye, TS., pp. 148, 149; Deussen, *Vedānta*, ch. xxviii; Garbe, *Sāṁkhya*, pp. 274 ff.

CHAPTER II

PERCEPTION

1. *Normal Perception.*

In its widest sense perception includes two things which differ in vital respects, the normal or human perception, which is transient, and the perception of God, which is immediate and eternal, and which possesses only so much in common with normal perception that, like it, it does not depend on any prior knowledge. Man, however, is not totally devoid of a perception which has in it something analogous to that of the deity, though unlike that it is transient and conditioned, but his normal perception stands on an entirely different basis, bringing him into immediate contact with the world of reality. Knowledge which arises from the contact of sense and organ is given by Gautama [1] as the meaning of perception; when not subject to error, when not requiring further determination, and when definite it reaches the standard of correct knowledge. Vātsyāyana [2] renders more precise the process of perception; the self is united with the mind, the mind with the sense, the sense with the object, with the result that perception thus arises. In doing so he definitely brings mind into the position of a quasi-sense, though in that quality it

[1] i. 1. 4: *avyapadeçyam avyabhicāri vyavasāyātmakam*; for the first epithet see Jacobi, JAOS. xxxi. 20, n. 2. The second excludes erroneous perception, e.g. of water in lieu of sun rays; the third cases of doubt.

[2] NBh. i. 1. 4; NS. ii. 1. 21; NV., pp. 40 ff.

appears neither in Gautama or Kaṇāda, and the former classes it among the category of objects of knowledge as opposed to instruments of proof. Despite, however, its connexion with the self and the mind in this manner, the proximate cause of perception is the sense, or more strictly its contact with the object, a distinction which permits the classification of the apprehension of pain or pleasure by the mind as perception, while excluding from the category other mental processes, such as inference, in which mind is active, but not as the proximate cause.

The place of mind in the process of perception is established by a series of proofs.[1] The self is all-pervading consciousness, but experience shows that, despite the presence of objects of sense and organs of sense, frequently perceptions do not result, a state of affairs which can be explained only on the assumption that there is requisite something to establish a special contact between the self and the sense organs with their objects. Again, the fact that we experience things not all at once, but in reality, as analysis shows, successively, proves the intervention of something between the self and the senses. Mind, however, has not merely this function of intervention: feelings like pleasure and pain are actually experienced just as much as sensations of colour and smell, and it is a fair argument from analogy to assume that there must be for their apprehension an instrument comparable with an organ of sense. The facts of remembrance[2] point in the same direction; if it is argued that feelings, thoughts, and volitions are directly present in the self, it is impossible to explain why they are not always and invariably presented, which experience shows not to be the case. Mind, therefore, has a double

[1] NS. i. 1. 16; ii. 1. 24; iii. 2. 60–3; VS. iii. 2. 1–3; vii. 1. 23; PBh., pp. 89–93; TC. i. 784 ff. Cf. Deussen, *Phil. of Up.*, pp. 273 ff.

[2] NS. iii. 2. 22–35; ÇV., p. 97.

function to perform; on the one hand it mediates between the senses and the self; on the other hand it plays the part of internal sense, and has as its objects the working of the mind. It is interesting to note that feeling and volition are thus ranked on a par with cognitions as the object of internal perception.

Further light is thrown on the definition by the discussion in the Sūtra[1] of the argument that perception is really inference since, when we see a tree, we really perceive only a part, the rest being supplied by inference, the part serving as mark of the whole. This view is rejected; it is pointed out that admittedly there is perception of a part, and that all perception is not inference, but it is further maintained that perception of the whole is real and direct, and is verified by our ability to hold and pull the tree or other object as a whole. The discussion is then linked to the dispute between Buddhism and the Nyāya on the relation of the whole to its parts, the Nyāya maintaining firmly the reality and distinct character of a whole. This passage makes it somewhat difficult to be assured of the correctness of the interpretation of the epithet 'not requiring further determination' in the definition as meaning 'not expressible by words' which Vātsyāyana and Uddyotakara give; other commentators, the latter tells us, interpreted the phrase as excluding inference, and indeed a perception, which is to be exempt from confusion of objects and to negative doubt, seems almost necessarily to involve expressibility in language.

The interpretation of the Sūtra was early affected by the necessity of bringing it into relation with the important doctrine of Dignāga, who, from the standpoint of a modified form of idealism, propounded the

[1] ii. 1. 30-6; below, ch. vii. § 2.

definition of perception as free from determination by imagination (*kalapanāpoḍha*),[1] which Dharmakīrti improved by adding that it must be correct (*abhrānta*).[2] As will be seen in dealing with his doctrine of inference, as a logician at any rate, Dignāga, followed by Dharmakīrti,[3] recognizes a perfectly definite distinction between the parts of sensation and imagination or intellect in perception; the former gives us absolute reality in momentary contact but a perception giving name, substance, quality, action, or class[4] is essentially the product of imagination synthetizing momentary impressions, a view obviously very different from that of the Nyāya with its realism, since all that is real in the full sense is the momentary sensation, which is absolutely inexpressible. A perception as opposed to a sensation gives the form of the object, but that is derived from the intellect, not from sensation. The distinction thus drawn between sensation and perception, with the allocation to the latter of the work of intellect was not accepted by Uddyotakara[5] or by Praçastapāda,[6] the argument of the former, whose attack on Dignāga is vouched for by Vācaspati,[7] being that a consistent sensationalism should be speechless and therefore unable to give the definition suggested,

[1] NV., pp. 44, 45; Stcherbatskoi, *Muséon*, v. 162–4; below, ch. iii, § 2.

[2] NVT., p. 102; TR., pp. 60, 61; *Mādh. Vṛtti*, pp. 69–75; NB., p. 103; NBT., pp. 4, 8, 15–20; SDS., p. 18; NSāra, commentary, pp. 84, 85; ṢDS., p. 30.

[3] In his *Saṁtānāntarasiddhi* (Bibl. Buddh. xix) he appears as an idealist *sans phrase*, denying the existence of cognizer or cognition; but the use of his logical view by Sautrāntikas (NVTP., pp. 152–4) and Vaibhāṣikas (SDS. *l. c.*), who were both realists, shows that his logic was compatible with realism, even if ultimately he himself meant to assign the sensation to the *ālayavijñāna* as its source.

[4] For the kinds of *kalpanā* cf. NV., p. 44; NSāra, commentary, *l. c.*; TR.; *l. c.*; NM., p. 93.

[5] NV., pp. 44, 45.

[6] p. 187; NK., p. 190; ṢDST., p. 67.

[7] NVT., p. 102.

or to describe perception as impermanent or a source of pain. If the terms of the definition mean only that the specific individuality of an object is inexpressible, that is true, since all things have a general and a specific character, and are expressible in the former aspect only, but this gives no real definition of perception.

With Trilocana, a predecessor of Vācaspati, of whom we know little else,[1] there seems to have been introduced into the school interpretation of the Sūtra the view that we must distinguish between two forms of perception, the first of which gives the bare knowledge of the class character of the object and is styled indeterminate (*a-* or *nir- vikalpaka*), while the second, in place of giving the bare qualification of the object (*viçeṣaṇa*) gives the determinate (*savikalpaka*) relation of qualified (*viçeṣya*) and qualification, whether the latter be strictly so called, i.e. something essentially coexistent with the thing qualified or an accident (*upalakṣaṇa*). The Sūtra must, it is held, refer to both, the latter depending on the former, which is inexpressible in words, like the cognition of children or those who do not know the correct term for a new experience, and therefore the first is understood by *avyapadeçya*, while the second by *vyavasāyātmaka*. This doctrine reappears in a classical form in Gañgeça,[2] who insists that the existence of this abstract or indeterminate perception is known by inference, since, unless it is postulated, there is an infinite regress, and we must therefore accept as final a direct perception of the class (substance, quality or action), which, however, always becomes concrete by application to the thing perceived, the two forms therefore not constituting distinct species;

[1] See Vācaspati on i. 1. 4. He is cited also, on other points, in TR., pp. 337, 356 (before Vācaspati); cf. on the Sūtra, pp. 63, 64.

[2] TC., i. 809 ff.; so TR., p. 64; NM., p. 97 ff.; TK., p. 8; NSM., pp. 13, 14; cf. *Padarthasratnamālā*, pp. 6, 7.

on the determinate perception follows the reference to self in the *anuvyavasāya*. At the same time the definition of perception is revised to run 'a cognition which is not brought about by another cognition', a definition [1] intended to meet the objection that the old definition really covered every cognition since organ was interpreted to include mind, that it omitted the divine cognition, and introduced the term organ whose extent could be decided only by perception itself. The new definition excludes inference, which depends on the perception of the invariable concomitance of the middle and major, and of the presence of the middle in the minor; analogy which rests on cognition of similarity; and verbal testimony resting on cognition of the meaning of words, a fact which also explains the primacy given to perception as a means of proof by the Sūtra.[2]

Another point of view, however, appears in Kumārila,[3] the *Nyāyasāra*,[4] and in recent Nyāya [5] doctrine. The Buddhist doctrine of the peculiarity (*svalakṣaṇa*) of the object in indeterminate perception was met on the one hand by the assertion of the Çābdikas [6] that it was the bare name which was thus apprehended, while others, the Vedānta, held that it was existence in its abstract form (*sattā*), views which Jayanta [7] rejects. Kumārila held that sensation set up a condition due to the thing in itself (*çuddhavastuja*) of observation like that of a new born child on perceiving reality, in which generality and

[1] TC., i. 552. Mathurānātha (i. 559) explains this as not inconsistent with God, being regarded as the final cause of all knowledge.

[2] NBh., p. 3; NV., pp. 14 ff.

[3] ÇV., pp. 87 ff.; v. 112 cited in TR., p. 64; NSāra, commentary p. 86; PSPM., pp. 37–9, agrees rather with TC.; PBh. with ÇV.

[4] pp. 8, 4. 84–6; the commentary takes the distinction of kinds as applicable to Yogins' perception only.

[5] TB., pp. 27, 28; TSD., § 42; SP., §§ 86, 166.

[6] TR., pp. 61, 62.

[7] NM., pp. 97 ff.

particularity are latent and which only later developed into determinate cognition, and the *Nyāyasāra* makes it clear that indeterminate perception gives only the mere existence (*vastusvarūpa-mātra*) of the object in the recognition that an undefined something exists on which determinate perception is built up. But, unlike Gañgeça, the indeterminate form is no mere inference: unobserved in practice it can be seen in any case of the acquisition of new knowledge. The latest development of this view definitely severs indeterminate perception from all other forms of apprehension at the root of which it lies, and thus approaches the psychological conception of sensation as opposed to perception.[1]

The validity of determinate perception is naturally assailed by the Buddhists, who deny that perception can give connexion of an object with a name, or that there is any generality which can be predicated of an individual thing, which is momentary in character. The Nyāya with Kumārila[2] refuses to accept these contentions; generality is directly perceived when an individual is apprehended, and can therefore be predicated of the individual, as in Aristotle being is predicable of the individual despite its unique character. The giving of a name is certainly not derived from perception, and a perfectly clear perception is possible, e.g. of musical notes, though we cannot name what we see whether from ignorance or forgetfulness. But the name can be supplied either on or after perception from memory or instruction; the giving of names is necessary for communication of knowledge and memory, but it is not in itself a source of error. Nor is perception merely due

[1] *Nīlakaṇṭhī* on TSD. *l. c.*; Athalye, TS., pp. 219, 220.

[2] VSU. viii. 1. 2; ÇV., pp. 97–116; on generality, pp. 201–17, 281–95, 464–8; cf. below, ch. iii, § 8; NSM., pp. 12 ff.

[3] Cf. Arist., *de Interpr.*, 16 a 19.

to the activity of memory; in our perception of any individual thing much is due to that source, but its distinct individuality and time relation are directly due to perception.

2. *The Forms of Perception and their Objects.*

The organs of perception are six in number, five external, those of seeing, hearing, tasting, smelling, and touching (a term which includes the temperature sense), and one internal, mind, and there are various ways in which the contact between the organ and the object which is the prerequisite of perception can take place.[1] These are conjunction (*saṁyoga*); inherence in that which is in conjunction (*saṁyukta-samavāya*); inherence in that which inheres in that which is in conjunction (*saṁyukta-samaveta-samavāya*); inherence (*samavāya*); inherence in that which inheres (*samaveta-samavāya*); and relation of predicate and subject (*viçeṣaṇa-viçeṣyatā*), and all that is the object of perception must fall within one or other of these modes of contact. The divergence of modes rests on ontological theories: the eye, for instance, as a substance can come into direct conjunction with another substance, but only indirectly with e.g. colour which inheres in that substance, and at a further remove with the class concept which inheres in the colour which inheres in the object with which the eye is in conjunction. The ear, again, is a portion of the ether, and sound inheres in it, and therefore is apprehended by the relation of inherence, while its class concept by the relation of inherence in that which inheres. The last class is intended to meet the special case of the perception of inherence and negation.

[1] Cf. VS. viii. 1. 3-11; NV. i. 1. 4; TC. i. 572 ff.; TA., p. 15; TB., pp. 28-30; TK., pp. 8, 9; TS., § 43; BP., 59-61; NSāra, pp. 2, 3, 74-80; ṢDST., p. 17; NSM., pp. 26-34.

Among the objects of perception the qualities of the self, such as cognition, pleasure, and pain are perceived by the mind, and the later Nyāya includes the self itself in that category, while the Vaiçeṣika accepts the doctrine that the self is only an object of inference.[1] Of the other objects, it is agreed that a substance having magnitude can be perceived by sight, provided, however, that it has a manifest colour[2]: the form of contact is literal conjunction, the object and the eye being deemed to come into actual effective contact. The modern school admits also the power of touch to perceive substance, provided that the substance has in it the quality of touch, while Viçvanātha, by an unhappy attempt at a compromise between the views, makes the power of touch to discern substance conditional on the substance having manifest colour. Quality and motion[3] again are perceived by the organs by means of the second form of contact, inherence in that which is in conjunction. Generality, the fourth of the Vaiçeṣika categories, is perceived by the second or the third of the forms of contact, according as the generality is that of substance or of a quality or action. Particularity, which resides in the atoms is necessarily immune from normal perception.

There remain the categories of inherence and non-existence, both of which the Nyāya holds to be perceptible, while the Vaiçeṣika restricts this power to

[1] iii. 1. 2; 2. 18; viii. 1. 2; NSāra, p. 36; TR., pp. 119, 120; NBh., p. 10, gives direct vision to Yogins only; below, ch. ix, § 1.

[2] VS. iv. 1. 6; below, ch. vii, § 2; ch. viii, § 2. Light, therefore, is necessary for visual perception, but as affecting the object, not the organ.

[3] Prabhākara denies perception, PP., pp. 78, 79; Kumārila accepts it, ÇD., p. 50. Deussen's denial (*Allgem. Gesch.*, I. iii. 309) that substance is perceived is an error; sight, touch, and mind see substance, NSM., pp. 22 ff. For the modern doctrine of the sensation of movement, cf. Wildon Carr, *Proc. Arist. Soc.*, 1915–16.

non-existence, and asserts that inherence is a matter of inference. In either case the contact of predicate and subject is held to apply, a view based on the fact that inherence and non-existence having no autonomous existence can be perceived only as attributes of some object in which they are found. In the case of inherence the conception, which is confined to the strict Nyāya view,[1] is at least simple, but the case of non-existence [2] presents obvious difficulties. As it is not a substance, it cannot be known by conjunction; as it is not a quality, activity, or class it cannot inhere in a substance, and therefore can be perceived only by its relation to that in which it does not exist. The perception of the non-existence of a pot on the ground involves, accordingly, first a contact between the eye and the ground, and secondly, a peculiar contact between the ground and the absence of the pot. This contact may be expressed in two forms, either as 'The ground is possessed of the absence of a pot' (*ghaṭābhāvavad bhūtalam*), the ground serving as the subject and the absence of the pot as the qualification, or as 'There is the absence of a pot on the ground' (*bhūtale ghaṭābhāvo 'sti*), in which case the relations are reversed. Thus the sixth form of contact consists of two distinct kinds, corresponding to the divergence in the form of proposition: in the first case, the negation forms the qualification of that which is in contact (*saṁyukta-viçeṣaṇatā*), namely the ground with the eye; in the second case the negation is to be qualified by that which is in contact (*saṁyukta-viçeṣyatā*). In

[1] TB., p. 30; cf. TC. i. 640 ff.; NSāra, pp. 3, 82; by inference only, TR., p. 162, but see NVT., p. 70; NV., p. 33; by both, PSPM., p. 89; cf. NSM., p. 30.

[2] VS. ix. 1. 1, 6–10; TB., pp. 29, 30; TK., p. 9; TS., § 44; NSāra, pp. 3, 79, 80; TR., pp. 103–16; NVTP., pp. 464–80; NV., p. 33; that it is inferred is the view in NBh., pp. 2, 101; NV., pp. 10, 279; PBh., p. 329 insists that inherence is inferable only.

the case of perception of a substance like a pot, however, there can be no such duality of form of contact; a pot we see in itself, but the non-existence of a pot can be perceived only in virtue of its relation to the ground, and it is in the double form of relation which is possible between the pot and the ground that there lies the reason for the double form of contact possible.

Non-existence, however, is not applicable to substance only[1]: the last form of contact, though it primarily refers to substance, is available to be brought into operation in cases where the positive element is established by any of the other modes of contact: thus the non-existence of a quality is established by a variety of the relation of subject and predicate applied to the second form of contact and so on.

This peculiar mode of contact assumed by the Nyāya is, not unnaturally rejected by the Mīmāṅsā, which, however, agrees with the Nyāya in the view that non-existence is the object of direct apprehension. Contact between an organ and non-existence is impossible, it is argued, because contact must be either conjunction or inherence. Conjunction is possible only between two substances, and non-existence is not a substance. Inherence signifies inseparable connexion, and no one can assert that of an organ and non-existence. Moreover, these conceptions have validity only for the world of existence, and should not be applied outside that sphere. They assert, therefore, non-perception (*anupalabdhi*) as a special independent means of proof, a view which the Nyāya rejects.[2] In doing so, however, it is compelled

[1] As Raghunātha (PTN., p. 48) holds. He also (pp. 76–8) claims that *vaiçiṣṭhya* is a special category. Cf. also *Padārtharatnamālā*, pp. 7, 8.

[2] TC. i. 673–92; TB., pp. 52–5; TK., pp. 17, 18; TSD., § 43; Kus. iii. 20–2; NSāra, pp. 33, 34, 241–6; TR., pp. 102–16; PSPM., pp. 72, 73; NSM., pp. 34–58; *contra* ÇV., pp. 243–52; ÇD., pp. 60–5. KKK. i. 355–64 ridicules the Nyāya view.

to make concessions, and to admit that non-perception is an accessory cause of the result. The mere vision of the ground does not suggest the absence of a pot: it can do so only when there was reason on other grounds to expect the presence there of a pot, and, when this expectation is defeated by our failure to see the pot, the basis is laid for the peculiar contact which in the Nyāya view is the cause of the perception of non-existence. But the Nyāya is careful to emphasize that non-perception, even as a subsidiary means, must be restricted to cases where perception is possible: thus the merit and demerit of good and evil actions is real in every sense, but it is not open to perception, and failure to perceive it is no ground for asserting that it does not exist. The controversy with the Mīmāṅsā thus reduces itself largely to a point of form, the Nyāya admitting non-perception as a subsidiary, while the Mīmāṅsā insists that it is the primary, cause of the perception of non-existence, and that it has the distinctive character of differing from perception, inference, or other proof.

Other difficulties regarding perception are raised and solved in the *Nyāya Sūtra*. An interesting suggestion of Dignāga that material contact is not the cause of vision is put forward, supported by the possibility of distant vision and of the eye seeing things larger and smaller than itself. The reply is that contact is effected by a ray from the eye, which, as possessing neither magnitude nor colour, is invisible; it is not merely overpowered by light, for it does not shine in the dark, though the ray in the eyes of cats suggests its presence in ours also. The obstructions met by sense prove also materiality; if glass, mica, crystal do not prevent vision it is simply because they are transparent; a wall does prevent it.[1] If contact, however, is necessary, it is

[1] NS. iii. 1. 30–50; cf. Kir., pp. 74–6; NK., p. 23; NV., pp. 35–8.

natural to suggest that there is but one sense organ, the skin,[1] and that all other senses are mere modifications of it. This, however, is contrary to the fact that objects are not perceived simultaneously, which argues a difference in their apprehension. Or again, if from the fact that all things perceived by sense have the common quality of being an object, it is argued that sense also is one, this view can be met by pointing to the different character of cognition in each of the five cases, the different location of the organ, the different process of its action, the different form of the organ, and its divergent constitution from atoms. Eye, nose, tongue, and skin are composed of atoms of fire, earth, water, and air, while the ear is a portion of the ether, and these elements have the characteristic qualities of colour, odour, savour, tangibility, and sound. It is true that all save air and ether possess more than one quality, but one predominates both in the atom and in the sense composed of atoms,[2] so that each sense apprehends one quality. On the other hand, no more than five senses are needed, for a separate sense is not required for the apprehension of distinctions within a genus.[3] Though the senses thus possess qualities they themselves are invisible, and their qualities must therefore exist in a latent state,[4] as must be the case if they are to perform their allotted function, a conception which has a remote affinity with the Aristotelian doctrine of sense as a

The rapidity of the ray prevents the observation of its successive action; its conjunction with points of space explains our sense of distance; cf. KKK. i. 111; SS. v. 104–8. Dignāga is quoted, *Padārtharatnamālā*, pp. 21, 22.

[1] Cf. NK., p. 45; a Sāṁkhya view, acc. to *Padārth. l. c.*

[2] NS. iii. 1. 51–8, 61–9; VS. viii. 2. 5, 6.

[3] NS. iii. 1. 59, 60; ÇV., p. 98.

[4] NS. iii. 1. 70–5; SP., § 125; TB., p. 67; TK., p. 3; ÇV., p. 169; Lakṣ., p. 8. Cf. Arist., *de An.*, ii. 6 ff.

potentiality, just as the doctrine of mind may be compared with that of the *sensus communis*. The organ is thus the place of contact between mind and the self; its existence, unlike that of external things, is proved like that of mind by inference alone, every agent requiring to work by means of an instrument. The ear, however, stands in a special position, as it actually is part of ether,[1] and possesses sound as a quality. Hence, in the perception of negation in the case of sound, what is perceived is not as, e.g. in the case of the negation of a jar, a qualification of an object, e.g. earth, but of the organ of sense itself.[2]

Keçava Miçra[3] is responsible for an effort to make precise the instrumentality of sense and the contact with an object in producing indeterminate and determinate perception respectively. Sense as the proximate cause (*karaṇa*) by its activity (*vyāpāra*), contact, gives indeterminate perception; contact as cause with indeterminate perception as activity gives determinate perception; indeterminate perception with determinate gives desire. But this refinement is not generally accepted.

3. *Transcendental Perception.*

Normal perception as described is essentially based on sensation, and there is therefore in it a substantial basis for the contention that the Nyāya-Vaiçeṣika system is comparable to the sensationalism of Locke.[4] It is true, moreover, that in its origin the doctrine was frankly accepted in its fullest extent by both schools: the Nyāya expressly lays down that inference depends on percep-

[1] This is denied by Kumārila, ÇV., pp. 418–21; cf. TC., i. 617 ff.; PSPM., pp. 60, 61; below, ch. viii, § 3.

[2] TC. i. 574 ff.; NSM., p. 35.

[3] p. 28.

[4] Athalye, TS., pp. 281, 282; Jacobi, NGWG. 1901, p. 464.

tion, and the same conclusion obviously follows for such knowledge as is obtainable by comparison. But it must not be forgotten that verbal knowledge in the Nyāya conception extended beyond this limit, and Praçastapāda accords decisive weight to the tradition handed down in the works of his master, Kaṇāda, neither view being in harmony with a pure sensationalism, and in perception we know generality as well as particularity.

The growing care with which the mechanism of proof was studied resulted, as was inevitable, in the definite attempt to provide a place for the ideal element which was plainly somewhat lacking in the older theory of perception. It was realized that to establish a universal proposition by mere empiric means was impossible: no summing of individual perceptions would give any assurance of legitimacy of reasoning. In the syncretist school, in Laugākṣi Bhāskara[1] and in Viçvanātha,[2] we find fully developed the conception of a supernormal or transcendental perception (*alaukika pratyakṣa*), which manifests itself in three different forms. The first, whose characteristic is generality (*sāmānya-lakṣaṇa*), is the knowledge which we possess from seeing an individual thing of the class to which it belongs, and of all the individuals of that class, not, however, as individuals, but as making up the class. This form of perception cannot be explained by any normal form of contact; it is to be interpreted as due to a connexion (*pratyāsatti*) between the mind and generality *sui generis*. A second form, whose characteristic is knowledge (*jñāna-lakṣaṇa*), is exemplified in the action of the mind which, when we, for example, perceive a flower brings before us the

[1] TK., p. 9; cf. VSV. ix. 1. 11; TSD., p. 45.

[2] BP. 62–6; for Gañgeça's view see TC. ii. 283 ff.; NSM., pp. 23 ff. Its place in inference is fully recognized in Kumārila, ÇV., pp. 201–7; NB., p. 103.

conception of fragrance as pertaining to it, though the flower itself is at such a distance that we have no possibility of actually experiencing the odour. The process demands, therefore, that we should already have framed for ourselves the connexion of the generic relation of odour and flower, which on the perception of the flower enables us to assert its odour, the process which lies at the root of inference. Under the same head fall the products of the creative imagination of the poet or thinker, and even such cognitions as deal with knowledge of the supersensible as 'I know an atom'.[1]

While these two forms of supernormal knowledge stand in close relation, and represent fundamental realities, the third, born of ascetic power (*yoga-ja*) [2] is peculiar to the system, and derives its existence from its acceptance of the power of seers to perceive in an intuitive vision the whole of truth. The exact cause of this power is asserted to be the contact of mind and the merit which the ascetic has acquired. In the complete ascetic the perception is ever present in its perfection; at a lower stage of merit it requires concentration of mind to achieve it.

Of these three forms it is clear that the first has close affinities with the simpler early doctrine that every sense can perceive directly generality by the use of the second and third forms of normal contact according as the generality is that of a substance, or quality, or activity. The modern school, however, has advanced beyond this doctrine by insisting on the peculiarity of

[1] NVTP., commentary pp. 466, 160, 161; cf. *Padārtharatnamālā*, pp. 6–8, where God's perception appears as one distinct class.

[2] VS. ix. 1. 11, 12. Hence NSāra, pp. 2–4, with a division into determinate and indeterminate applicable to the lower form (*ayuktāvasthā*), and the indeterminate only in the *yuktāvasthā*; see ch. ix, § 2. Cf. SS. i. 90, 91; TR., pp. 59, 60 with commentary; NBh., p. 10; ÇV., p. 72; PBh., p. 72, has *ārṣa*. Cf. KKK. i. 29; NK. p. 197.

the form of contact and accentuating the part played by mind, which in the first form of supernormal knowledge frames the general concept, and in the second is responsible for the association of ideas which constitutes it. There need be little hesitation to ascribe to the influence of Buddhist logic with its insistence on the part of imagination in the framing of ideas the growing appreciation in the Nyāya-Vaiçeṣika of the active part played by mind in the development of knowledge.

The conception of the perception enjoyed by ascetics is also found in Dignāga and Dharmakīrti,[1] who provides for four classes of perception—sense perception, mental perception, self consciousness, and the perception of ascetics. The second and third classes in his division fall into the sphere of activity of mind in perception in the Nyāya-Vaiçeṣika theory. Dharmottara[2] adds that the perception of ascetics is essentially indeterminate.

[1] NB., p. 103. [2] NBT., pp. 7–16.

CHAPTER III

INFERENCE AND COMPARISON

1. *The Development of the Doctrine of Inference and Syllogism.*

THOUGH Gautama stands at the head of the school of Nyāya, on the essential doctrine which is normally associated with logical inquiries he has extremely little to tell us, but his testimony is the more valuable in that it shows the gradual development from mere dialectics to logic. Vātsyāyana stands on the same level as his master; in his exposition of the process of reasoning as described by Gautama,[1] he asserts that the process of reasoning is extremely subtle, hard to understand, and only to be mastered by one of much learning and ability. The admission is important, as it makes it easy to realize how difficult were found the first steps to understand the real nature of logical reasoning even when the formal procedure was well established as it was in Gautama's time.

Gautama[2] lays down that there are five members (*avayava*) of a syllogism, namely the proposition (*pratijñā*), the reason (*hetu*), the example (*udāharaṇa*), the application (*upanaya*), and the conclusion (*nigamana*). But Vātsyāyana reveals that others raised the number of members of the syllogism to ten, and it is probable enough that this represents a view prevalent before Gautama, and that his contribution to the de-

[1] i. 1. 34-8; NBh., p. 43. [2] i. 1. 32.

velopment of the topic included the removal of these members which in the conclusion have, as his commentator observes, no just place but pla a part in the discussion of a topic. These are the desire to know (*jijñāsā*), the doubt (*saṁçaya*), the belief in the possibility of a solution (*çakyaprāpti*), the purpose in view in attaining the conclusion (*prayojana*), and the removal of doubt (*saṁçaya-vyudāsa*). With its full ten members [1] we have before us in miniature the course of the kind of discussion which preceded the development of formal investigation of the logical process, and we can recognize the substantial improvement involved in omitting all that did not directly bear on the attainment of the conclusion.

In the later logic of the schools the scheme of Gautama is illustrated by the formal syllogism

The hill is fiery
Because it has smoke
Whatever is smoky is fiery, like a kitchen
So is this hill (smoky)
Therefore is the hill fiery.

The argument, therefore, rests on a general assertion of the concomitance (*vyāpti*) which exists between smoke and fire. But can this generalization be attributed to Gautama himself? The answer must assuredly be in the negative. The only principle laid down by Gautama is as follows [2]: The reason proves what is to be established through its similarity with the example, not through dissimilarity. The example has the characteristics of the thing because of its similarity with it, or has not the characteristics, because of dissimilarity.

[1] Cf. Bhadrabāhu's 10-member argument for Jainism; *Med. Log.*, pp. 6 ff., which, however, is very different.

[2] i 1. 34–6; Athalye, *TS.*, p. 279; Jacobi, NGWG. 1901, pp. 469, 477; Gāṅgānāth Jhā, NS. i. 385 n.; NBh., pp. 42, 43.

It is impossible to resist the conclusion that the third member of the syllogism is nothing more than an example, and that the original process knew no formulation of a general rule. This conclusion is supported not merely by the fact that the term example is only with great difficulty to be reconciled with a real general proposition, but by the form of the syllogism in its fourth and fifth members, which run in the original: 'Thus is this' (*tathā cāyam*), 'Therefore thus (is it)' (*tasmāt tathā*). The summing up in the application is expressly said by Gautama to be dependent on the example, and this is entirely borne out by the word 'thus' which can only be referred to the word 'as' in the example 'as a kitchen' (*yathā mahānasaḥ*) as the example originally ran.[1] Similarly the 'thus' in the fifth member of the syllogism is only to be explained as a reference to the 'as' of the third. In both cases, however, if the third member had the full form which it possesses in the later system, the reference would be unintelligible. With this conclusion accords perfectly the literary use of the syllogism: the last two members are not used, and the third appears merely in the reduced form of the example, while in Vātsyāyana, where, if it had existed, the general proposition would have been expected to appear it is never found; although he frames many syllogisms especially in Āhnika I of Book V in his commentary, the most that he does is to adopt the form: 'It is observed that the kitchen has smoke and also has fire'. The fact that reasoning can only be by means of a general proposition had thus not yet been appreciated in the school, for this reasoning still was from particular to particular by analogy in the manner approved by J. S. Mill. The origin of the syllogistic

[1] Originally presumably *tathāyam*.

form can then be recognized as arising from the effort to expound a proposition to another: the proposition is stated; the reason for it is asked; the ground is given; its validity is called in question; an example familiar and therefore cogent is adduced, and the similarity of the subject to the example is emphasized, and the conclusion is finally drawn. It is characteristic of the conservatism of the schools that the scheme was retained long after it had ceased to be the real form of the reasoning employed.

The other important contribution by Gautama to the theory of the syllogism is contained in the solitary aphorism[1] devoted to the conclusion, which thus fares badly compared with the members of the syllogism to which eight aphorisms are devoted, while fallacious reasons have six. There inference is declared to be dependent on perception (*tat-purvākam*), and to be of three kinds—*pūrvavat*, *çeṣavat*, and *sāmānyato dṛṣṭam*. These phrases are in themselves hopelessly obscure, and Vātsyāyana gives two explanations of fundamentally different character, a fact which may be interpreted either as indicating that even before Gautama there were different views prevalent in the school, or that there intervened a considerable interval between Gautama and his follower, during which conflicting interpretations of his aphorisms had come into vogue. According to the first of these interpretations inference *pūrvavat*, 'as formerly', is inference from cause to effect: thus from the sight of clouds it is inferred that rain will fall. Inference *çeṣavat* is from effect to cause, as when from the swelling river it is inferred that rain has fallen.

[1] i. 1. 5. Other views are given by Vācaspati and by Uddyotakara, *l. c.*, who prefers the idea that it is inference from something commonly seen, e. g. water from the presence of cranes; cf. SBH. viii. 3. The reading '*dṛṣṭam* is impossible.

Inference *sāmānyato dṛṣṭa* is illustrated by such a case, differing from the two previous as that in which from observing the different positions assumed in the course of the day by the sun we conclude by analogy of ordinary motion that it moves, although such motion is not open to our perception. The second explanation offered by Vātsyāyana makes *pūrvavat* an inference based on previous experience of the concomitance between two things, such as smoke and fire, which we still therefore accept later on when we no longer have the actual perception of the concomitance before our eyes. *Çeṣavat* is proof by elimination; thus sound can be proved to be a quality by showing that it must be either a substance, quality, or activity, and that it can be neither the first nor the last, and therefore must be the second. *Sāmānyato dṛṣṭa* is an inference in which, the relation between the reason and the consequence not being a matter of perception, something which is not perceptible is proved to exist by virtue of the abstract similarity with something else of the reason, a definition which is rendered more intelligible by the instance adduced which shows that the self or soul is proved to exist by the fact that desire, &c., are qualities, and that qualities must abide in some substance, namely, the self.

It is doubtful whether either of these theories has any claim to represent the true state of affairs, for in an obscure aphorism in a later part of his work[1] Gautama refers to objections to inference based on the fact that it sometimes misleads: thus to the argument that, if we see a river swollen, we infer that there has been rain may be objected that the cause may be an embankment;

[1] ii. 1. 37, 38; Jacobi, NGWG. 1901, p. 478; NBh., pp. 86, 87; NV., pp. 253–5. The answer insists on the specific character of the facts on which inference is based.

to the argument that, if we see ants carrying off their eggs, we infer there will be rain, may be objected that the real cause is that some one has damaged their nest, while, if we infer from the scream of a peacock the coming of rain, we may really be hearing a human cry, from which no such inference can be drawn. It can scarcely be denied that the three instances given must be deemed to correspond with the three forms of inference previously defined, and in that case it is clear that to Gautama inference *pūrvavat* is from the later to the earlier, from the effect to the cause, and that *vice versa* inference *çeṣavat* is from the earlier to the later, but the precise sense of *sāmānyato dṛṣṭa* must remain obscure, perhaps denoting similarity as a basis of inference. It is difficult to doubt, however, especially in view of the tradition and the use of the phrase later, though in a different context, by Praçastapāda, that the term applied to some abstract form of reasoning in which perception could not directly be applied.

This conclusion receives reinforcement from the further development given to the scheme at some later period, for which we have the solitary testimony of Vācaspati Miçra in his exposition of the Sāṁkhya system.[1] The decisive advance made is that the three forms are reduced to two classes: the first of these styled direct (*vīta*) comprises *pūrvavat* and *sāmānyato dṛṣṭa*; the second styled indirect (*avīta*) is comprised by *çeṣavat*. The latter is a means of proof by elimination, and is used to establish, for example, the Sāṁkhya doctrine of the pre-existence of the effect in the cause; the clay and the pot are one, because neither the relation of union or separation between them is possible; for, if they were different, then they must either be in a relation

[1] Bürk, VOJ. xv. 251–64; cf. the use of *vīta* and *avīta* in NV., p. 126; Vijñānabhikṣu, SS. i. 103.

of union like the pot and its contents, or in one of separation, like two mountains; neither of these conditions is the case; therefore clay and pot are one.[1] In the same way the existence of the soul is established by the argument that if it did not exist there would be no self consciousness, which is manifestly contrary to fact. Between the two forms of direct proof the difference consists in the nature of the knowledge which results, not in the process itself. In *pūrvavat* that knowledge is concerned with a general principle which is perceptible; in *sāmānyato dṛṣṭa* the peculiar nature of the knowledge involved lies in the fact that the general relation exists, but is not open to perception (*adṛṣṭasvalakṣaṇa-sāmānya* as opposed to *dṛṣṭasvalakṣaṇa-sāmānya*).[2] The form of inference *pūrvavat* is of minor importance to a system which is concerned with higher things than those of sense: the other form of direct proof is invaluable to establish such things as the existence of the soul. All that has the characteristics of joy, sorrow, and confusion, it is argued, is guided by another, like a chariot by the driver; all the world has those characteristics; therefore all the world has a ruler. Or, again, thus we can prove that the perception of colour requires sight; perception of colour requires an instrument, namely sight, for it is an activity; every activity requires an instrument, as felling trees requires an axe; perception of colour is an activity; therefore perception of colour requires an instrument. The skilled use made of the arguments is obvious, but it must remain doubtful to what school is to be ascribed the adaption to this end of the older division of the Nyāya. It is plain that it existed before Vācaspati Miçra, and it may be[3] that it was devised by some member of the Nyāya before it was

[1] Cf. NV., p. 234, which favours the early use of the argument.

[2] Cf. PSPM., pp. 47, 48.

[3] *Contra* Vācaspati on i. 1. 35.

adopted by some adherent of the Sāṁkhya. The failure of the doctrine to become accepted in either school is clearly remarkable, for it plainly offered a convenient means for giving effect to the traditional theory more explicitly than was done by the contending view of its significance. But, of course, it would be a mistake to seek to find in it the parallel of the distinction between induction and deduction in the terminology of formal logic[1]: the character of the reasoning corresponds strictly neither to deduction or induction, and the distinction between these two forms, in itself of no ultimate importance, is not reproduced in any form of the Indian doctrine. To Gautama it is clear the distinction could not possibly have occurred, content as he was with reasoning by analogy from particular instances.

The terminology of Gautama and of Vātsyāyana naturally reflects the stage of their researches: the normal terms of the later logic, *pakṣa*, *pakṣadharmatā*, *vyāpti*, *anvaya*, *vyatireka*, and *parāmarça*, are unknown to the Sūtra, and the term *sādhya*,[2] which later denotes the conclusion to be proved of the subject, has the not unnatural sense of the subject itself as that of which an attribute is to be established.

If the early Nyāya school had made little progress in the scientific examination of its subject, it is not surprising that Kaṇāda, whose interest was essentially in reality, has little to add to the doctrine of inference. The fact that he mentions in the chief passage in which he touches on the matter the technical term *avayava*,[3] which denotes a member of the syllogism, and in the

[1] Jacobi, *Gött. Gel. Anz.* 1895, p. 204; Garbe, *Sāṁkhya*, pp. 153, 154; Bürk, VOJ. xv. 262, 263; Max Müller, *Six Systems*, pp. 496–500; Suali, *Intr.*, p. 414.

[2] Cf. Gaṅgānātha Jhā, NS. i. 483; NBh., p. 41.

[3] ix. 2. 1, 2; cf. iii. 1. 7–14.

context has the meaning example, is a clear indication that he contemplated logical doctrine much as it stands in Gautama. His own interest is devoted to a statement of the real relations which afford the basis of the logical relation between reason and consequent. They are enumerated as cause and effect, conjunction, opposition, and inherence: inference can be from the effect to the cause or *vice versa*.

2. *Praçastapāda and Dignāga.*

In Praçastapāda's exposition [1] of Kaṇāda's doctrine of inference an advance of first rate importance is made. The attempt at an exhaustive enumeration of real relations as a basis for inference is abandoned in favour of the wider conception of concomitance (*sāhacarya* in his terminology, as opposed to the later *vyāpti*) between the ground (*sahacarita*, *avinābhūta*, later *vyāpta* or *vyāpya*) and the consequence. He does not, however, admit that this is an innovation; he claims that Kaṇāda's list of real relations is not intended to be complete but illustrative, every form of relation being meant to be included. His own doctrine is simple [2]; if anything is indissolubly connected with another in time or space it is legitimate for us, finding ourselves confronted with one of the two, to conclude the existence of the other also. The affirmative judgement is therefore analysed as follows: a man first takes cognizance of the connexion of fire and smoke expressed in the propositions, 'Where there is smoke, then there is fire; in the absence of fire there is no smoke', and when he sees smoke so as to have no doubt of its existence, he proceeds to conclude the presence of

[1] Jacobi, NGWG. 1901, pp. 479 ff.; Stcherbatskoi, *Muséon*, v. 133 ff.

[2] p. 205; cf. Kumārila, ÇV., pp. 202 ff.; NSāra, p. 5: *samyagavinābhāvena parokṣānubhavasādhanam anumānam*; PSPM., pp. 43 ff.

fire. There is no departure from the realism of Kaṇāda, but the precise list of real relations which he expounded has proved to be too limited to meet all needs, and a more general relationship has been propounded, which covers such cases as the appearance of one set of lunar mansions at the setting of the other, or the inference of the presence of water from the sight of cranes.

In close connexion with the new conception stands the account given by Praçastapāda of the conditions for the validity of the reason or middle term as a means of proof. In his account he cites[1] as a view of Kāçyapa the rule that 'that middle term is capable of producing a correct conclusion which is connected with the major, present in similar cases, and absent in dissimilar cases', a classification on which a theory of fallacies is based. This theory goes, it is certain, far beyond Kaṇāda who knows two kinds of fallacy only, but later tradition assumes that Kāçyapa[2] is a reference to Kaṇāda by his family name, and it may be regarded as proved that Praçastapāda intends us to accept the view set out as Kaṇāda's. What remains doubtful is whether in this he is deliberately attributing to the Sūtra a view, which he desired to read into it, or whether the process of change dates from before his time. It is a point in favour of the latter theory that he himself puts forward four classes of fallacy, but this is not of decisive weight. It is of importance, however, that, concomitantly with the doctrine of defects of the middle, appears one of defects of thesis and conclusion, a treatment which is almost peculiar in the school to Praçastapāda.

A further important innovation is the appearance of the distinction, wholly unknown to Gautama and Kaṇāda, of the process of inference for one self (*svaniç-*

[1] p. 200. [2] Cf. TR., p. 144.

citārtha) and for another (*parārtha*). The distinction is one which is accepted by the syncretist school, though not adopted by commentators on the Nyāya like Uddyotakara and Vācaspati Miçra, who remain faithful to the texts they explain. It is clear that for him the inference for oneself was the only true form of inference: after defining it, he proceeds to show that the other means of proof beside perception and inference allowed by the Nyāya and Mīmāṅsā schools have no claim to separate rank, and can be included in inference. This form of inference he divides into two classes,[1] in contradistinction from the three which the Nyāya set up, namely *dṛṣṭa* and *sāmānyato dṛṣṭa*. The former is the form of inference, when the middle term and conclusion[2] are not heterogeneous; the latter is the form when they are heterogeneous, and the result depends on an idea common to the reason and the conclusion. The distinction, though far from clearly expressed, is evidently between matters of inference which fall under the sphere of sense perception, and those which escape that test, and therefore must rest on abstract reasoning. The definite acceptance of this doctrine by the Vaiçeṣika stands in harmony with the acceptance in place of the crude realism of Kaṇāda of the wider idea of logical connexion, with a more vaguely conceived physical counterpart.

The inference for another is definitely identified with the five-member syllogism, which in Gautama forms a category, and is not classified formally as a means of proof, though inference itself is so classed. The names

[1] p. 205; so NSāra, pp. 5, 93 ff.

[2] Jacobi (NGWG. 1901, p. 481) and Suali (*Intr.*, p. 417) render *prasiddhasādhyayoḥ* as referring to the subject and example, but this is contrary to the analogy of *sāmānyato dṛṣṭa* in the Nyāya: cf. *apratyakṣe liṅgaliṅginoḥ saṁbandhe*, NBh., p. 14; cf. ÇV., p. 195, vv. 92, 93; in pp. 201 ff. the double division is discussed; TR., pp. 81, 82; PSPM., pp. 47, 48.

of the five members, however, differ from those given in the Nyāya school. They appear as *pratijñā*, *apadeça*, *nidarçana*, *upasaṁdhāna*, and *pratyāmnāya*, the first alone therefore coinciding with the Nyāya names. It is not probable that the new terms were the invention of Praçastapāda; the second, the name for the reason, is given by Kaṇāda[1] himself. The different terminology may be interpreted as denoting some measure of independence of the Nyāya in the development of logic in the Vaiçeṣika school, but too much stress cannot be laid on this conclusion; the influence of the Nyāya is plain on Praçastapāda; he divides the example into the two cases of similarity and dissimilarity,[2] which precisely reproduces the older division of the Nyāya and follows its precise terminology. But the treatment shows one great distinction which is the inevitable result of the new conception of invariable concomitance. In the third member of the syllogism the principle is expressly set out, and the example sinks to the level of an illustration, though not until the last days of the schools was the further step taken and the example omitted as superfluous.

With these changes the whole system of the Nyāya appears transformed; what was a mere technical discipline has been changed into a deliberate effort to formulate the principles involved in inference, and the result achieved is largely adhered to by the following authors of both schools. As yet, however, the terminology of Praçastapāda differs largely from the later norm: nothing shows this more clearly than his avoidance[3] of the terms *vyāpti*, *vyāpaka*, and *vyāpya*, or *pakṣa*, *vipakṣa* and

[1] iii. 1. 14.

[2] This the Mīmāṅsā rejects, PSPM., p. 51; ÇD., p. 44.

[3] Jacobi, NGWG. 1901, p. 482; Stcherbatskoi, *Muséon*, v. 152, n. 3, 155, n. 2.

sapakṣa, though the ideas with which later these terms are connected are, as has been seen, familiar to him; *anvaya* and *vyatireka* occur once[1] each only; the doctrine, later a commonplace, of *kevalānvayin* and *kevalavyatirekin* is not accepted, and *sādhya* is still sometimes[2] used for the subject of the syllogism.

What, it is natural to ask, were the causes which produced so great a development in the analysis of the logical process? The assumption that the growth of logical doctrine took place without external influence within the school itself is *prima facie* natural, and has been strongly maintained. But there are substantial arguments which may be adduced to prove that the contrary was the case, and that the new development of Indian logic was directly caused by the influence of the Yogācāra or idealist school of Buddhism, and in particular of the logical writings of Dignāga. That scholar directed against Vātsyāyana a strong attack, to which a reply in due course came from Uddyotakara; to Uddyotakara an answer was given by Dharmakīrti, whose *Nyāyabindu* expresses the views of Dignāga, and who was fortunate to find a commentator of capacity in Dharmottara whose *Nyāyabindu-ṭīkā* is happily extant along with the work on which it comments. Dignāga's own works[3] are preserved, so far as they are extant, in Thibetan translations: among them were the *Pramāṇasamuccaya* with a commentary by the author himself; the *Nyāyapraveça*;[4] the *Hetucakrahamaru*[5]; the *Alambanaparīkṣā*, with his own commentary, and the *Pramāṇaçāstrapraveça*, and enough is known of them to confirm the view that the *Nyāyabindu* expresses with adequate

[1] p. 251. [2] NK., p. 203; so NB., p. 104.

[3] Vidyābhūṣaṇa, *Med. Log.*, pp. 80 ff.; on Dharmakīrti, pp. 103 ff.; on Dharmottara, pp. 130 ff. Cf. Pathak, JBRAS. xix. 47-57.

[4] JASB. iii. 609-17; but see Ui, p. 68, n. 2. [5] JASB. iii. 627-32.

accuracy his tenets. Some of his precise arguments are also given in Uddyotakara's commentary, the attribution to Dignāga being vouched for by Vācaspati Miçra, so that it is possible to form a definite view of his contributions to logical theory.

The date of Dignāga is obviously of the greatest importance for this question, but it is involved in obscurity. The tradition of his life preserved in the Thibetan Lama Tārānātha's History of Buddhism ascribes his place of birth to Kāñci, now Conjeeveram in the Madras Presidency, and makes him the son of a Brahman. Taught by Nāgadatta of the Vātsīputrīya sect, he became expert in the doctrines of the Hīnayāna school of Buddhism, but later acquired from his teacher Vasubandhu, the brother of Asañga, knowledge of the doctrines of the Mahāyāna school and in special of the idealism (Vijñānavāda) of which Asañga and Vasubandhu were the leading representatives. He defeated his opponents in disputes at Nālandā, travelled widely in Mahārāṣṭra and Orissa, and finally died in the latter country. If the record has any claim to truth, it enables us to assign to Dignāga a date shortly after the *floruit* of his teachers, and in fact on the strength of arguments, which seem to make A. D. 480 a plausible date for Vasubandhu, Dignāga has often been assigned to the early part of the sixth century A. D.[1] This view, however, can hardly now be maintained, for there are strong reasons to suppose that Vasubandhu can more safely be dated in the first half of the fourth century A.D.[2] so that Dignāga may have flourished before A. D. 400. A famous verse of the *Meghadūta*[3] has been interpreted by the ingenuity

[1] Takakusu, JRAS. 1905, pp. 1 ff.

[2] N. Peri, *Bull. de l'École française d'Extrême-Orient*, xi. 355 ff.; cf. Keith JRAS. 1914, p. 1091.

[3] i, 14.

of commentators as a reference to the logician's heavy hand, and, if the tradition is accepted, it would tend to confirm the date suggested for Dignāga, since Kālidāsa is more probably to be dated at the end of the fourth than of the fifth century. But there is no cogent ground for accepting the tradition. It is, however, clear that, so far as chronological grounds go, there is nothing to prevent the supposition that Praçastapāda was indebted for his system largely to Dignāga, whose fame is attested not merely by the attacks of the Nyāya school, but by the onslaught of Kumārila Bhaṭṭa, the famous Mīmānsist, and his commentator Pārthasārathi Miçra, and the criticisms of Jain writers like Prabhācandra and Vidyānātha.

The *Pramāṇasamuccaya* in his treatment of topics already presents a close similarity to Praçastapāda. It is divided into six chapters, the first dealing with perception; the second with inference for oneself; the third with inference for another; the fourth with the three characteristics of the reason or middle term and the claim of comparison to be a separate means of proof, which is disallowed; in the fifth verbal testimony is similarly rejected; and in the last the parts of a syllogism are treated of. The *Hetucakrahamaru* contains an interesting examination of the different forms of syllogism with a view to determine which are valid, and the *Nyāyapraveça* illustrates fully the different forms of fallacy.

The essence of the doctrine of Dignāga is the exposition of a theory of logic, in modification of the established doctrine of the Nyāya, to harmonize with the fundamental idealism of the school of Asañga. The views of Asañga were historically a modification of the extreme scepticism and nihilism of the doctrine of vacuity (*çūnyavāda*), which is associated with the name of

Nāgārjuna.[1] While Nāgārjuna deduced from the utter incompatibility of our ideas that there was no reality either beyond them or in them, the new doctrine was compelled to admit that so radical a doctrine contradicted experience too widely to be acceptable, and it fell back on the theory that, while there were no realities external to the mind, nevertheless thought itself was not unreal, though in accordance with the essential tenets of Buddhism they could not admit the existence of a soul or self. This thought for them assumed two forms: consciousness proper (*ālaya-vijñāna*), which lasts until the individual reaches Nirvāṇa, and which serves in lieu of the substantial soul, and the thoughts of the individual about things (*pravṛtti-vijñāna*).[2] It seems, however, that Dignāga's[3] logic went beyond this standpoint: his doctrine of perception manifests elements which are not in harmony with the view that all reality is thought. As has been mentioned, he distinguished perception sharply and definitely from imagination, and declared that what it gave was what was without name, class, &c., an idea which recurs in the indeterminate perception of the schools. Whereas on a strictly idealistic theory in the ultimate issue perception should not have remained distinct from other mental processes,[4] he appears to have held the view that in it man came into contact with a reality which though lasting but an instant (*kṣaṇa*) was in truth real (*vastu, paramārthasat*), but at the same time, because of its momentary character, was

[1] *Mādhyamika Sūtra* (Bibl. Buddh. iv); M. Walleser, *Die mittlere Lehre des Nāgārjuna*, Heidelberg, 1911, 1912.

[2] Asañga, *Mahāyānasūtrālaṁkāra* (ed. and tr. S. Lévi, Paris, 1907, 1911), ii. 20; SBE. xxxiv. 403, 427; de la Vallée Poussin, *Bouddhisme*, p 202.

[3] Stcherbatskoi, *Muséon*, v. 162–4; NBT., pp. 4, 14, 20; above, ch. ii, § 1.

[4] SSS. iv. 2. 5–9; ÇV., pp. 121 ff., 169 ff.; *Mahāyān.*, xi. 1 ff., 15 ff.; i. 18.

never knowable. For the actual formation of any idea, to the datum of perception or sensation there fell to be added the working of imagination (*vikalpa*), a conception which is, certainly not without justice, to be compared with the Kantian doctrine. In a similar strain Dharmakīrti develops a doctrine of perception which he defines, like Dignāga, as distinct from imagination, but qualifies as without error (*abhrānta*).[1] In perception there is a two-fold object, that which is immediately apprehended, or contributed by the datum (*grāhya*), and that which results from the operation of thought (*niçcaya*) set to work by the force of the apprehension. The first corresponds to the momentary element, the second to the series of momentary impressions (*kṣaṇa-saṁtāna*) as they are worked up by thought into a unity, and this is what is known, not the momentary impression which lies beyond knowledge.[2] According to the proximity or remoteness of an object of perception the perception varies: this is its peculiar characteristic (*sva-lakṣaṇa*), and proves it to be a reality (*paramārthasat*), and it shows that it possesses practical efficiency. In this view there is further advance towards an assertion of the reality of something beyond thought, but the position is not inconsistent with that of Dignāga;[3] and it is clearly analogous to the view of the Vaibhāṣikas, who appear in the *Sarvadarçanasaṁgraha* as adopting the terminology of Dharmakīrti.

For Dignāga, therefore, the whole of knowledge, despite its contact at one point with an unknowable reality, is made up of ideas involved in both perception

[1] NB., p. 103; cf. on *kalpanā*; NV., pp. 43–5; TR., pp. 60, 61; above, ch. ii, § 1; SBNT., pp. 32–6

[2] NBT., p. 16.

[3] Cf. Jacobi, JAOS. xxxi. 8. n. 1, whose view that the *kṣaṇasaṁtāna* is *paramārthasat* seems to be untenable; *svalakṣaṇa* is not the *saṁtāna*, NBT., p. 17; NV., p. 44.

and inference: these ideas are the product of our mental activity (*prāpaṇaçakti, prāpaka-vyāpāra*),[1] and are not created by any external cause. In a passage happily preserved for us by Vācaspati Miçra[2] he denies emphatically that there can be any real thing indissolubly connected which can be the logical ground of anything, since the relationship of logical reason and consequent does not depend on external reality, but on the relationship of attribute and subject which is a creation of the mind. The ideas thus obey laws of connexion not imposed by reality, but by the action of our own thought (*buddhy-ārūḍha, niçcayārūḍha*[3]), and thus *a priori* in character. The nature of these laws is further made explicit by the division of the syllogism on the basis of the relations of identity, cause, and negation. It is impossible to ignore the principle underlying this division: it corresponds to a classification of judgement based on the relation of subject and attribute, first into positive (*vidhi*) and negative (*anupalabdhi* = *pratiṣedha*), while the positive judgement is then divided according as it is based on identity, i. e. is analytic (*svabhāvānumāna*), or is based on causality, empiric (*kāryānumāna*). Reduced to a Kantian form we can recognize, without too much pressing, the ideas *a priori* of substance and attribute, being, non-being, identity, and cause, a list which has sufficient affinity with the Kantian categories to be more than a mere curiosity of speculation. All

[1] NBT., p. 18; cf. p. 16: *saṁtana eva ca pratyakṣasya prāpaṇīyaḥ.*

[2] *sarvo 'yam anumānānumeyabhāvo buddhyārūḍhena dharmadharmibhāvena na bahiḥsattvam apekṣate*, NVT., p. 127; with °*nyāyena* in *Kāçikā* on ÇV. *Nirālambanavāda*, 167, 168 (JBRAS. xviii. 230): Kumārila's reference is clear. For the Sautrāntika and Vaibhāṣika views see SDS., pp. 14ff., 18; SSS. iv. 3. 1–7; 4. 18, 19. The parallelism with the former (de la Vallée Poussin, *Muséon*, ii. 67) seems less than with the latter, who appropriate Dharmakīrti's definition of perception; cf. NBT., pp. 16–20.

[3] NBT., p. 30. Cf. Berkeley, *Siris*, § 305.

our ideas or the objects which we know are indissolubly linked with one another, since they are either inferable from them by means of analysis, or related as cause and effect. The real relations between the unknown things which lie beneath our knowledge are indifferent to us, and have no part in forming our ideas.[1]

The division of the syllogism in this way is not recorded of Dignāga and by Sureçvara[2] is expressly attributed to Dharmakīrti. This view is confirmed by a passage from Dharmakīrti quoted by Çrīdhara,[3] where it is said: 'The rule according to which there exists an indissoluble connexion between ideas or objects does not arise from observation or non-observation, but from the laws of causality and identity, which have a universal application.' There is, of course, nothing inconsistent here with the view of Dignāga, which rather acquires greater precision by the new matter thus added.

The theory of the ideal nature of the indissoluble connexion which lies at the base of reasoning thus presented stands in close relation to the idealist view of the world of the Yogācāra school, and therefore there is *a priori* no ground for supposing that the idea was borrowed by Dignāga from Praçastapāda or from one of his predecessors. In truth it is obviously easier given an idealistic hypothesis to conceive an indissoluble connexion which it lies in the power of the mind to impose than to arrive at such a result from the standpoint of realism. How can it possibly be said on the basis of our imperfect experience that things are indissolubly connected?

[1] Stcherbatskoi, *Muséon*, v. 144. Cf. SDS., p. 6; Kant, *Kritik der reinen Vernunft*[1], pp. 80 ff., 235 ff.

[2] *Bṛhadāraṇyakavārttika*, ch. vi; Pathak, JBRAS. xviii. 92; so Munisundara, ibid. xix. 57. It is criticized in TR., pp. 82–4.

[3] NK., p. 207; *Muséon*, ii. 56; TR., p. 82; SDS., p. 5; Deussen's rendering (*Allgem. Gesch.* I. iii. 204) is impossible; cf. *Padārtharatnamālā*, p.

Praçastapāda does not attempt to answer this problem: the theory of a peculiar variety of perception (*jñāna-lakṣaṇa*) is a later effort to meet the need of an explanation of how a universal connexion can be assumed from experience. *A priori*, therefore, it is more reasonable to assume that Praçastapāda owes the principle to a school in which it had a natural right to exist.[1] The argument[2] against this view that, had the Buddhists invented for themselves the concept of indissoluble connexion they would never have set up the real categories of identity, causality, and non-existence, which on the other hand are comparable with the older Vaiçeṣika list of Kaṇāda, loses all its force when the true nature of these divisions is realized; moreover, the argument is based on ignorance of the fact that the doctrine as it first appears in Dignāga has not this addition.

There is, however, positive evidence that the introduction of the idea of indissoluble connexion was recognized in the Nyāya school as due to Dignāga. Uddyotakara[3] carefully refutes a doctrine which attributes the name of syllogism to the demonstration of something as indissolubly connected with something else by one who has certain knowledge. Uddyotakara objects that, as in the Buddhist view everything is indissolubly related to everything else, the knowledge in question of a thing as indissolubly connected is no more than knowledge *sans* phrase, and not inference. Now not only have we the assurance of Vācaspati[4] that Uddyotakara's criticisms are usually directed against Dignāga, but he actually assigns the doctrine impugned to that authority,

[1] Stcherbatskoi, *Muséon*, v. 134-45.

[2] Jacobi, NGWG. 1901, p. 483.

[3] NV., p. 56. Cf. the Sāṁkhya definition, SS. i. 100; an older definition is given in NV., pp. 59, 60.

[4] NVT., pp. 1, 127; NVTP., p. 28.

and explains that it stands in close relation to his theory of knowledge, which admits as the basis of reasoning the power which the understanding has to create its own objects, distinguishing in them the aspect of subject and attribute, while not dealing with real relations. It is significant that here and elsewhere Uddyotakara [1] admits that there are exceptions to the rule of indissoluble union even in the case of smoke and fire, since not only does fire occur without smoke, as is generally admitted, but also smoke without fire, which contradicts the fundamental assumption of the stock syllogism of the schools. In yet another place Uddyotakara,[2] dealing with inference from effect to cause, discusses and rejects the idea of indissoluble connexion, and Vācaspati [3] again attributes the doctrine to Dignāga, and emphasizes its accordance with the Buddhist theory of knowledge. There is also a significant verbal similarity in the account of indissoluble connexion given by Praçastapāda [4] with that of Dignāga as reported by Uddyotakara.

In Dignāga [5] and in Dharmakīrti [6] we find clearly expressed the three conditions which must be fulfilled by the middle term if the syllogism is to be correct, the conditions being further used for the purpose of explaining the classes of defective middle term. We find the fact recognized clearly in Uddyotakara,[7] who criticizes the doctrine evidently, as Vācaspati [8] assures us, as he found it in Dignāga himself. The formula runs, 'The middle term must be present in the subject, also in similar cases, and be absent in dissimilar cases.' The

[1] NV., p. 53; cf. Sureçvara in JBRAS. xviii. 92, v. 2.

[2] NV., pp. 52–4.

[3] NVT., pp. 120–2.

[4] p. 205; *prasiddhasamayasya* (*prasiddhāvinābhāvasya*, NK.) = *tadvidaḥ* (i. e. *nāntarīyakavidaḥ*, NV., p. 56).

[5] *Med. Log.*, pp. 91 ff.

[6] NB., pp. 111 ff.

[7] NV., pp. 58, 59.

[8] NVT., p. 127.

critic objects that the language should have made it clear that the middle term must be present in the whole extent of the subject, and not in part alone; that, while it must only appear in similar cases, it need not appear in each of them; and that it must be absent from all dissimilar cases. The nuance indicated is expressed in Sanskrit by the word *eva*, and Vācaspati assures us, what would otherwise be plausible, that the formulation of the doctrine of the three conditions has been affected by the Buddhist doctrine of the negative or rather relative signification (*apoha*)[1] of words. On this view a word has not the power (*çakti*) attributed to it by the Mīmāṅsā to communicate to objects the verbal form under which we conceive them, or to express the real nature of anything: it merely serves to distinguish it from other things, and in a proposition, in view of the necessity of making clear the precise implication of terms, it is usual to append *eva* to the word to which special significance attaches as a mode of reminding the hearer or reader of the need of attending to the implication. Now it is recorded that in this special case Dharmakīrti criticized Dignāga, apparently because the latter held that one *eva* was sufficient to bring out the full implication of the rule regarding the three conditions of the middle term, while Dharmakīrti held that in each case the important term must be stressed in this manner, and in face of this fact Uddyotakara's criticism reveals clearly its Buddhist origin, which is the less surprising since we now know that Dharmakīrti and the Uddyotakara were contemporaries.

Yet a further proof of the dependence of Praçastapāda on Dignāga may be derived from the fact that the

[1] Ratnakīrti, *Apohasiddhi*, SBNT., pp. 1–19; Stcherbatskoi, *Muséon*, v. 105-7; ÇV., pp. 295–328; NK., pp. 317–20; *Ātmatattvaviveka*, pp. 35, 48, 51; NVT., pp. 340 ff., NBT., p. 74; NV., pp. 324 ff.

distinction of reasoning for oneself and reasoning for another, which gives syllogism, is present in Dignāga, and is expressly stated by Dharmottara in his commentary on Dharmakīrti[1] to have been introduced by him, and to stand in relation to his theory of the function of language in knowledge. Denying as Dignāga did the authority of either the sacred scriptures or even of a master, he reduces the authority of verbal testimony to its true character. In the *Pramāṇasamuccaya*[2] the rejection of verbal testimony as a separate and independent source of knowledge is based on the argument: does credible testimony mean that the person averring it is credible, or that the testimony is credible? If the former, it is mere case of inference from the credibility of the speaker: in the latter, it is a case of perception. In the work of Dharmottara[3] the same view of the credibility of testimony is emphasized in a new form; testimony is a product of the true external fact, with which it is immediately connected. Thus the syllogism, in so far as we draw from it true knowledge, is not a source of knowledge by reason of its words, but by reason of the facts on which these words rest: a syllogism, therefore, is a source of knowledge only in a metaphoric sense (*aupacārika*), for it is the facts, not the words, which are the source of knowledge. Praçastapāda's debt to Dignāga in this regard is clear, despite his slight change in terminology,[4] which may legitimately be attributed to a desire to conceal his borrowing, for he retains in practice, if not in theory, verbal testimony as a separate means of proof, while adopting the principle

[1] NBT., pp. 46, 47.

[2] *Med. Log.*, pp. 88, 89; criticized in NV., p. 63. Cf. NSāra, commentary p. 94.

[3] NBT., pp. 63-5: *kāryaliṅgajam anumānam pramānaṁ çābdam*: cf. PBh., p. 213.

[4] *svaniçcitārtha* in lieu of *svārtha*; NSāra, p. 3, has *svārtha*.

of distinction between reasoning for oneself and reasoning for another, which in truth rests on the fact that verbal testimony is no true means of proof at all.

The same dependence of Praçastapāda on the Buddhist logic can be traced in detail in the doctrine of fallacies, and it is significant that he alone accepts the fallacies of the subject and of the example which play a marked part in the logic of Dignāga. Nor is it fanciful to ascribe to the same influence the adoption by Praçastapāda of the form of exposition which he uses, and which makes no effort in the manner of Vātsyāyana to follow the order of the text of the original Sūtra. So deeply indebted was Praçastapāda to Dignāga that to ascribe this point also to his influence is natural and convincing.

To preserve the theory of the priority in invention of the conception of invariable connexion to the Vaiçeṣika school we should be compelled to postulate its appearance in that school at some period before Dignāga, and assume that the tradition of its discovery had been lost so early that Vācaspati Miçra found no trace of it in the works which he could use in compiling his treatise on the Nyāya. The conjecture, in the absence of any positive evidence, would be unsatisfactory, and the originality of Dignāga is supported by the fact that we can trace in his immediate predecessors an interest in the problem which suggests that it formed the subject of investigation to an extent likely to result in the precise formulation of the true doctrine. Thus from Chinese sources we know that Maitreya, who is stated to have been a teacher of Asaṅga, framed the syllogism as follows:

Sound is non-eternal
Because it is a product
Like a pot, but not like ether
A product like a pot is non-eternal
Whereas an eternal thing like ether is not a product.

Asaṅga himself framed the fourth and fifth of these clauses differently so as to run:

Because a pot is a product, it is non-eternal; so is sound because it is a product

Therefore we know sound is non-eternal.[1]

To Maitreya, therefore, the argument was simply from instance to instance: the form accepted by Asaṅga, though it still is based on the example, shows a clear effect to attain the general principle which alone is effective as a reason. In Dignāga's[2] formulation the syllogism runs:

The hill is fiery

Because it has smoke

All that has smoke is fiery, like a kitchen, and whatever is not fiery has no smoke, like a lake.

The retention by Dignāga of the homogeneous and heterogeneous examples is interesting: it recalls the rule of Gautama, and is re-echoed by Praçastapāda.[3]

A further step is taken by Dharmakīrti,[4] whose exposition in the *Nyāyabindu* is divided into three parts only in lieu of the six of the *Pramāṇasamuccaya*, namely, perception, inference for oneself, and inference for another. He maintains that the example is no real part of the syllogism, since it is implicit in the middle term. In the reasoning 'The hill is fiery, because it is smoky, like a kitchen', the term 'smoky', which implies fire, includes a kitchen and other smoky things, and the example is all but unnecessary. Nevertheless the example has so far value in that it points out in a

[1] *Med. Log.*, pp. 74 ff.; Sugiura, *Hindu Log.*, pp, 30 ff.

[2] *Med. Log.*, pp. 95, 96. The thing to be proved in his view is the hill as possessed of fire, a view rejected in NV., pp. 52–4, in favour of smoke qualified by fire; so PSPM., p. 45, as opposed to Kumārila.

[3] How far Vasubandhu anticipated Dignāga's doctrine of *vyāpti* does not appear from our scanty information; *Med. Log.*, p. 77.

[4] *Med. Log.*, pp. 114. 115.

particular and therefore more impressive manner what is implied in the general proposition.

With Dignāga and Dharmakīrti the progress in logic made by the Buddhists appears to have come to a head: it was the logic of Dignāga which was carried to China by the famous pilgrim, Hiuen-tsang, who acquired it in the course of his long stay (A.D. 630–45) in India, and introduced into Japan by a Japanese pupil of his, the monk Dohshoh.[1] In India the Nyāya school was driven by the necessity of making headway against the new doctrine of the heretical school to revive the study of logic, the movement taking form in the elaborate commentary of Uddyotakara, in which he sought to refute Dignāga. The work, however, is not confined to this end: it takes into account, as was inevitable, the views of Praçastapāda on logic, and it marks a definite stage in the process of amalgamation of the schools. Dharmakīrti answered Uddyotakara, but after him no new element of vital importance appears to have been introduced into the study.[2] The questions which have occupied the earlier writers were the subject of minute examination: difficulties real and fancied were developed and explained in abundance, and the doctrine received in Gañgeça's *Tattvacintāmaṇi* its final form save in detail. It was in this shape that the doctrine passed into the syncretist school of Nyāya-Vaiçeṣika; all of whom save Çivāditya accepted the Nyāya logic as the basis of their system without substantial change.

[1] Sugiura, *Hindu Log.*, pp. 38 ff.

[2] Dignāga and Dharmakīrti were much criticized in other schools, e. g. by Kumārila and Sureçvara. The Mīmāṅsā school in logic and metaphysics alike shows abundant traces of Nyāya-Vaiçeṣika influence. Prabhākara's date is unfortunately uncertain; the tradition (e.g. SSS. i. 19; vii. 15) of his posteriority to Kumārila is unplausible; PSPM., pp. 11–17. Uddyotakara (e. g. NV., pp. 55, 56) criticizes views like his on inherence (PSPM., pp. 89, 100) but not so as to prove his priority.

3. *The Final Form of the Doctrine of Inference.*

Inference in the normal definition of the modern school[1] is the proximate cause of the inferential judgement or knowledge (*anumiti*), and this knowledge is of a special character, distinct from that attained in perception. To Buddhist logic[2] the distinction lies in the fact that perception gives, though inexpressible in words, the peculiar character (*sva-lakṣaṇa*) of the momentary object, while inference deals with the ideal generality (*sāmānya-lakṣaṇa*), but this view is not, as has been suggested, that of the Nyāya. In the strict sense of the term, as Uddyotakara[3] points out, the peculiarity of the object is inexpressible, for all the terms denote at once generality, individuality, and form. Moreover,[4] the doctrine of perception insists that in it we grasp at once generality and individuality in the determinate form, which is the only one known to us, and all means of proof give us knowledge of generality, particularity, and that having it. The distinction between the knowledge we obtain by perception and that given by inference rests, therefore, on the fact that in perception we know the individual in its concrete detail as well as its generality, &c., in inference we deal with generality, &c., in an abstract form alone; we have on the one hand before us the crackling fire; on the other hand we infer the existence of fire past, present, or future as a generality connected

[1] TC. ii. 1 ff.; SP., §§ 142-53; TA., pp. 17-19; TB., pp. 31-42; TK., pp. 10-12; TS., §§ 44-51; BP. 66-70, 142, 143; TR., pp. 65-70.

[2] NB., p. 103; *Madh. Vṛtti*, pp. 59, 60, 261; Jacobi, NGWG. 1901, p. 462, n. 2.

[3] NV., pp. 44, 45.

[4] NV., p. 5; NVT., pp. 12-14; NVTP., pp. 139-50; PBh., p. 186; NK., pp. 189, 190; ṢDST. 67; cf. ÇV., pp. 282-93, 332-4; PSPM., p. 95.

with smoke, and the precise detail of the fire which causes the smoke never appears to us.

As the nature of the knowledge obtained by inference differs from that gained in perception, so the inferential process differs from the process of perception. An inferential judgement is defined as the knowledge which is due to reflection or consideration (*parāmarça*), and consideration in its turn is defined as the knowledge that the reason is an attribute of the subject and is invariably connected with the conclusion which is to be proved of the subject. The definition of consideration is of first importance in the doctrine of inference, and this is emphasized in an early doctrine recorded in Uddyotakara,[1] which defines inference as consideration or reflection regarding the reason (*liṅga-parāmarça*). The process as explained by Keçava Miçra is as follows: the first stage in the operation leading to inferential judgement is the perception of the invariable connexion between smoke and fire, a result due to frequent observation of the concurrence of the two in a kitchen or elsewhere. Then smoke is observed arising on the mountain. Thirdly, through remembrance of the relation which perception has established between the smoke and the fire, there arises reflection in the form that there is on the mountain smoke, which is always accompanied by fire, upon which supervenes the inferential judgement, 'The mountain is fiery'.

The value of the conception of inference as a mental process is obvious, and is enforced with minute detail by the school. Merely to set the two premisses, 'The mountain is smoky; Smoke is always accompanied by fire', side by side, would amount only to the assertion of

[1] NV., p. 47; cf. Udayana in TR., p. 65; TB., pp. 31, 35, 36; or *tṛtīyaliṅga*°, the first and second stages being knowledge of smoke in the distance, then knowledge of the concomitance, NSM., p. 88.

a perception actually present and the result of past perception.[1] The second premiss again must be made an attribute inherent in the first, if there is to be any result, for the middle term or reason must be brought into direct connexion with the subject[2] to be proved, if there is to be any inference. It is not enough that the invariable concomitance should be made an attribute of the reason, as in fact of course it is true that the reason and consequence are invariably connected, but the mere fact is not enough for inference. There the knowledge of the concomitance must be simultaneous with the perception of the smoke on the mountain : in other terms, the concomitance must be an attribute of the perception of the smoke on the mountain and not of the smoke in itself. Similarly, from another point of view, stress is laid on the fact that the subject (*pakṣa* in the new terminology) cannot be a thing *per se*: it must be something regarding which there is a desire to establish something else (*siṣādhayiṣā*), for only then does it come within the sphere of inference. The desire may of course be for one's own sake or for the sake of some one else, and it does not matter that we may have the same knowledge from some other source, as long as we have the desire to establish it by inference.

This recognition of the mental activity of inferring[3] as the decisive feature in inference leads to an important discussion between the older and later schools as to the precise factor which is to be deemed the proximate cause of inferred knowledge, or in other words what precisely is to be deemed the inference as a process. The answer obviously depends in part on the meaning assigned to

[1] Cf. TS., § 44, with Athalye's note.

[2] *pakṣadharmatā*; cf. TC. ii. 407-41; NSāra, p. 6. The reason is styled *liṅga*, *hetu*, or *sādhana*.

[3] Cf. the modern doctrine, e.g. Bosanquet, *Logic*, Book II, ch. vii.

proximate cause (*karaṇa*). Its sense in the normal use of language is instrument, and therefore one definition of *karaṇa* makes it to be a cause possessing an activity (*vyāpāravat kāraṇam*), that is to say a cause which, by means of its function or activity, produces a result. Accepting this definition two interpretations of what is the real cause of inferential knowledge are possible. In the first place, the view, which is more or less clearly expressed by Kaṇāda[1] and emphasized in his commentators, that the cause is the reason or middle term may be held, subject to the correction that the knowledge of the reason (*liñga-jñāna*) must be substituted for the reason (*liñga*). This view is, however, rejected for the obvious reason that mere knowledge of the reason produces no inference: it is only knowledge of the reason as existing in the subject and invariably concomitant with the consequence. In the stock example, mere knowledge of smoke as such or as existing on the mountain yesterday is no ground for the inference of fire on the mountain to-day: the smoke is gone and cannot, therefore, since it has ceased to be, become the instrumental cause of anything. The other alternative which is the view of the older Nyāya, followed by Viçvanātha,[2] is to treat the knowledge of the invariable concomitance as the proximate cause, assigning to it as its function the reflection (*parāmarça*), which in that case must be regarded as consisting of the knowlẹdge of the presence of the reason in the subject (*pakṣadharmatājñāna*). The more recent theory is that adopted by Çivāditya,[3]

[1] iii. 1. 14; ix. 2. 1; PBh., p. 201; TA., p. 17; cf. *liñgadarçana* as one view in NV., p. 47; conceivably a reference to PSPM., p. 48.

[2] BP. 66; cf. *liñgaliñgisaṁbandhasmṛti*, or that aided by perception of the concomitance, as views in NV., p. 47.

[3] § 146; see NV., pp. 47, 48. when this aided by. recollection of concomitance (*liñgaliñgisaṁbandha*) is accepted.

Gañgeça,[1] Annam Bhaṭṭa[2] and Laugākṣi Bhāskara, who adopt the view that the cause is that which immediately and always precedes the effect: the reflection therefore which regards the middle term as an attribute of the subject and invariably concomitant with the consequence is, therefore, the cause of inferential knowledge, a view which is supported by an appeal to the facts of language: the term instrument applies naturally to some material thing which can possess an activity, not to knowledge whether of the reason or of the invariable concomitance.

The view, however, which thus insisted on a mental activity as the essence of inference was not accepted universally; the Mīmāṅsā adopted a view more akin to the concept of formal logic which sets the major and minor premisses side by side without insisting on the mental act of combination. But this view the Nyāya decidedly[3] objected to, and definitely rejected, on the simple, but conclusive, ground that the mere setting together of propositions gave no result, and that equally the memory of the concomitance and the perception of the presence of the reason in the subject remained fruitless, unless they coalesced in a single mental act.

The essence of inference therefore rests on the invariable concomitance (*vyāpti*) between the reason or middle term (*vyāpya*) and the consequence or major (*vyāpaka*), terms which, if perhaps in origin having a real inference,[4] are developed as logical, for the school abandons any idea of setting out in detail the real relations at the basis of inference. But reality[5] underlies inference, and we must

[1] TC. ii. 2: *vyāptiviçiṣṭapakṣadharmatājñānam.*

[2] TS., § 47.

[3] NSM., pp. 86, 87.

[4] The *vyāpaka* need not be more extensive than the *vyāpya*; 50 is *vyāpaka* of 100.

[5] PBh., p. 201; TC. ii. 27 ff.; TR., p. 65; TK., p. 11; TS., § 44.

ask, how is the invariable concomitance known? In the first place we must admit that mere observation of concomitance in a special case or a few cases is not enough for logical purposes: to attain certainty the knowledge of coexistence must be accompanied by the absence of knowledge of any contrary case, i.e. we must use the method of positive and negative instances. If a discrepancy can be adduced or is suspected, then it must either be shown to be merely apparently an exception, or the doctrine of concomitance must be admitted to be conditional (*aupādhika*) and therefore useless for logic. If, however, no concrete case is adduced, but it is argued on general grounds that not even all the cases which have been observed, though numerous, are enough to give certainty of universal concomitance, the only reply is to show that a contrary instance is really impossible. This may be done by careful examination of the concomitance itself, which may prove to be irresistible, or it may be shown by the use of the *reductio ad absurdum* (*tarka*).[1] The man who denies that from smoke we can infer fire is confronted with the result that he must contend that there are cases in which smoke is not connected with fire, but arises from some other cause, which is contrary to all experience, and he is driven to admit that after all we are entitled to deduce fire from smoke. So for the moment we escape the danger of arguing in a circle, which is obvious if we try to show that it exists because it is found in so many cases, since for such an inference as for all others a concomitance is an essential prerequisite, and *ex hypothesi* no concomitance has yet been established. It is obvious, however, that the question is not yet solved, for the validity of our indirect proof in the ultimate issue rested upon concomitance,

[1] Above, ch. i, § 3.

in this case a negative one, so that the real character of concomitance is as far from solution as ever.

The definitive reply to the question of the mode in which a concomitance is known is, therefore, based on the view expressed in Gautama[1] that inference depends on perception, but the crude idea which doubtless dominated the earlier view has made room for a more subtle doctrine, in which supernormal or transcendental (*alaukika*) perception takes the place of the simple contact of organs of sense and object. When we see any object we see also its generality (*sāmānya*), including all other possible members of the class: thus by this peculiar mental contact (*sāmānyalakṣaṇā pratyāsatti*) we appreciate the generality of smoke and of fire. Further by yet another contact, whose characteristic is knowledge (*jñāna-lakṣaṇā*),[2] we realize the universal concomitance of the two, smoke and fire, so that the moment we see smoke we at once have knowledge of fire as connected with it. This is not a process of inference, for there is no possibility of the operation of reflection (*parāmarça*) in its production, and it differs from ordinary perception, as there is not a connexion between the object and the senses in all the times and places in which the former exists. The nature of the *reductio ad absurdum* now becomes plain; it does not serve to prove or create the knowledge of the universal concomitance; it is only accessory or contributary to remove doubts and to make the knowledge of the concomitance free from uncertainty. Nor, again, is

[1] i. 1. 5; cf. ÇV., pp. 68 ff., 200 ff.; ṢDST., pp. 61, 62. Proof by positive and negative instance is applied to every conceivable topic. Cf. SS. v. 28 ff. Cf. B. Seal, *Positive Sciences of Ancient Hindus*, ch. vii.

[2] Above, ch. ii, § 3. Pañcaçikha is credited in SS. v. 32–6 with a view suggesting that concomitance is a mental concept imposed on things, not an expression of a reality, but the value of so late evidence is minimal. The perception of generality is accepted in Mīmāṅsā; PSPM., p. 95. Cf. NSM., pp. 81 ff.

the generality which we perceive a mere mental figment in the view of the school of this period; it is an absolute reality,[1] but it exists only in the individuals in which it appears, and is not hypostatized as something apart from the individual substances or attributes or activities in which it resides.

The concomitance,[2] as we have seen, can be either positive or negative, and in the normal case in regard to a subject and an attribute it is possible to establish both relations. Thus in the judgement, 'Where there is smoke, there is fire', we have a positive concomitance, to which there is the negative counterpart, 'Where there is no fire, there is no smoke'. The rule of the school to append the examples of both to the statement of concomitance is duly carried out in both cases; a similar case (*sapakṣa*) is a case in which the conclusion, i. e. fire, is present, but, as smoke need not be present with fire, a concomitance must be illustrated by something more, a demonstrative example (*dṛṣṭānta*),[3] that is one in which not merely fire but smoke is present, as in the kitchen. The counter-case (*vipakṣa*) does not admit of such duality: it includes all that has no fire, and therefore all that has no smoke.

In other cases we do not find the possibility of positive and negative concomitance. In the proposition, 'The pot can be named, since it is knowable', the concomitance can be positive only (*kevalānvayin*), since while it is true that 'What can be known can be named', the proposition, 'What cannot be named cannot be known' cannot be established, since no probative example can be adduced for it, seeing that only of what can be known

[1] *sāmānyasya vastubhūtatvāt*, TB., p. 31; *svābhāvikas tu saṁbandho vyāptiḥ*, ibid., p. 35; below, ch. vii, § 3. Cf. ÇV., p. 212.

[2] Not in NS., but in NV., p. 48; TC. ii. 735 ff.

[3] Only this is recognized as valid for reasoning by PSPM., p. 51; ÇD., p. 48.

can anything, *ex hypothesi*, be known. On the other hand, in the proposition, 'Living organisms have souls, since they possess animal functions', there can be a negative concomitance only (*kevala-vyatirekin*), since the proposition, 'What has no soul has no animal functions' can be illustrated by the case of the pot, but the positive proposition, 'That which has animal functions has a soul', cannot be illustrated, since the conclusion has precisely the same extension as the subject, and cannot therefore be found anywhere outside it. In the case of negative concomitance only it is, therefore, impossible to adduce any example (*sapakṣa*); in the positive concomitance only it is impossible to adduce any counter example (*vipakṣa*).

The relations thus stated may be illustrated by the accompanying diagram:[1]

The circle S represents the subject, the circle M the reason, and the circle P the conclusion (*sādhya*). The space between the circumference of S and that of P represents the whole field of examples, part of which falls within, part without the circle M, the former alone giving the probative example (*dṛṣṭānta*). All the space outside P represents the counter-examples (*vipakṣa*). In

[1] Jacobi, NGWG. 1901, p. 466.

the normal concomitance, which is at once positive and negative (*anvaya-vyatirekin*) we have the positive sphere, 'Where M, there P'; and the negative, 'Where no P, there no M'. To represent the purely negative concomitance it is necessary to assume that S expands to the dimensions of P, in which case, of course M must expand likewise; there then remains no room for an example, and only a counter-example is possible. To illustrate the purely positive concomitance it is necessary to assume that the circumference of P disappears and the possibility of a counter-example is abolished.

In place of basing the distinctions of positive-negative, positive only and negative only on the concomitance, it is also possible to classify the middle terms on the same principle,[1] a procedure which does not differ in substance from the more natural one here adopted, of treating the concomitance as the seat of the distinction. Applied to the inference or the middle term, however, the scheme tended to produce results, which were early criticized, and which, though ascribed by Çrīdhara [2] to Praçastapāda would apparently not have been accepted by that author.[3] It is a less serious matter that the positive inference operates with a conclusion which is co-extensive with existence, and thus departs widely from the normal form of conclusion.[4] The objections, however, to the purely negative inference (*kevala-vyatirekin anumāna*) are overwhelming. All the terms in it have the same extension, and thus the essential characteristic of inference, the use of a general principle to demonstrate something, disappears as there is no particular case to

[1] TC. ii. 735–9.

[2] NK., pp. 203, 204; *Muséon*, v. 152, n. 3.

[3] At p. 239, however, he seems to admit a *kevalavyatirekin* argument; all appear in NSāra, p. 6; TR., pp. 70–80; below, ch. iv, § 2; NV., pp. 123–32 elaborately justifies all the cases.

[4] NSM., pp. 67 ff, replying to Mīmāṅsaka and Buddhist views.

which the principle can be applied. Moreover, to arrive at a positive conclusion from a negative is in itself an unusual procedure, and if Praçastapāda denied that either form was a correct syllogism, he had much reason to support his action. The Nyāya contends, indeed, that as every negation has a positive opposed to it, there is sufficient positive element available to produce a reflection (*parāmarça*) and to induce a result, but the effort is plainly unsatisfactory and unconvincing. But the doctrine [1] was held firmly against the contention of the Vedānta and the Mīmāṅsā [2] that, in such a case there was to be recognized the mental process, constituting a separate means of proof, called presumption (*arthāpatti*). The stock example of this is the inference, 'Devadatta, though he is fat, does not eat during the day, and therefore must eat at night.' The Nyāya formulates the proposition as a purely negative inference, 'Devadatta eats at night, because he is fat without eating in the daytime.' The positive concomitance, 'He who is fat without eating during the day eats at night,' cannot be observed, but the negative proposition, 'He who never eats is never fat' falls under our immediate experience. Similarly the *reductio ad absurdum* in its formal aspect is defended by the Nyāya as an example of the purely negative inference.

The validity of inference was assailed by the Cārvāka school who maintained the impossibility of legitimately establishing an invariable connexion; the Buddhist reply rests on an ideal construction as expressed in the concomitance, not on a real relation. A somewhat similar view is attributed in one version of the *Sāṁkhya*

[1] TC. ii. 582 ff., 645 ff.; NSāra, pp. 32, 33, 237-42; TR., pp. 96-101; Kir., p. 104; Kus. iii. 19; NSM., pp. 87, 89; cf. KKK. i. 347-55.

[2] ÇV., pp. 230-43; VP., p. 14; PSPM., pp. 70, 71, bases presumption on doubt, ÇV. on inconsistency; Keith, JRAS. 1916, p. 370.

Sūtra to Pañcaçikha, probably without regard to historic fact, as that author was probably anterior to the period of the discussion of concomitance. The Sūtra itself assumes an innate power in the things which are concomitant. Çañkara also admits the validity of inference, subject however to the superior authority of scripture which alone gives us absolute truth, while the Nyāya contends for the absolute value of inference as based on perception.[1]

4. *The Final Form of the Doctrine of Syllogism.*

The syncretist school[2] follow without question the doctrine of Praçastapāda that there is a fundamental distinction between inference for oneself which is true inference, and inference for another which is styled inference therefore only by an analogy. Inference[3] for another is the exposition by means of a proof consisting of five members of a thing which has already been ascertained for oneself. Or, in other words, as stated by Dharmottara,[4] the inference for oneself is notional (*jñānātmaka*), as opposed to that for another which is verbal (*çabdātmaka*), though, unlike the Buddhists, the logicians do not carry the concept to the natural result of recognizing that there is no place in their system for the concept of verbal testimony as a special kind of means of proof. Syllogism, therefore, is inference in a modified

[1] ṢDS., ch. i; KKK. i. 181 ff.; SDS.. ch. ii; SS. v. 27 ff. with Aniruddha; BS. ii. 1. 11; *Bhāmati*, pp. 293, 561; NV., pp. 190, 192; NK., p. 255; Kus. iii. 6-8; NSM., pp. 76 ff.; JBRAS. xix. 54-6.

[2] TB., pp. 37, 38; TS., § 45; TC. ii. 689 ff.; cf. ÇV., pp. 182-207; PSPM., p. 48.

[3] PBh., p. 231; NSāra, p. 5. Max Müller's ascription of the distinction to rhetorical ends is erroneous (*Six Systems*, pp. 567 ff.); cf. NSM., pp. 117, 118.

[4] NBT., p 21.

and secondary sense, since it is the cause which produces in the mind of the hearer or reader the knowledge of the universal concomitance, which is the true base of inference. In the Nyāya view there is an essential distinction between the effect of verbal testimony and that of syllogism; in the first place the information imparted is accepted without any activity on the part of the hearer: in inference as communicated by the syllogism the hearer must perform the necessary mental operation, which the teacher has already performed, and which he now aids by syllogistic exposition the hearer to perform for himself. There can, therefore, be no vital distinction in principle between inference and syllogism: any inference can be thrown into syllogistic form for one's own satisfaction if desired, and it must be so treated if it is to be communicated to another. The difference therefore reduces itself to a difference of aspect, the one deals with the process of inference, the other with its formal expression, or as Çivāditya[1] has it the one is characterized by substance (*artharūpatva*), the other by sound or words (*çabdarūpatva*).

Syllogism, which bears the name *nyāya*, then consists of a collection of propositions arranged in due order, or in the formal definition of Gañgeça[2] is an exposition which produces a verbal knowledge whence arises in the hearer the knowledge of the invariable concomitance and of the presence of the characteristic in the subject, knowledge which is the last cause of inferential knowledge. The number of members remains fixed at five as in Gautama, with the traditional names of proposition (*pratijñā*), which states the subject with the conclusion as an attribute; reason (*hetu*), which ascribes to the subject the middle term which serves as the means of

[1] SP., § 154.

[2] TC. ii. 691, 692. For *Nyāya* as reasoning generally cf. NV. iv. 1. 14.

connecting it with the conclusion; example (*udāharaṇa*), in which the concomitance is given in full with an example, either positively or negatively; the application (*upanaya*) in which there is attributed to the subject the middle term characterized as being a member of the concomitance; and the conclusion (*nigamana*), in which it is declared that the consequence is an attribute of the subject. The purpose of the five members is stated formally[1] to be to teach the knowledge of the subject; the syllogistic mark; the knowledge of the concomitance; the knowledge of the syllogistic mark as an attribute of the subject; and that there is nothing opposed to the final result reached in the conclusion. In its typical form the syllogism is thus exemplified:

The mountain is fiery
Because of smoke
Where there is smoke there is fire, as in a kitchen, or
Where there is no fire, there is no smoke, as in a lake,
And so (i. e. provided with smoke which is invariably accompanied by fire) is this (mountain)
Therefore is it so (i. e. provided with fire).

In the example,[2] now misnamed, the concomitance may be expressed in two ways: either as given above or in the adjectival form, 'Whatever has smoke, that also has fire', or 'Whatever has the absence of fire that has also the absence of smoke'. The latter mode of expression is the more frequent in harmony with the tendency of the language to nominal expression. The application and conclusion in Sanskrit are framed in the enigmatic *tathā cāyam* and *tasmāt tathā*, the historic ground of which we have already seen. The scheme which is normal must be modified slightly for the purely positive and the purely negative inferences, since in these only

[1] Cf. NBh., p. 45.
[2] T.C. i. 740 ff.; NSāra, pp. 12. 135-8; TR., p. 180.

one form of concomitance can appear under the example, and in the latter a negative is necessary in the second last member of the syllogism.[1]

The characteristics of the syllogism are obviously not without relation to the nature of the Sanskrit language. The preference carried out to the full extent of a positive result is rendered easy by the fact that every proposition can be thrown into a positive form by the simple expedient of using the qualification of non-existence (*abhāva*), and saying that the mountain possesses absence of fire in place of saying that the mountain is not fiery. Similarly no hypothetical result is necessary; as we have seen, the concomitance can be expressed in the form of two correlative clauses, but it can be easily, and is more frequently, expressed in adjectival form. The subject is capable of wide extension thanks to the power of the language; where a thing is not a convenient subject, a place or time may be converted into one. But the subject must either be individual,[2] or a class denoted by a class name and capable of being considered as a single object. If a number of things do not form a real class,[3] there cannot be any single judgement about them; there can only be a series of judgements arising from a series of independent inferences regarding each individual.

An inference, again, as we have seen, must correspond to reality, and there can be no formal correctness, as opposed to real representation of truth. This demand excludes partial or in the school terminology contingent (*aupādhika*) judgements, which would not correspond to

[1] Jacobi, NGWG. 1901, p. 470, says in the fourth and fifth members, but this would give a negative conclusion; cf. NSāra, pp. 7, 108, 110; TR., pp. 75–7. The negative form is sometimes adopted, however; e. g. TB., p. 89; cf. NBh., p. 48; Colebrooke, i. 315, 316; *Padarthāratnamālā*, p. 54.

[2] NS. ii. 2. 66.

[3] Below, ch. vii, § 3.

reality, for in the Nyāya view the knowledge that some S is P is not true knowledge, which would require a knowledge of exactly what S were P.

The similarity of the syllogism of the Nyāya to that of formal logic is as obvious as the dissimilarity,[1] and the cause of the difference is plain. The Nyāya syllogism represents the form developed in discussion. The proposition which heads it represents the starting-point: without something to represent the object of a desire (*ākaṅkṣā*) to obtain information no discussion can begin. The reason is the answer to the question why the proposition is asserted: the example, or rather the statement of concomitance, replies to the question why the reason is sufficient to produce the conclusion, the general statement being made clear by an example. It remains then only in the two last members of the syllogism to apply the general rule to the particular case, and then to express the conclusion, which thus appears at the end of the syllogism not as a mere idle repetition, but as the assurance of a reasoned conclusion. What is remarkable, however, is the fact that the example remains almost to the last an essential part of the system, indeed in practice it is the example which is given rather than the formal statement of concomitance: it remained for Laugākṣi Bhāskara in his comment, the *Nyāyasiddhāntamañjariprakāça*[2] to say that the use of the example is conventional and not essential.

While in practice the Nyāya syllogism is frequently reduced to the first three members, the third in the mere form of the example as in 'The mountain has fire, because it has smoke, like a kitchen', the Mīmāṅsā formally reduces the number to three, namely the first set of three; another view accepted the second, third,

[1] Athalye, TS., pp. 286 ff., 265 ff. [2] Ibid. p. 281.

and fourth members as adequate, while the Vedānta was satisfied either with the first or the last three.[1] The later Buddhist view accepted as necessary only the third and the fourth (*udāharaṇa* and *upanaya*). Dharmakīrti's[2] view, differing from that of Dignāga,[3] treats the proposition and the reason, in which the example is included, as sufficient for inference. The Vaiçeṣika agreed with the Nyāya, though the tradition of the distinguishing names given by Praçastapāda was preserved.

5. *Analogy or Comparison.*

The Nyāya school[4] and the authorities of the Nyāya-Vaiçeṣika, with the exception of Çivāditya, treat analogy or comparison (*upamāna*) as a third means of proof, the establishment of something unknown through its similarity to something already known. The stock example of the process is already given by Vātsyāyana; a man who has never seen a buffalo is told by a forester, who as an expert is worthy of credence, that it resembles a cow. On entering a woody region he sees a strange animal, whose shape reminds him of a cow, and there comes to his remembrance the name buffalo taught by the forester. The essence of the process involves both the knowledge imparted by the forester, and the perception of similarity in the object presented, and there is a direct divergence of opinion between the ancient and modern schools[5] on the part played by these two factors

[1] VP., p. 14; TC. ii. 689 n.; PSPM., p. 49; ÇD., p. 44.

[2] NB., p. 118; cf. NBT., p. 90.

[3] His acceptance of these members is criticized, NV., p. 141.

[4] NS. i. 1. 6; ii. 1. 44–8; TC. iii. 1-101; TA., p. 20; TB., p. 45; TK., p. 16; TS., § 58; BP., 79, 80; TR., pp. 85–94; cf. ÇV., pp. 222–30; ṢDS., p. 70.

[5] NKoça, p. 147; the first view in NBh., pp. 21, 22; the latter, NV., pp. 60, 61; NSM., pp. 20–3 follows NBh.

in the production of the result. The older view holds that the immediate cause of the knowledge obtained by comparison is the verbal knowledge given by the forester, while the perception of resemblance is but an accessory cause of the result. The modern school inverts the relationship, thus laying greater emphasis on the similarity which lies at the bottom of the process, but without fundamentally altering the view of the process. Similarity, however, is not to be deemed the only cause of knowledge of this kind; dissimilarity or a peculiar property may serve the same end; thus a man may recognize a camel because, unlike a horse, it possesses a humped back and a long neck, or a rhinoceros by the single horn which adorns its nose.

There is disagreement also between the ancient and modern schools as to the precise nature of the judgement in which the process of comparison results. The older view, held also by Keçava Miçra, Laugākṣi Bhāskara, and Annam Bhaṭṭa, gives the judgement as an assertion that the animal perceived bears the name buffalo. The more recent opinion of Viçvanātha treats it as a recognition that the thing seen is an individual of the species buffalo, and this accords with the fact that the result of the experience is to enrich the subject of the experience with the recognition by its name of a new animal species.

The weakness of the Nyāya concept was not ignored by the rival school. Vācaspati Miçra,[1] in expounding the Sāṁkhya doctrine, which does not admit comparison as a separate means of proof, analyses the process, and proves that there is nothing permitting of the setting up of comparison as a special means of attaining knowledge. The instruction of the forester falls in the sphere

[1] *Sāṁkhyatattvakaumudī*, 5; cf. PSPM., p. 69.

of verbal knowledge[1] as a means of proof; similarity is recognized by perception, and inference accounts for the rest. The Vaiçeṣika school include comparison in inference[2]: the syllogism runs: 'This object is to be styled buffalo, since it is like a cow, and whatever is like a cow bears the name buffalo.' The reply of the Nyāya[3] is an appeal to experience which shows that in ordinary life judgements of comparison are formed without going through the process indicated, a reply which shows a complete inability to distinguish between a logical and a psychological analysis, and to the conservatism of the Nyāya rather than any other cause must in all likelihood be attributed the maintenance even in the latest state of the school of a distinction between inference and comparison as fundamentally different modes of proof. The whole subject receives elaborate discussion by Udayana,[4] who rejects the Vedānta and Mīmāṅsā defence which regards the instrument in comparison as the cognition that this animal is like a cow, and the conclusion as the judgement, 'The cow is like this buffalo'. He defends comparison on the ground that it implies more than verbal testimony, which only teaches us that the term 'buffalo' is applicable where likeness to a cow is found; comparison, on the other hand, gives us the knowledge that the term 'buffalo' applies to a species, which we comprehend from perceiving a specimen in quite a different manner from our previous knowledge based on verbal testimony. Comparison, therefore, teaches us the direct signification of a word; it does not teach anything about the existence or non-existence of anything; hence

[1] In NSāra, pp. 30-2, 222-37, it is reduced to verbal testimony.

[2] VSU. ix. 2. 5.

[3] *Nīlakaṇṭhī*, p. 116.

[4] Kus. iii. 8-12; cf. TC. iii. 40 ff.; TR., pp. 92-4; the Mīmāṅsā (PSPM., p. 68) makes likeness a separate category, a view refuted both in SS. v. 94-6 and by Kumārila.

if there is an attempt to prove the non-existence of a creator by the comparison, 'Whatever is like the omniscient individual soul is not omnipotent, and this being which is like the individual soul is what is meant by the name God', the reply is that the use of comparison as means of proof in this way is invalid.

In the *Nyāya Sūtra*[1] itself the case for comparison is defended against a difficulty made as to the possibility of argument from mere similarity by the statement that the reasoning is based on recognized and patent similarity. Against the argument that it, like inference, leads to the establishment of what is not perceived by means of what is perceived, it is urged that it is the perception of the buffalo which leads to the result of the comparison, and that the verbal expression of a comparison diverges from that of an inference, whence the difference of the things follows.

[1] ii. 1. 44–8; NBh., pp. 90, 91; NV., pp. 258–60. Cf. KKK. i. 319–35.

CHAPTER IV

LOGICAL ERRORS

1. *The Origin and Development of the Doctrine of Fallacies.*

THE treatment of fallacies in both the *Nyāya Sūtra* and the *Vaiçeṣika Sūtra* is brief and simple, standing in curious contrast to the elaboration of this topic by the later texts. Fallacies rank as one of the categories of of Gautama,[1] but, in accordance with the lack of development of any theory of the true nature of inference, there is no attempt to explain the reasons underlying the classes of fallacies enumerated. Naturally enough, the commentators find in the list the prototype of the scheme which they recognized in the contemporary syncretist school, but it is difficult to believe that this view had any legitimacy. Of the list of five given the first and second alone are named with familiar terms: the first is *savyabhicāra*, 'discrepant', which is defined as a reason which leads to more conclusions than one (*anaikāntika*), and this definition applies to the form of fallacy throughout its history. The second is the contrary (*viruddha*), which is marked by the fact that the reason leads to a result opposite to that which is established, and it also—though with change of sense—passes into the later terminology. The third, *prakaraṇasama*, seems by its literal sense, 'equal to the question', to mean a reason

[1] i. 2. 4-9; cf. TR., pp. 216 ff.

which provokes the very question which it was intended to answer; the later view classes it as equivalent to the counterbalanced reason (*satpratipakṣa*), but with doubtful propriety, for it may equally well be equated to the contradicted reason (*bādhita*), or more probably differ from either.[1] The third form, styled 'equal to the conclusion' (*sādhyasama*), is explained as one in which the reason is as much in need of proof as the conclusion: later it is classed among the unreal reasons (*asiddha*). The last is 'that for which the time has gone by' (*kālātīta*): on one interpretation, which Vātsyāyana rejects, it applies to a fault in the form of the syllogism, when the reason is adduced in the wrong place in the order of propositions. This interpretation, however, is open to the objection that mere formal order is not essential to the meaning of a Sanskrit sentence, and that the misplacement of any member of the syllogism is described in the Nyāya as falling under a special form, 'the untimely' (*aprāptakāla*) of the category styled 'Occasions for Rebuke' (*nigraha-sthāna*).[2] The accepted explanation,[3] however, is hardly easy to believe. It is based on the view that an effort is made to argue the abiding character, and therefore eternity of sound from the fact that it is manifested by union (e.g. between a drum and the rod), just as colour, whose existence is admitted, is manifested by union with light. The fallacy lies in the fact that the manifestation of sound is not due to the union, but takes place at a subsequent moment (*kālātīta*) after the union has ceased. The later doctrine forces it into the category of contradicted reason, but manifestly without plausibility. Indeed, in no part of Gautama's

[1] Cf. NBh., p. 53; NV., pp. 175, 176.

[2] NS. v. 2. 11.

[3] NV., p. 177; NBh., p. 54; NVT. gives the later view that it = *bādhita*.

system is there more clear proof of the lack of an authentic tradition of his meaning, unless perhaps in the confusion as to the significance of the three kinds of inference which he recognizes.

The case with Gautama is very different from that with Kaṇāda.[1] The doctrine of Kaṇāda as now restored to the text of the Sūtra is perfectly plain: it states a definition of a fallacious reason or non-reason (*anapadeça* in his terminology, in which *apadeça* replaces *hetu*) as that which is unproved (*aprasiddha*), that is which is not shown to be in invariable concomitance with the consequence. Of the fallacious reason two species are mentioned, the unreal (*asat*), and the doubtful (*saṁdigdha*), which correspond accurately enough to the later *asiddha* and *savyabhicāra*. The examples given are for the unreal the argument, 'Since it has horns, it is a horse', for the insufficient[2] reason, 'Since it has horns, it is an ox'. A horse of course is not horned, but there are other animals besides an ox which are so adorned. As the traditional text stands, this clear outline has been brought into confusion by an interpretation which may probably enough be little if at all anterior to Praçastapāda himself.[3]

2. *Dignāga and Praçastapāda.*

The evidence already adduced in the account of the development of inference gives ground to suppose that Dignāga can claim to have enunciated the principle of invariable concomitance as the fundamental principle of the syllogism. The investigation of this question

[1] iii. 1. 15–17.

[2] *anaikāntika* evidently = *saṁdigdha*.

[3] *aprasiddho 'napadeçaḥ*; *asan saṁdigdhaç ca* is the original text; Praçastapāda (p. 204) read it as one Sūtra.

inevitably led to the exposition of the conditions which must mark the middle term if it were to serve the purpose for which it was destined, and the *Nyāyapraveça*[1] lays down the three essential conditions in explicit terms. The whole of the subject must be connected with the middle term; all things denoted by the middle term must be homogeneous with things denoted by the major term; none of the things heterogeneous from the major term must be a thing denoted by the middle term. Dharmakīrti in the *Nyāyabindu*[2] reproduces the same rules for the three characteristics of the middle term; it must exist in what is to be inferred (*anumeye sattvam eva*); it must exist in things only which are homogeneous with the major term (*sapakṣa*); and it must not exist in things heterogeneous with the major term (*vipakṣa*). The division of fallacies in both is based on the principle that, if one or more of these rules is violated, there arises a fallacious reason. Three classes of such fallacies are recognized by Dignāga, the unreal (*asiddha*), the indeterminate (*anaikāntika*), and the contrary (*viruddha*) as they are styled by Dharmakīrti, who follows with modifications and improvements the scheme set out by his predecessor. Four subdivisions of the unreal reason are recognized: when the unreality is recognized by both parties to the discussion; when it is conceded by one party only; when its reality is called in question; and when it is doubtful whether the middle term can be predicated of the subject. Of the indeterminate there are six forms: when the middle term abides both in the major term and in the opposite, which is the too general middle term of later logic (*sādhāraṇa*); when the middle term abides neither in the major nor its opposite, the too restricted (*asādhāraṇa*) form of later logic; when the

[1] *Med. Log.*, pp, 93 ff.; NV., pp. 58, 59.
[2] NB., pp. 114 ff.; ṢDST., pp. 44–6.

middle term abides in some of the things homogeneous with, and in all of the things heterogeneous from, the major term; when the middle term abides in all the things homogeneous with, and some of the things heterogeneous from, the major term; when the middle term abides in some things homogeneous with, and some heterogeneous from, the major term; and lastly the contrary but not discrepant (*viruddhāvyabhicārin*) middle term, that is when a thesis and its contradictory are both supported by equally valid reasons. The stock example of the last is the argument adduced by a Vaiçeṣika to prove that sound is not eternal because it is a product; while the Mīmāṅsā responds that it is eternal, because it is audible. Finally, there are four[1] subdivisions of the contrary, according as the middle term contradicts the major term, or the implied major term, or the minor term, or the implied minor term. Of these the fallacy which is contrary to the implied major term is akin to the contrary but not discrepant, since it depends on the fact that it is contrary to a principle of the school by which it is used, and it is therefore termed 'that which cuts across one's principles (*iṣṭavighātakṛt*)'. The example given by Dignāga is the argument that the eyes, &c., are of service to some being, because they are made of particles, like a bed, seat, &c. Here the major term 'of service to some being' is ambiguous: its apparent meaning is 'of service to the body', but the implied meaning is 'of service to the soul'. But the Sāṁkhya system holds that, though things made of particles are of service to the body, they are not of service to the soul which has no attributes. Hence the middle term contradicts the implied term as understood by the Sāṁkhya.

[1] Kumārila, ÇV., pp. 195–7, clearly refers to this view, and the *iṣṭavighātakṛt*.

Dharmakīrti [1] presents us with the same classification but with a diminution in the subdivisions. The four of the unreal reasons remain, but of the indeterminate only the first two are kept, the too general and the too restricted, and the contrary, likewise, is reduced to two varieties, depending on the fact of the existence of the middle term in what is heterogeneous from the major, or its non-existence in what is homogeneous with the major. It is of interest that he recognizes and disallows the two varieties of contrary but not discrepant, and that which cuts across one's principles. The former he holds not to concern inference at all, as it arises from the fact that the two different sides in such a case rest on the authority of scripture, and this is for him, as in theory it was for Dignāga, no true source of knowledge.[2] The latter he dismisses because it is included in the general conception of contrary, which indeed in the definition of Gautama is that which is contrary to the principles admitted by the reasoner.[3]

In the case of Praçastapāda the question is complicated by the existence of the *versus memoriales* which he cites as embodying the views of (Kaṇāda) Kāçyapa, and in which the division of fallacies is based on the conditions for the correctness of the reason for inducing proof. They [4] run: 'That mark is the means of inference which is connected with that which is to be inferred, is known to exist in that which is accompanied with that

[1] NB., pp. 111-15; so the Mīmāṅsā, ÇV., p. 217. For the unreal see ÇV., pp. 192, 193.

[2] NB., p. 115. It is retained with the other two in ÇV., p. 193.

[3] NB., p. 113; NS. i. 2. 6.

[4] p. 200:

anumeyena sambaddhaṁ prasiddhaṁ ca tadanvite
tadabhāve ca nāsty eva tal liṅgam anumāpakam
viparītam ato yat syād ekena dvitayena vā
viruddhāsiddhasaṁdigdham aliṅgaṁ Kāçyapo 'bravīt.

which is to be inferred, and does not exist at all where that does not exist. That which departs therefrom in one or two points is declared by Kāçyapa to be no reason, as contrary, unreal, or doubtful'. The similarity of the statement of the three conditions (*trairūpya*) of the middle term to that in the Buddhist formulation is obvious, but it is important to note that the parallelism is not complete as regards the first essential condition. In the case of the Buddhist formula this condition is stated as the connexion of the middle term with the subject (*anumeya*), the sense of the latter term being made clear by its definition, in the *Nyāyabindu*, as the thing possessing an attribute (*dharmin*), whose peculiarity is to be known (*jijñāsita-viçeṣa*).[1] It is natural to read the same meaning into the *versus memoriales*, and this has been repeatedly done,[2] but only at the cost of complete disregard of the language. While that which is to be inferred (*anumeya*) can, like *sādhya* in its earlier sense, denote the subject of the inference, it equally easily and naturally like *sādhya* is employed of the conclusion, and that this is here the sense is proved by the expression 'which is to be accompanied by that' for the 'that' (*tad-anvite*) can only refer to *anumeya* which precedes it, and it is of course common ground that the characteristic of the similar instance (*sapakṣa* in the *Nyāyabindu*, here *tadanvite*) is to present the major and middle terms, not the middle term and the subject. The apparent objection that thus the reference to the subject is omitted must be recognized, but the remedy is not to read[3] into the verses

[1] NB., p. 101; this view as in Dignāga is controverted in NV., pp. 52-4, where (p. 122) PBh., p. 200, seems to be referred to. Dignāga's own case is given in *Padārtharatnamālā*, p. 13. Cf. p. 109, n. 2.

[2] Jacobi, NGWG. 1901, p. 480; Stcherbatskoi, *Muséon*, v. 146; Suali, *Intr.*, p. 393; Faddegon, *Vaiç. System*, p. 303. But cf. ṢDST., p. 44.

[3] Athalye, TS., p. 282; but cf. SBH. vi. 285; Garbe, trans of SS., p. 58; Gañgānātha Jhā, NS. i. 346.

the qualification that the first condition, connexion with the conclusion, is to exist in the subject, which of course begs the question. The Vaiçeṣikas deliberately adopted the view that the knowledge of the middle term was the proximate cause of inference, and were criticized by their opponents precisely because thus they failed to emphasize the element of existence of the middle term in the subject. The explanation of their attitude is perfectly simple: the three conditions as set out represent a precise statement of the third member of the syllogism, the example (*udāharaṇa*) when completed as it was in Praçastapāda's time by the enunciation of the general proposition. Of the first part of the example we have a reflection in the first condition, the invariable concomitance between the middle term and the major term, between smoke and fire, 'Where there is smoke, there is fire'; the second condition corresponds to the affirmative example of the concomitance of smoke and fire as in a kitchen; the third with the negative example of the absence of smoke when there is no fire, as in a lake. The reference to the subject is of course implicit: the conception of a middle term is essentially relative to a subject on the one hand and a major term on the other. In the Buddhist formulation in its turn there would be inadequate reference to the invariable concomitance as a principle if it were not that the middle term is essentially relative to the major and is related to it, in the view of Dharmakīrti, by way of identity, cause and effect, or non-existence. The divergence of emphasis, however, is very far from diminishing the probability of borrowing on the part of the Vaiçeṣika: it is in entire accord with the natural wish of a school, when it has to appropriate fruitful ideas from another to disguise and adapt them in form if not in substance.

The impression of borrowing is confirmed by the fact

that Praçastapāda, or some predecessor, if we admit that the *versus memoriales* were really composed before him, thought it necessary to remodel the text of the *Vaiçeṣika Sūtra* in order to bring the new doctrine into harmony with the accepted text. The correction was ingenious: the two aphorisms of the original text, which, as we have seen, defined fallacy and set out two classes, were combined into a single clause and read as giving the varied classes of fallacies. But the complication did not end there, for it was not sufficient to Praçastapāda to establish three classes of fallacies: he had to assume that the enumeration gave room for the four classes which he himself accepted. The terms of the text as changed gave the old classes of unreal (*asat*), doubtful (*saṁdigdha*), and also *aprasiddha*, a new term, while the *versus memoriales* gave *asiddha*, *viruddha*, and *saṁdigdha*, and Praçastapāda added the *anadhyavasita*, or void reason. To effect a harmony between these views and the Sūtra Praçastapāda[1] declared the identity of *aprasiddha* with *viruddha* and his new addition, regardless of the utter violence he thus did to the text. A later hand[2] endeavoured at least to avoid the incoherence thus created in the Sūtra by the interpolation of a word at the end of the second of the two aphorisms which Praçastapāda read as one: the text thus gave once more two clauses, but in lieu of a definition of fallacy, followed by an enumeration of two classes, we have first the statement that the *aprasiddha* is a fallacy, and then that the unreal and the doubtful are fallacies, the absurdity of which is self evident.

Praçastapāda[3] himself gives in prose practically the

[1] pp. 238, 239. [2] Jacobi, NGWG. 1901, p. 481, n. 2.

[3] p. 201: *yad anumeyenārthena deçaviçeṣe kālaviçeṣe vā sahacaritam anumeyadharmānvite cānyatra sarvasminn ekadeçe vā prasiddham anumeyaviparīte ca sarvasmin pramāṇato 'sad eva tad aprasiddhārthasyānumāpakaṁ liṅgam.* For my interpretation cf. NV., p. 122.

same account of the conditions affecting the reason or middle term: the mark must be associated in respect of time or place with the thing to be inferred, be found in all or one case where the attribute to be inferred is present, and be proved to be non-existent in everything opposite from what is to be inferred. The slight divergence of wording brings out clearly the essential realism of the system, the reason is a reflex of reality. At the same time the wording confirms the view that the first condition refers to the relation of middle term and major, not of middle term and subject: the thing to be inferred is the fire on the mountain, not the subject which is not a thing to be inferred, but a thing whose attribute is to be inferred from the mark. In the second condition a new element appears, which forms also the subject of observation by Uddyotakara in his examination of the formulation of the subject of the three conditions of the reason by Dignāga: it is expressly recognized that the extension of the middle is not equivalent to that of the major: fire may exist without smoke. This point the earlier formulation ignored, for the simple reason that it was irrelevant to the business in hand: the third member of the syllogism must give an affirmative example, and it is irrelevant to note that the major may exist without the middle term.

On the basis of the threefold conditions of the reason Praçastapāda bases his division of fallacies: departure in one or two points brings about the invalidation of the reason to attain the conclusion, just as in the Buddhist view. Moreover, the divisions of the unreal reason are similar to those which were already given by Dignāga, from whom he doubtless borrowed them.[1] But in the other categories there is a significant variance which can

[1] Stcherbatskoi, *Muséon*, v. 168, 148–58; *contra*, Faddegon, p. 322.

hardly be deemed due to anything save a deliberate effort to improve on the Buddhist scheme which he really takes as the basis of his own. The antinomic reason, contrary but not discrepant, which Dignāga had classed among the indeterminate reasons, would normally fall into the class of doubtful reasons, which takes the place of that category in Praçastapāda's scheme. But Praçastapāda divides the cases covered by it into two, assigning one part to the category of contrary reasons, and the other to the new class of void reasons, which is his own invention. The explanation of the reference of the antinomic reason to the category of contrary pure and simple is easy; to Dignāga,[1] if a thesis were supported by one school on the strength of their scriptures and a contrary thesis were set up by another school on the strength of their scriptures, the result was that the middle term, being denied or asserted on equal authority, fell into the category of doubtful: more consistently still, Dharmakīrti[2] ruled out the reason altogether as falling outside the subject-matter of inference; Praçastapāda,[3] on his part, who accepted the binding force of the declarations of Kaṇāda, treats a view which is contrary to the tenets of his school as downright contrary (*āgama-bādhita*). Similarly, of course, the variety *iṣṭa-vighātakṛt*, which Dharmakīrti also rejected as a distinct species of contrary falls under the general head.

The other part of the antinomic reason as classed by Praçastapāda under the new class of void reasons consists of cases in which two arguments cancel each other, and there being no means of decision between them the reason which it is desired to set up is null and void. The rest of this class is made up by the too restricted form of the doubtful reason of the Buddhist system, in

[1] NBT., p. 85. [2] NB., p. 115.
[3] p. 239; NV., p. 171.

which the middle term is present neither in the major term nor in its opposite. The stock example is the reasoning, 'Sound is eternal, because it is audible'. Dharmakīrti,[1] however, classifies in the same count the argument which the Nyāya and Vaiçeṣika accept, 'Living bodies have a soul, because they have animal functions', which the later theory makes an inference with purely negative concomitance (*kevala-vyutirekin*).[2] It is not certain how far Praçastapāda would have accepted the classification of these two kinds under the same head, for, though he does not actually recognize the classes of purely positive and purely negative inference, he appears [3] to admit the truth of the argument, 'Sound is a quality, because it is audible', or 'Sound differs from other things, because it is audible'. The distinction between the two instances is plain: in the first the major term 'eternal' is wider in extension than the subject and the middle term, which are of equal extension, sound alone being audible; in the second, the three terms are all of like extension, and in the later view at least the conclusion is legitimate. Whether in any case the too restricted reason is deemed doubtful or void seems little more than variation of terminology designed to mark the independence of the new writer. The distinction is the more noteworthy in that Praçastapāda himself records an objection to this view in the fact that Kaṇāda [4] in treating of sound appears to have reckoned the too restricted reason as a source of doubt, although Praçastapāda [5] has not much difficulty in explaining away this seeming obstacle to his theory. It is in keeping with his determination to avoid too close

[1] NBT., p. 79; NB., p. 114. [2] NV., p. 125.

[3] p. 239. On the validity of this form cf. TR., pp. 77, 78, 219; PSPM., p. 47, disallows it. Cf. also Faddegon, pp. 307, 323.

[4] ii. 2. 21–3. [5] p. 239; NK., pp. 245, 246.

adherence to his predecessor that he never mentions the name of the antinomic reason, despite his elaborate discussion of its character.[1]

3. *The Final Form of the Doctrine of Fallacies.*

In the syncretist school [2] the classes of fallacies (*hetvābhasa*) depends on the correctness of the middle term, but the number of conditions has been increased to five in lieu of three. A middle term to be valid must be found in the subject (*pakṣa*), that is the thing in which the existence of what is to be ascertained (*sādhya*), e.g. fire, is doubtful; be found in the similar instances (*sapakṣa*), in which the existence of the thing to be ascertained is already known, e.g. a kitchen; be absent from the contrary instances (*vipakṣa*), in which the absence of the thing to be ascertained is already known, e.g. a lake; not be contradicted (*bādhita*) by the facts; and not be counterbalanced by another proof (*asatpratipakṣa*). If any of these conditions is not complied with in the ordinary inference the reason is only apparently a reason (*hetvābhāsa*), but in the purely positive inference the third condition, and in the purely negative inference the second condition are *ex hypothesi* excluded. An apparent reason is a faulty reason (*duṣṭa-hetu*), and much subtlety is wasted in making precise the definition of a fault in a reason (*hetu-doṣa*). Annam Bhaṭṭa declares it to be that which is the object of a correct knowledge which prevents an inferential judgement;

[1] The void reason in six varieties appears in NSāra, pp. 10, 11, 124-6. PSPM., pp. 46, 47, has only the too general, too restricted, unreal, and *bādhita* in the sense of *viruddha*.

[2] SP., § 157 ; TK., p. 13 ; TB., p. 101 ; the five conditions in lieu of three appear to have been due to Udayana's *Ātmatattvaviveka*, TR., pp. 177-9, 217 ; NV., pp. 165 ff., has three only, but NVT. has five. The Buddhist list is followed, not PBh.

Laugākṣi Bhāskara more generally as that which is the object of a knowledge which renders impossible the inferential judgement or the process which leads up to it, the latter phrase being wide enough to cover what is held on any of the theories to be the proximate cause of inference, whether knowledge of the middle term, knowledge of the concomitance, or the reflection (*parāmarça*). Annam Bhaṭṭa [1] insists on requiring that the knowledge should be correct, since otherwise in the familiar reasoning, 'The mountain has fire, because it has smoke,' a fault might be suggested through the erroneous perception of the absence of fire on the mountain.

The classes of fallacies are also increased to five, an artificial symmetry designed doubtless to imitate the Buddhist system, which recognizes three conditions and three sets of fallacies. Presumably the increase in the number took place first in the classification of fallacies, and thence was extended to the number of conditions. The five classes are in the order of Gāngeça [2] the discrepant (*savyabhicāra*), which is also styled indeterminate (*anaikāntika*); the contrary (*viruddha*); the counterbalanced (*satpratipakṣa*); the unreal (*asiddha*); and the contradicted (*bādhita*), but they may be examined in the order of the Buddhist list with the addition of the two new members of the series.

I. The indeterminate or discrepant,[3] which is styled in the Vaiçeṣika terminology the doubtful (*saṁdigdha*) lies in the fact that one or both of the second and third conditions is violated, whence the conclusion ceases to

[1] TS., § 52.

[2] T.C. i. 762 ff.; NSāra, p. 7, keeps Gautama's names, but adds a sixth; TR., *l. c.*, follows Gautama. KKK. i. 365 ff. refutes them all.

[3] SP. § 160; TC. i. 784–841; TA., p. 19; TB., pp. 44, 107, 108; TK., pp. 13, 14; TS., § 53; BP. 72–4. Keçava omits the third form; so also TR., pp. 217–20; NSāra, pp. 7, 10, 123–6, makes eight varieties: the first two are in NV., p. 173; PSPM., p. 46.

possess any certainty, and remains therefore an object of doubt. It falls into three species:

(1) The too general reason (*sādhāraṇa*) is found not only in the similar instances, but also in the opposite instances: the possession of horns does not make an animal an ox, nor has the mountain fire because it can be known.

(2) The too restricted reason (*asādhāraṇa*), on the other hand, offends against the second condition, for it occurs nowhere outside the subject itself. Its absence from the opposite instances or counter examples tends to establish the validity of the conclusion, but its absence from the similar instances or examples tends to invalidate the result which remains therefore a matter of doubt. 'Sound is eternal, because it is audible' is the standing example; as we have seen, the fallacy is distinguished in the modern school from the purely negative inference by reason that in the fallacy the major term has greater extension than the other terms, while in the inference which is valid all three terms have the like extension.

(3) The reason which does not subsume (*anupasaṁhārin*) is that which is alleged of a subject which is so extensive as to permit neither of examples or counter examples, as in 'All is eternal, because it can be known'. The nature of 'all' forbids the possibility of any universal concomitance, and thus prevents either the second or the third of the conditions being complied with. Or equally well the opposite argument can be used, 'All is transitory, because it can be known'. The modern school[1] object that the individual things of this world might serve as examples, and therefore define the fallacy as one in which there exists only a positive connexion between reason and consequence, a definition which is open to the

[1] Athalye, TS., pp. 303, 304.

retort that it covers the case of the purely positive inference which the modern school accepts as valid as does the older school, as in 'All can be named, because it can be known'. There exists, however, a clear difference between the last proposition and those quoted to illustrate the fallacy: in the latter there is a real ground of connexion between naming and knowledge, in the former it is not so, and the test of reasoning is always in the school correspondence with reality.

II. The contrary reason (*viruddha*)[1] is one which serves to prove exactly the opposite of the thesis it is adduced to establish. It thus does not exist in examples, but does exist in counter-examples, and so violates the second and third conditions alike. Sound is not eternal, because it is a product, nor is an animal a horse because it has horns.

III. The unreal reason (*asiddha*)[2] falls into three species in accordance with the three factors involved in the reflection (*parāmarça*) which brings about inferential knowledge; the subject, the relation of the middle term

[1] SP., § 159; TC. i. 842-64; TA., p. 19; TB., pp. 44, 107, 108; TK., p. 14; TS., § 54; BP. 74; NSāra, pp. 7, 9, 119-23, gives eight varieties; TR., p. 224, gives the same definition as NSāra and TB. In NB., NV. i. 2. 6, it still is really a *bādhita*; the new sense is in NVT.

[2] SP., § 158; TC. ii. 897-937; TA., pp. 19, 20; TB., pp. 42-4, 102-6; TK., pp. 14, 15; TS., § 56; BP. 75-7. NSāra, pp. 7-9, 113-9, gives fourteen divisions (twelve in commentary) defining it as *aniçcitapakṣavṛtti*; TR., pp. 228-8, follows Udayana's *Lakṣaṇamālā* (according to the commentary) in the threefold division, but adds a fourth class of *ajñānāsiddha* (in three varieties) and mentions five of Bhāsarvajña's as subvarieties. Both record the more general divisions of *ubhayāsiddhi* and *anyatarāsiddhi*. NV., p. 177, has a triple division with divergent names for (2) and (3); but NVTP. recognizes the new names, while NVT. has four classes (*svarūpa*, *ekadeça*, *āçraya*, *anyathā*); PBh., p. 238, has *anumeya*, *tadbhāva*, and two varieties of what is equivalent roughly to NB., p. 112, ll. 2-7, where three varieties occur; NB. has also *dharmy-* and *saṁdigdhāsiddha*.

to the subject, and the relation of the middle and major terms.

(1) The subject may be unreal in either of two ways: it may be a wholly imaginary thing, as in the case of the reasoning, 'The sky lotus is fragrant, because it is a lotus', where the unreality of the subject renders the conclusion, which else is necessary, impossible. Or the subject may be deprived of the essential characteristic which makes it fitted to be a subject of a syllogism, the desire to establish some proposition of it; if we have the inference, 'The cylinder is round, because it is round' we merely prove what is proved (*siddha-sādhana*). The modern school, however, decline to reckon this a fallacy, and include it instead under the category of Occasions for Reproof (*nigraha-sthāna*). In either case the reflection on the elements of the syllogism is impossible, since unreal things or things already known cannot be made the objects of such reflection. Hence this species ranks as 'unreal as regards the substratum' (*āçrayāsiddha*).

(2) The unreal in itself (*svarūpāsiddha*) is that reason which does not exist in the subject, and therefore cannot afford the basis of any reasoning, as in the proposition, 'The lake is a substance, because it has smoke'. With the usual needless love of subdivision this is again subdivided, six kinds being given by Keçava Miçra.

(3) The reason which is unreal in regard to the concomitance (*vyāpyatvāsiddha*) is one in which the concomitance between the middle term and the consequence does not present itself as inevitable and invariable. The similarity of this case to the variety of indeterminate reason called too general (*sādhāraṇa*) is obvious, but there is a real distinction of nature. In the former case there is a clear disturbance of the universal concomitance necessary for a conclusion; in the latter the concomitance is absent, or at least is not known certainly to exist.

There are two forms of this class: in the first the concomitance simple does not exist; in the second there is concomitance but only a conditional (*aupādhika*) one, which is of no value for inference. In the first case we have such inferences as 'The mountain has fire, because it has golden smoke', for the addition of golden destroys the concomitance, since golden smoke does not, in the Indian view, exist. Even if we substitute black for golden, the older school denies the validity of the inference, though the modern school admits it, apparently on the ground that otherwise it might be thought that the quality black formed a necessary part of the concomitance which is between the smoke and fire as such. More interesting is a third example: the reasoning, 'Sound is momentary, because it exists', which represents the Buddhist view is rejected because it involves the proposition that all which exists is momentary, and the Nyāya-Vaiçeṣika insists that a sound lasts for three moments, that of its production and that of its destruction with that intervening between them.

The conditional concomitance [1] is illustrated by such a case as the argument, 'The mountain has smoke, because it has fire'. The proposition is conditioned by the fact that there is no universal concomitance between fire and smoke, but only between fire produced from wet fuel and smoke. Laugākṣi Bhāskara and Annam Bhaṭṭa treat this as a fallacy, and indeed Annam Bhaṭṭa's definition of the third form of the unreal reason seems strictly speaking to cover the conditional concomitance only. On the other hand, there exists a view which declines to accept such a case

[1] On *upādhi* see TC. ii. 294–406; TB., pp. 43, 44, 106; TK., pp. 15, 16; TSD., § 56; BP. 138–40; VSU. iii. 2. 14; TR., pp. 65–70. Max Müller's view (*Six Systems*, pp. 570, 572) is clearly wrong. Cf. NSM., pp. 110–16.

as fallacious, since it does not fulfil the requirement of a fault in reasoning, namely that it should prevent the taking place of the reflection (*parāmarça*). In truth if the condition is borne in mind, it is possible to reason accurately. Thus we can reason correctly, 'If the lightning were to fall on a heap of hay, it would give out smoke', since in such a case the condition for the truth of the concomitance would actually be verified. This is an interesting example of the effort to extend the process of inference beyond the bounds imposed upon it by the demand that nothing save an absolutely universal concomitance should be taken as a basis of reasoning.

IV. The counter-balanced reason (*satpratipakṣa*)[1] is one for which there exists another reason which proves the contrary of the consequence. The later texts apply to it also the term *prakaraṇasama* taken from Gautama, equating the two ideas by interpreting the *prakaraṇasama* as a reason which, though intended to give a certain proof, leaves us with the desire for án argument to establish the conclusion, and hence is called 'like an argument' (*prakaraṇasama*). This form of reason differs from the contrary, because in the latter the reason in itself proves the opposite of what was intended, while in this case the reason is simply rendered inconclusive by the existence of an argument opposed to it of equal weight. In the contradictory reason (*bādhita*) again, the consequence is in flat contradiction with the truth, and this contradiction may be proved not merely by argument, but by direct perception or other recognized

[1] SP., § 163; TC. ii. 865-96; TA., p. 19; TB., pp. 44, 45, 108, 109; TK., p. 14: TS., § 55; BP. 77; the view of NSāra, pp. 7, 12, is refuted in TR., pp. 221-3; when the *viruddhāvyabhicārin* appears as a variant of this form, while Bhāsarvajña seems to reduce it to an *anyatarāsiddha* (otherwise the commentary, pp. 133-5). The identification with *prakaraṇasama* is in NVT. i. 2. 9.

means of proof. Again, to make this case of fallacy, there must be equal weight in the two reasons which can be opposed: in the triple division suggested by Keçava Miçra the first two cases where the first or the second is of prevailing weight cannot be properly reckoned here. If there is scriptural authority for either argument, it must prevail, and the reason would become not counter-balanced, but contradicted.

V. A reason is said to be contradicted (*bādhita*)[1] in the definition of Keçava Miçra when by means of another proof, perception, or otherwise, it can be established that there is present in the subject the negation of the consequence which the argument is intended to establish. It can be illustrated, therefore, by such a proposition as 'The fire is cold, because it is a substance, like water', while for the counter-balanced reason we must have resort to such arguments as 'The mountain is fiery, because it has smoke' opposed to 'The mountain is not fiery, because it is bare rock'. With the contradicted reason the later school identifies the *kālātīta* fallacy of Gautama, on the ground that it is inopportune and intempestive (*kālātīta*) to adduce a reason of this sort to prove a conclusion which other evidence has already established the contrary conclusion.

From this general classification and description none of the syncretist writers departs in substance, though Keçava Miçra omits entirely the non-subsuming variety of the indeterminate reason. Çivāditya,[2] however, increases the number of classes to six by accepting as a separate class the void reason (*anadhyavasita*) of Praçastapāda, which he defines much as in that writer,

[1] SP., § 162; TC. ii. 938-82; TA., p. 20; TB., pp. 44, 45, 109, 110; TK., p. 15; TS., § 57; BP. 78; NSāra, pp. 7, 11; TR., pp. 229-31.

[2] SP., § 161. The NSāra, pp. 7-12, has the old five of Gautama and the void reason as a sixth; the last TR., pp. 235, 236, rejects.

showing that at his early date the fusion of the Vaiçeṣika views was not yet completely carried through. The earlier Vaiçeṣika, too, had not recognized the classes of counterbalanced and contradictory reasons as such: Çañkara Miçra[1] tells us that they were interpreted into the text of the Sūtra by a Vṛttikāra, or writer of a commentary, but the identity of this author is wholly unknown. There is, of course, a rough distinction between the new classes and the old, but it can hardly be contended[2] that the Vaiçeṣika school acted on an attempt to distinguish between formal and material fallacies in omitting them, for, as we have seen, there were approximations to these classes in the classification of Praçastapāda. Thus the contradicted reason figures in Praçastapāda as part of the contrary (*viruddha*) in the shape of the reason contradicted by the text of the school (*āgamabādhita*), and this can be traced further back to the antinomic reason (*viruddhāvyabhicārin*) of the Buddhist logic. The counter-balanced reason (*satpratipakṣa*) again figures with Praçastapāda as part of the void reason (*anadhyavasita*), and again can be traced to the antinomic head of the Buddhists. Nor in truth is it really possible to attempt a serious distinction of formal and material in fallacies, since the Indian logic is never formal but always realistic.

It is characteristic that there should have been made a serious effort to induce the categories set up by Gautama to enter into the new division, nor is it at all unlikely that the fivefold classification was stereotyped precisely in order to suit the fivefold classification of the *Nyāya Sūtra*. The efforts to equate *prakaraṇasama* and *satpratipakṣa*, *kālātīta* and *bādhita* have been mentioned; the compilers ignored the fact that Gautama's

[1] VSU. iii. 2. 17. [2] Athalye, TS., p. 300.

contrary (*viruddha*) is really equivalent to contradiction by scripture (*āgamabādhita*) or Dignāga's *iṣṭavighātakṛt*, and equated it with the later *viruddha*. The *sādhyasama* was equated with the unreal reason;[1] but the divisions of that head may be traced in part through Praçastapāda to the Buddhist logic, though the details are dubious.[2]

4. *Other Logical Errors.*

On the theory of the Buddhist logic a train of reasoning is fallacious, not only if the middle term is defective, but also if the subject-matter or thesis cannot be sustained, that is, if it is refuted in advance by the proof of the opposite, or if the examples which serve to show the correctness of the middle term are not valid, being badly chosen. On this basis are set up fallacies of the thesis (*pakṣābhāsa*) and fallacies of the example (*dṛṣṭāntābhāsa*), details of which we have both from Dignāga[3] and from Dharmakīrti.[4] It is significant that Praçastapāda[5] accepts the whole theory, and follows closely the Buddhist model even to the extent[6] of closely copying, but with characteristic variation of phraseology, the description given of the defective thesis. The doctrine,

[1] NV., p. 177.

[2] Stcherbatskoi's views (*Muséon*, v. 169, 170) are open to doubt. The decisive approach to the modern view is in NV., pp. 176, 177.

[3] *Med. Log.*, pp. 90 ff., 96 ff.; Sugiura, *Hindu Log.*, pp. 59 ff., 68 ff.

[4] NB., pp. 111, 116 ff.

[5] pp. 234 ff., 247 ff.

[6] *avirodhi* (p. 231) replaces *anirākṛtaḥ*, NB., p. 110; Stcherbatskoi, *Muséon*, v. 158. Dignāga's definition (cf. NV., pp. 119, 120) was *sādhyatvenepsitaḥ pakṣaḥ, viruddhārthānirākṛtaḥ*, the last half being condemned by NV. Subandhu (not Vasubandhu) seems to have defined it as *pakṣo yaḥ sādhayitum iṣṭaḥ* (NVT., pp. 184, 186). Gaṅgānātha Jhā's view (NS. i. 441 n., 454 n.) that he is the author of the *Vādavidhāna* (NV., pp. 120, 156) is improbable, in view of the positive evidence of the Thibetan trans., JRAS. 1914, pp. 601, 602.

however, is foreign to the Nyāya [1] or the Vaiçeṣika or to the combined school, and only the Jains [2] agree with the Buddhists and Praçastapāda in recognizing it. The reason is clear: as Uddyotakara [3] and Vācaspati Miçra [4] plainly say, if the theses are to be deemed as in themselves true or false, there would be no purpose served in recourse to the middle term, and an examination of the fallacies adduced in the Buddhist school shows that the division involves useless repetition. Vātsyāyana [5] and the schools after him accept clearly the doctrine that the thesis is neither true nor false in advance; it is a subject of doubt which is resolved by the use of the middle term, or, as Annam Bhaṭṭa [6] has it, the subject (*pakṣa*) is that which possess the conclusion in a doubtful form (*saṁdigdhasādhyavān*). So little, indeed, did Praçastapāda impress the doctrine he had borrowed on his school that Vācaspatimiçra [7] ascribes the fallacies of thesis and example to the Buddhists without hinting that he knew that Praçastapāda himself had adopted the principle. The possibility of borrowing [8] by Buddhism must therefore be entirely negatived.[9]

On the other hand, the syncretist school [10] treats errors in the definition (*lakṣaṇa*) as being closely connected with errors in the reason or middle term. A definition may be too general (*ativyāpti*), and include the characteristics which are found in other things than the subject of the definition, as in 'The cow is a horned animal'. This form can be compared with the unreal reason in respect of concomitance (*vyāpyatvāsiddha*) or

[1] Save Bhāsarvajña, NSāra, pp. 13, 14, 138–44; cf. PSPM., p. 50.
[2] Siddhasena, NA. 21, 24 : Māṇikya, PMS. vi. 12, 40.
[3] NV., pp. 116–20.
[4] NVT., p. 32.
[5] NBh. i. 1. 1.
[6] TS., § 49.
[7] NVT., p. 239.
[8] Jacobi, NGWG. 1901, p. 483.
[9] Stcherbatskoi, *Muséon*, v. 156–8.
[10] TB., pp. 110, 111; TK., p. 21; TSD., § 3.

the too general form of the indeterminate reason. Or a definition may be too narrow (*avyāpti*), as when a cow is defined as tawny, and other coloured cows are excluded. Or the definition may be impossible (*asaṁbhava*) as when the cow is defined as whole hooved, both this and the preceding being varieties of the unreal in respect of the substratum. A correct definition is negatively defined as one which is free from any of these three faults, and more positively by Vātsyāyana[1] as an attribute which differentiates what is defined from all things other than itself. This characteristic results in the definition of the schools being largely reduced to the statement of the specific difference possessed by any thing, and in many cases definition takes place by negation of certain attributes within a wider conception.[2]

In addition to fallacies Gautama devotes three other categories to logical errors, but the later texts treat them with as scanty consideration as they deserve. The first is the fraud or cheating (*chala*), which consists merely in the giving of false interpretations to the words of an adversary in discussion. The forms of this device are three; a word may be understood in the sense which appertains to another word of the same form, as for instance *nava* may be meant as 'new' and interpreted as 'nine'. Or the word may be given too wide a sense (*sāmānyachala*), or a metaphorical expression may be interpreted literally (*upacārachala*).[3]

The second class consists of futile objections (*jāti*),[4] of

[1] NBh. i. 1. 2.

[2] TR., pp. 75, 76, shows that a definition is really a purely negative inference.

[3] NS. i. 2. 10–17 with commentary; NSāra, pp. 16, 17, 161–6; TB., p. 111; TSD., § 81; GSAI. xix. 342 ff.; NSāra, pp. 16, 17, 161–6; TR., pp. 239–46.

[4] NS. v. 1; NSāra, pp. 17–23, 167–91; TB., pp. 111, 112; TSD., § 81; ṢDST., pp. 81–7; TR., pp. 247–317.

which Gautama enumerates twenty-four, while the syncretist texts barely mention them. The examples given show clearly enough their nature: to serious arguments, the opponent replies by other reasons analogous in character, but lacking the serious nature of true inference. Thus, if it is argued that the soul is inactive, because it is all-pervading like ether, it may be answered that it is active, because it is the seat of union like a pot. Or if it is said that sound is non-eternal, because like ether it is a product, the reply is that it is eternal, because as an object of auditory perception it is dissimilar to a pot. It is characteristic of the nature of Gautama's work that Chapter I of Book V of the *Nyāya Sūtra* should be devoted to the detail of this topic.

The third class consists of Occasions for Reproof (*nigraha-sthāna*)[1] of which Gautama enumerates and defines twenty-two in the next chapter of Book V. They represent occasions when a disputant exposes himself to rebuke and humiliation by committing some error of an obvious character, such as arises when a man allows himself to wander from the subject or be distracted from the matter under discussion. Thus a man may be guilty of giving away in the example his own proposition (*pratijñā-hāni*), of departing from it (*pratijñāntara*), of opposing it (*pratijñā-virodha*), of renouncing it (*pratijñā-saṁnyāsa*), of shifting the reason (*hetv-antara*) or of shifting the topic (*arthāntara*). His remarks may be meaningless, unintelligible, incoherent, or inopportune; he may say too little or too much. Or he may repeat himself or be reduced to silence or to display ignorance, when an argument has thrice been repeated before him under the eyes of the assembly. Again, he may show lack of ingenuity (*apratibhā*), or evade discussion on

[1] NS. v. 2; NSāra, pp. 23-8, 191-8; TB., pp. 112, 113; TSD., § 81; ŞDST., pp. 87-93; TR., pp. 318-64.

plea of business, or admit a defect on his own side while criticizing one on the other, or fail to censure an error or censure what is correct, or depart from a tenet which forms the basis of reasoning (*apasiddhānta*), while the fallacies proper are naturally included as a specially appropriate occasion for rebuke.

These miscellaneous classes have, it is clear, for the most part but little direct connexion with logical errors, and fall rather within the sphere of dialectic. Strictly logical are only such cases as those of inconsistency with the proposition in its various aspects or the shifting of the reason enunciated in the second member of the syllogism by the use of a different reason in the third member. In cases such as the *regressus ad infinitum* (*anavasthā*), the reasoning in a circle (*cakraka*), the *ignoratio elenchi* (*ātmāçraya*), and others,[1] the errors which occur can be regarded as series of syllogisms partly invalid. Nor is it difficult, if it were worth while, to show that the various sorts of logical errors can be reduced to the violation of one or other of the five conditions laid down for the correctness of the middle term.

From the Nyāya school it is at least probable that the other schools borrowed their criticism of invalid reasoning. It is true that the claim has been made by competent authority[2] that the conception of the *regressus ad infinitum* as a means of argument is to be referred to the Sāṁkhya school. But already in Gautama[3] the principle is adduced in the discussion of the indivisibility of atoms to which exception is taken on the ground that, if each atom is capable of division, the process will continue *ad infinitum*, which involves a *regressus ad*

[1] Cf. KKK. ii. 218 ff.

[2] Garbe, *Sāṁkhya*, pp. 157–60 (cf. ed. 2, pp. 216 ff.); *contra*, Suali, *Intr.* p. 117.

[3] iv. 2. 25.

infinitum and, as such, is not permissible. The doctrine, however, on which the conception is based is not expounded by Gautama: perhaps to him it seemed obvious that such a conception was not permissible, and the possibility that an explanation could only be found in a perfectly coherent system did not occur to him or his successors.

CHAPTER V

THE NATURE AND AUTHORITY OF SPEECH

1. *The Nature of Speech.*

THE recognition by the Nyāya and of the syncretist school, save Çivāditya, of verbal knowledge (*çabda*) as a means of proof imposed upon them a careful survey of the nature and origin of language, in which, however, their freedom of thought was strictly limited by the presuppositions which they inherited. Each word has, they hold,[1] a significance (*çakti*), which is the convention (*samaya*) made by God that such and such a meaning should be understood from such and such a word. All language is, therefore, conventional, but the modern school varies the rigour of the ancient by admitting in the case of proper names the exception that the convention is imposed by human instrumentality, while some supporters at least of the older view argued that, though the immediate instrument was man, yet in giving a proper name the father was obeying the command of scripture to assign a name to his son, and therefore the action was ultimately divine, a subtlety which even Viçvanātha rejects. Of more value is the further definition of significance given by Annam Bhaṭṭa, which makes it that relation between word and object which serves to call the object to memory when the word is spoken. The nature of significance, as the power in

[1] TK., p. 16; TS., § 59; SM. on BP. 81; NSāra, pp. 29, 209–19.

words to convey the sense imposed upon them by convention, human or divine, is not further elucidated in the Nyāya, which rejects, however,[1] the Mīmāṅsā doctrine of the existence of a special category of power (*çakti*), taking just exception to the multiplication of entities which would result if every capacity of a substance were thus given the rank of a category.

Freed from the burden of a binding tradition the Nyāya was able to deal more effectively with the problem of the precise denotation of words. To the Mīmāṅsā a word denotes the class (*jāti*), and the notion of the individual (*vyakti*) arose from necessary implication only, an opinion shared by the schools of grammar and rhetoric.[2] The modern Nyāya, for its part, adopted the other extreme view: the word denoted the individual concrete object, its attributes coming in by implication alone. The Vedānta sought to combine the opposing views by a distinction between the express and latent signification of the word, which was deemed primarily to refer to the class concept, but only to do so in virtue of its acknowledged connexion with the concrete objects included in the class. The Buddhist view was very different: faithful to the opinion that the true nature of anything cannot be known, but merely its differentia, they held that the signification of a word was merely expressive of distinction from other things (*apoha*). To the ancient Nyāya,[3] which Annam Bhaṭṭa and Viçvanātha follow, the word, denotes at once the individual object, the class of which it is a member, and the distinctive property of the class (*ākṛti*).

[1] TC. iv. 1. 460 ff.; ÇV., pp. 347 ff.; SS. v. 97; TR., pp. 163, 164, quoting the *Prameyapārāyaṇa*; PSPM., p. 90; ibid., pp. 54–8, refutes the convention theory.

[2] TC. iv. 1. 556 ff.; Müller, *Six Systems*, pp. 530 ff.; Pāṇinidarçana, SDS., ch. xiii; PSPM., pp. 153–6; Çaṅkara, BS. i. 3. 28

[3] NS. ii. 2. 60–8; TC. iv. 1. 589 ff.; NBh., pp. 121 ff.; NV., pp. 314 ff.

While the meaning of language is conventional, the modes of acquiring it are various. The Vedānta lays stress on the use of gesture: objects are pointed out to the child and the names given. Other sources given by the Nyāya include the usage of life, in which the child by hearing the same word used in different contexts gradually comes to learn its sense; grammar, which teaches the meaning of roots, terminations, and cases; dictionaries; instruction by experts; comparison; explanation by synonyms; context and contiguity, the former applicable in the case of a word of generic meaning whose precise sense is thus indicated, and the latter serving to make clear the meaning of an unknown word by its proximity to others already familiar.

The sense of the words thus acquired is the primary or direct sense as opposed to the secondary of implied signification (*lakṣaṇā*).[1] The primary sense, however, may bear various relations to the etymology of the term. It may remain true to its root meaning (*yaugika*), as in 'cooker' from 'cook'; it may have a customary sense (*rūḍhi*), as in *ghaṭa*, 'pot', which, even if it is to be traced, as held by one school of Indian grammar to a root, still bears no obvious connexion with it; or it may without sacrificing its etymological sense be restricted by custom to one only of the objects to which it might apply (*yoga-rūḍha*), as in the case of *hastin*, 'elephant', where usage has confined the term 'possessing a hand' to one only of the animals which might thus have been styled. More artificial is a fourth class (*yaugika-rūḍha*) mentioned by Jagadīça[2] and Viçvanātha, which includes words whose sense might be explained equally well either as etymological or customary.

[1] TC. iv. 2. 660 ff.; cf. *Padārtharatnamālā*, p. 16.

[2] TA., p. 21; cf. TC. iv. 2. 591.

The implied sense falls in the view of the ancient Nyāya into four subdivisions: in the first the original sense is merged in the implied meaning as in 'the tribunal applauds'; in the second the original sense remains, but something further is suggested, as in 'Guard the ghee from the crows', where the command is understood to apply also to other birds; in the third, a part of the primary sense is left out, and a part retained, as in the Vedānta doctrine 'That thou art', where 'that' denotes the unqualified absolute, and 'thou' the qualified soul, which, divested of its qualities, is the absolute; fourthly, by a process of implication on implication, the term *dvirepha*, 'having two r's', originally applied to the word *bhramara*, 'bee', is used of the bee itself. This last class is rejected by the modern school,[1] which attributes it to the Vedānta. The modern school differ also from their predecessors in their view of the cause which gives rise to implication; the latter assert that it arises from the inapplicability of the primary sense in the context, but the modern school with more justice claim that it depends on the purpose of the speaker, for in some cases there is no apparent incompatibility between the literal sense and the context to give rise to implication.

Govardhana[2] gives a different division of the implied sense into primary (*çuddha*), and secondary (*gauṇī*), the former of which includes the first two of the divisions ordinarily accepted. The secondary form of implication covers such a case as *Gañgāyām ghoṣaḥ*, 'the cowherds' station on the Ganges', where the qualities of coolness and holiness which mark the current of the sacred river are attributed to its bank. The doctrine is important,

[1] It is given by Viçvanātha only; cf. NKoça, p. 639; Jayadeva on TC. iv. 2. 660.

[2] On TS., § 59.

for it is part of the reply of the Nyāya to the doctrine of suggestion (*vyañjanā*) on which from the eighth century onwards an important school of poetics was founded.[1] Suggestion based on words (*çābdī*) was classed by the Nyāya as secondary implication: suggestion based on thought was included under inference. Thus when the maiden says

Go, if thou wilt, beloved; safe be thy journeying;
There may rebirth be mine, where thy journey endeth,

the intimation that parting will cause her death is attributed by the theory of poetics to suggestion, but by the Nyāya is regarded as merely inference. The theory which reduces suggestion to inference has its classical exponent in Mahima Bhaṭṭa, and formed the subject of an elaborate refutation by Mammaṭa, but his arguments failed to persuade the Nyāya school of the untruth of their theory.

Words, however, by themselves alone convey no meaning; they derive their signification from their serving as members of sentences (*vākya*), a term which in the Nyāya view applies not merely to propositions containing verbs, but to any collocation of words, such as a noun and adjective, which has a definite sense. In this view the Nyāya conflicts as often with the Prābhākara Mīmāṅsā,[2] which finds that words have significance only when constructed with a verb, which lends significance to the subject, object, or other qualification of the action which it expresses. In the Nyāya view no such primacy belongs to the verb or any other part of speech: the meaning is conveyed by the collective sense of all

[1] Jacobi, ZDMG. lvi. 396 ff.; NGWG. 1908, pp. 1 ff.; *Vyaktiviveka* (Trivandrum S.S. 1909), pp. 2 ff.

[2] PSPM., p. 63; Kumārila allows of significance in words; NV., p. 315, is directed, acc. to NVT., against the Prābhākara view; cf. NSM., pp. 161 ff.

the words taken together.[1] But it is not every collocation of words that can give a meaning: there are three requisites which must be fulfilled to secure this result. The first is, as viewed from the standpoint of the listener, expectancy (*ākāṅkṣā*)[2]: the word *ghaṭam*, accusative of 'jar', by itself is unintelligible: it requires its complement in *ānaya* 'bring', where the root *ā-nī* is expressed in the second person imperative; from the point of view of the word it, and each element of it, demands supplementing by another word or words. Secondly, there must be compatibility (*yogyatā*)[3] between the meanings of the words: 'water burns' is syntactically possible, but contrary to reality and, therefore, meaningless. In the third place, the words must stand in proximity (*saṁnidhi, āsatti*). A word itself consists of a number of sounds, each of which exists for three moments only, that of its production, of its perception, and of its passing away, so that the perception of a word bears a similarity to the process of recognition: the sense is apprehended at the last moment when the final sound is heard, and the earlier sounds remain only in memory.[4] In a series of words if there intervenes too long an interval between any of them they cannot be apprehended as a single whole, and therefore reasonable proximity is necessary, whether the words be spoken or arranged in writing. It is not enough, however, that these conditions should be fulfilled for the meaning of a sentence to be appre-

[1] TC. iv. 1. 460 ff.

[2] TC. iv. 1. 185–244; TA., p. 20; TB., pp. 47–9; TK., pp. 16, 17; TS., §§ 60, 61; BP. 84.

[3] TC. iv. 1. 245–85: TA., &c., *u.s.*; BP. 83.

[4] TB., pp. 49, 50; NBh., p. 121; NV., p. 314, negative the *sphoṭa* theory which denies to letters the power of denoting things and invents an intermediate entity, a sound, whence knowledge of things is derived; see SDS., ch. xiii; YS. i. 52; *contra*, SS. v. 57; Çaṅkara BS. i. 3. 28.

hended: their existence must be recognized by the hearer or reader, for, if he does not do so, he will misunderstand the sense, while, on the other hand, even if they are absent, he may by conceiving them to exist read a possible sense into the words.[1]

A further condition is, however, laid down by Gañgeça,[2] Viçvanātha, and Jagadīça, and implied in the view of Annam Bhaṭṭa. They require knowledge of the intention of the speaker (*vaktṛ-tātparya-jñāna*) by which means alone, for example, can one distinguish between the two senses of the words *saindhavam ānaya*, 'bring my horse' and 'bring salt'. But serious objections are urged against this view, on the ground that words which convey a definite sense may yet not be uttered with the purpose of conveying that sense. Thus a fool may utter words which he does not understand, or a parrot repeat a sentence without knowing its meaning, and it is not a sufficient reply to argue that such sentences are apparent only, not real. A Vedic text must have a definite meaning, yet it may be recited by a man who does not understand a word of it, it may be wrongly expounded by a teacher, or it may be read in a book. In the last case there is no speaker whose intention can be understood: in the two former the speaker does not intend to express what is really the meaning. If the orthodox view is adopted, which attributes to God the authorship of the text, so that the intention to be known is his, there is the fatal objection that the meaning of Vedic sentences may perfectly well be understood by those who reject the view that God is their author. A very different definition of intention is, therefore, given by the *Vedāntaparibhāṣā*,[3] which makes it consist

[1] TC. iv. 1. 286–318; TA., &c., *u. s.*

[2] TC. iv. i. 319–74; TA., p. 20; BP. 84; TSD., § 59.

[3] p. 20.

in the fitness of words to express a particular meaning, there being no utterance with the intention to convey a different sense, the proviso being intended to cover the case of equivocal terms like *saindhavam*, where the intention of the speaker is to convey one sense only.

Propositions fall into three classes, command (*vidhi*), prohibition (*niṣedha*), and explanation (*arthavāda*).[1] A command is a sentence which conveys knowledge which forms a base for action as in 'Let him who desires the heaven offer the Jyotiṣṭoma sacrifice'. It takes the two forms of a categorical imperative (*niyoga*), applicable to rules which must be obeyed in every case, or of a permission (*anujñā*), as in the case of rites, the performance of which is optional. A prohibition affords knowledge of an act which as injurious is to be avoided, while an explanation covers the rest of the field of propositions, and includes whatever serves to make clear the meaning of a text. These divisions primarily apply to Vedic texts, but are transferred also to profane works.

2. *The Authority of Speech.*

The exact nature of verbal knowledge as a means of proof is a matter of some difficulty, and there appears to have been a diversity of opinion between the older and the modern school. Annam Bhaṭṭa[2] defines verbal knowledge as the knowledge of the meaning conveyed by the whole sentence, and ascribes as its proximate or special cause the spoken word (*çabda*), by which the sense was conveyed. This view is consistent in taking the unit of understanding as the sentence, and it is unnecessary to suggest that Annam Bhaṭṭa may have

[1] TK., p. 17; NS. ii. 1. 63 divides into *vidhi* (TC. iv. 21 ff.), *arthavāda* (ibid. 460 ff.), and *anuvāda*. Cf. TSD., § 81: PSPM., pp. 110 ff.

[2] TS., § 63; NVT. i. 1. 3 emphasizes that knowledge is of the things denoted by the sentence.

been prepared to accept the theory as applicable to individual words. On the other hand, the definition, viewed in the light of the proximate cause assigned, leaves no room for written works. The defects of this view are avoided in the definition of Viçvanātha,[1] who makes the knowledge of words (*pada-jñāna*), not words, the proximate cause, on which supervenes the comprehension of their signification, the final result being verbal knowledge. This view, which is that of the modern school, is supported by a quaint argument: if the word alone were the proximate cause of verbal knowledge, how could a verse written by a dumb man be understood as it is in fact?[2]

The *Nyāya Sūtra*[3] establishes the authority of verbal testimony as the assertion of a trustworthy person against the claim that it is inference in a manner which seems largely to give away the case. It admits that, as in inference something unseen is inferred from what is seen, and as in inference we argue from a sign, e.g. smoke to a conclusion, e.g. fire, so in verbal testimony we draw an inference from a word to a thing, signified by it. But the answer is that there is reliance in the matter signified by a word because the word is used by a reliable person (*āpta*). There is no perception of connexion between a word and its sense such as we find at the basis of inference. There is indeed a connexion, but it is conventional, as is seen in the actual facts of speech, where diverse peoples use diverse words for the same thing. The further objections[4] to the authoritative character of the Veda based on its falsehood, contradiction, and tautology are refuted by arguing that the alleged untruths are due to some defect in the rite,

[1] BP. 81.

[2] NSāra, p. 210, gives gesture and writing as equivalent to speech.

[3] ii. 1. 49–57.

[4] ii. 1. 58–69.

performer, or instrument, through which the hoped for result of sacrifice, e.g. the attainment of a son, is unattained; that the contradictions are merely cases of alternatives permitted; and that the alleged tautology is really useful repetition. The Veda, therefore, is accorded authoritativeness like the spell and medicine because of the authority of their authors; the Sūtra leaving it uncertain whether it ascribed the Veda to God. The *Vaiçeṣika Sūtra*[1] stands in much the same position. It asserts the conventional character of language, and declares the composition of the Veda to have been due to intelligence. Moreover, it seems to assert that the assignment of names is a proof of the existence of beings distinguished from ordinary men, a statement which, if it does not point to the recognition of God as the giver of names, does indicate the recognition of seers.[2] Further doubt is created by the twice[3] repeated assertion that scripture is authoritative, because it is proclaimed by God or proclaims the duty of man, as the terms *tadvacanāt* are variously, and not without a plausible ground in either case, explained, the former version having the authority of Praçastapāda, though it suffers from the disadvantage that God is not directly referred to anywhere in the Sūtra. The claim of verbal testimony to be a separate proof is disposed of by the assertion that it is explained by inference,[4] which gives us either the argument that the conclusion is inferred from the fact that scripture is authoritative as proclaimed by God, or from the fact that it is authoritative as proclaiming the sacred law. In any case scripture is freely used by Kaṇāda to confirm his arguments as it is used by Gautama.

The view of the Nyāya is followed by the syncretist

[1] ii. 2. 14–20; vi. 1. 1–4.
[2] ii. 1. 18.
[3] i. 1. 3; x. 2. 9.
[4] ix. 2. 3.

school, which in this measure formally departs from the Vaiçeṣika proper, which rejected verbal knowledge as a separate means of proof just as it rejected comparison, including both under inference. When words are pronounced, they argued,[1] and their meaning is recollected, there takes place an inference which may be formulated thus: the meanings of the words which are heard are connected with one another, because they are brought to my recollection by the aid of words, which are connected by relations of expectation, compatibility, and proximity. More simply the argument may be put thus: before a man can utter words he must appreciate the connexion between the ideas which he is about to express in language, as is shown by their possessing expectancy, &c., and it is not language which establishes this connexion. The reply of the Nyāya-Vaiçeṣika, as given by Annam Bhaṭṭa,[2] rests, as in the case of comparison, on a psychological ground: the consciousness resulting from verbal knowledge as a means of proof is asserted, with truth, to be different from that obtained from the use of formal inference, but this reply does not meet the real point at issue. Udayana[3] attempts a more formal answer: taking the syllogistic form of the Vaiçeṣika argument, he seeks to demonstrate that the premisses do not warrant a certain conclusion, while anything else than a certain conclusion is of no value.

In the Vaiçeṣika view, as presented by Praçastapāda,[4] it is probable that we must recognize the influence of the Buddhist logic which declined to accept verbal knowledge as a separate source of proof, on the ground

[1] TC. iv. 1. 22 ff.; PSPM., pp. 63–6, rejects human testimony as not in itself valid, but only if we believe the speaker to be truthful.

[2] TSD., § 68; cf. NSM., pp. 136–44.

[3] Kus. iii. 13. Cf. NSāra commentary, p. 209; ÇD., p. 51. The whole view is refuted, KKK. i. 335–46.

[4] p. 206 ff.; above, ch. iii, § 2, pp. 106–8.

that it was itself merely an effect of the reality which it represented. Just as when we see smoke we deduce the presence of fire, so when we hear a true word we deduce the reality which it stands for: every word then is a causal conclusion, the thing it represents being the cause, and the word the consequence of the cause which is the real fact. The place of verbal knowledge, therefore, in the view of Dignāga is to be found only in the syllogism as reasoning for another, not as an independent means of proof. Praçastapāda, however, departs from the spirit of the Buddhist theory by his acceptance of the authority of the master, Kaṇāda, as decisive, and in effect the conception of authority nominally rejected by the Vaiçeṣika, thus reappears in full strength. It is easy, therefore, to understand how the syncretist school accepted the Nyāya [1] view without question, since in recognizing the validity of the dicta of Kaṇāda Praçastapāda in effect rendered the refusal to accept verbal knowledge as a means of proof meaningless. Vyomaçiva [2] indeed accepted formally verbal testimony as a means of proof.

Not all propositions of course are authoritative: that character applies only to Vedic texts, and to the utterances of a man worthy of credence, and a man's credibility depends in the ultimate issue according to Annam Bhaṭṭa [3] on the fact that he speaks the truth, or according to Keçava Miçra [4] that he describes things as they really

[1] Bhāsarvajña (NSāra, p. 29) holds that the validity of verbal testimony is established by experience of its truth in practice (e.g. the result of sacrifice) and the absence of ground for disbelief in one thus competent to declare unseen things, which are the main sphere of verbal testimony.

[2] ṢDST. 67; cf. SSS. v. 33.

[3] TSD., § 59.

[4] TB., p. 46; TR., pp. 94, 95: *yathāvasthitārthadarçī yathādṛṣṭārthavādī cāptaḥ*. The divine authority is dealt with, ibid. pp. 12, 58.

are. In both cases the Nyāya view accepts the utterances as correct on the ground that it believes for reasons which it thinks sufficient that they do reveal the truth of the universe: there is here no question of faith in revelation contrary to the claims of reason: *credo quia incredibile* is not the attitude of any adherent of the Nyāya; what is revealed forms a complete system of coherent truth.

The Veda, however, is not all of equal authority: it is divided in the later Nyāya into the four classes of Çruti, Smṛti, Itihāsa, and Purāṇa in a descending order of value. Çruti is the primary fountain of knowledge: Smṛti is available only when it does not contradict it, or when Çruti is silent on the point at issue; the other two sources are of inferior importance. Çruti again includes the four Vedas, each with its subdivisions of Saṁhitā, Brāhmaṇa, and Āraṇyaka, including Upaniṣad: Smṛti is represented by the law books, and Itihāsa and Purāṇa by the epic and the Purāṇas. The Çruti alone is treated as divine in origin, and therefore unconditionally worthy of credence: the other authorities have human authors, and therefore are liable to be erroneous.[1]

The claim, however, that the Çruti is the work of God is assailed by the Mīmāṅsā,[2] which urges the view that the Veda is not the work either of man or of God, but exists for ever in its own right. How, they ask, could God, who as incorporeal has no organs of speech, utter the words which make it up? If it be argued that he assumed a human form for the purpose of revelation, the

[1] Athalye, TS., p. 350; PSPM., pp. 128 ff.

[2] ÇV., pp. 35 ff., 358, 553–5; SDS., p. 104. Cf. the Sāṁkhya view, SS. v. 42, 45 ff., where the authorship and eternality of the Veda are denied, but its self-proved authority upheld; PSPM., p. 66. For God's authorship see Kus. ii and iv.

answer is that by such assumption he would lose his power of revelation, being subjected to all the limitations of material existence. Moreover they deny that there is any tradition of either divine or human authorship: the sages mentioned apparently as authors did no more than apprehend the hymns and hand them down in schools. Positively they adduce passages which assert that the Veda is eternal and uncreated. Against them the Nyāya [1] urges that other passages assert the creation of the Veda, but it also adduces more effective arguments. All propositions which we know of have authors, as in the case of those we ourselves enunciate or those of the *Mahābhārata*. To the Mīmāṅsā retort that the argument applies only to works whose authorship is known as in the case of the epic, the Nyāya replies that the authorship of God is assured for the Veda by the testimony of Gautama, in whose school it has been handed down. Moreover if the Vedas were eternal, the sounds in them would coexist from eternity, and it would be impossible to arrange them in the deliberate order which alone permits of their being a means of verbal knowledge. The Vedas, then, must have an author, and their transcendental wisdom forbids our supposing that any man could have excogitated them, leaving us no option but to ascribe them to God.

The Mīmāṅsā, however, has no hesitation in asserting that sound is eternal: [2] it is a quality of the ether, and like it eternal; the beating of a drum reveals it to our ears, but does not call it into being; when any letter is

[1] TC. iv. 1. 83 ff.; TSD., § 62, with Nīlakaṇṭha's commentary; NSāra, pp. 29, 214–16.

[2] MS. i. 1. 6–23; ÇV., pp. 408–85 (words), 486–552 (Veda); PSPM., pp. 56–61; cf. Çaṅkara, BS. i. 3. 28. Müller's theory (*Six Systems*, pp. 196 ff., 520 ff.) of the word as a creative power is clearly not in the texts.

pronounced in our hearing we recognize it at once with absolute certainty, which would be impossible if its existence were momentary only as the Ṇyāya believes. The Nyāya rejects the doctrine of the eternity of sound: Gautama[1] gives three reasons for this view; that sound has a beginning; that it is perceived by an organ of sense; and that like any other product it has attributes. If we recognize as we do a sound like *ga* when pronounced by diverse persons at diverse times, it is because of the identity of the specific character (*jāti*) of the sound which always accompanies it whenever it is uttered, or in a homely simile it is like the flame of a lamp which, relit after being extinguished, is nevertheless regarded by us as the same as the flame which originally stood in its place.

The Veda, then, is for the Nyāya a divine revelation of eternal truth, but it is supplemented by the statements of men whose knowledge of the truth confers upon them a right to our belief.[2] Such men are Gautama and Kaṇāda, the founders, according to tradition, of the Nyāya and the Vaiçeṣika systems, and it is in the light of this position that the importance of verbal knowledge becomes clearly revealed. The aim of philosophy is not to discover a theory of the universe: it has the more modest aim of enabling us to understand as a reasoned system those truths which are revealed for us by scripture or discerned by seers with the superhuman power of direct perception which such men, as we have seen, command. It is not enough that man should accept tradition alone, for his beliefs then would be blind and inaccurate: he must study the lines of reasoning laid down in the systems which establish how the truth of

[1] NS. ii. 2. 14–59; TC. iv. 1. 375–464; NSāra, pp. 29, 216–19.
[2] TC. iv. 1. 88 ff.

the revelation can be apprehended. But, if man were to attempt this study without the aid furnished by the declarations of the seers, his chance of success would be negligible: mere ordinary reasoning and perception do not avail in the doctrine of the schools to seize the fundamental truth of the universe.

CHAPTER VI

THE DIALECTICAL CATEGORIES

THE categories of Gautama are essentially nothing more than the headings of chapters of a handbook of logic and dialectics, and they agree thus in nothing save the name with the serious attempt in the Vaiçeṣika system to afford a classification of all existence. The first, the means of proof (*pramāṇa*) would normally be expected to contain the whole theory of knowledge, but it must be supplemented by the third, which treats of doubt (*saṁçaya*), the fifth and seventh which treat of the example (*dṛṣṭānta*) and the members of the syllogism (*avayava*), the eighth which deals with *reductio ad absurdum* (*tarka*), and the last four of the sixteen which cover the topics of fallacies (*hetvābhāsa*), fraud or travesty (*chala*), futile objections (*jāti*), and occasions for reproof (*nigrahasthāna*). The second category, on the other hand, which deals with objects of proof (*prameya*) contains the metaphysics of the Nyāya and corresponds roughly with the Vaiçeṣika categories, while the fourth category, purpose (*prayojana*) deals with the motives of activity and falls therefore in the same sphere. There remain, therefore, five categories which do not enter into the spheres proper to the doctrine of knowledge or metaphysics, but have greater affinity with the former, since they deal with dialectical discussion and debate. These are the investigations of the nature of principles of discussion (*siddhānta*), which forms the sixth category; of determination (*nirṇaya*), the ninth category; of formal discussion (*vāda*), the tenth category; and of wrangling (*jalpa*), and cavilling, (*vitaṇḍā*), which are the eleventh and twelfth in the series.

With the advance of the philosophical character of the school these dialectical categories became of less and less importance, and in the syncretist texts which adopt as a rule the order of topics suggested by the Vaiçeṣika categories they are little noticed. But Keçava Miçra respects the order of the Nyāya, and from him and his commentator Govardhana it is possible to gather some knowledge of the development in conception of these categories which took place between the time of Vātsyāyana and the modern school. It is of some interest that, while Keçava Miçra tends to accord with Vātsyāyana, his commentator follows the views which also find expression in Viçvanātha's commentary on the Sūtra.

This division of opinion is specially marked in the case of the category of principle or dogma (*siddhānta*), which Gautama [1] describes and subdivides into four classes, but with such vagueness of expression as to leave full room for the ingenuity of commentators. Its real sense is doubtless that of a tenet considered as part of the system of a school: in the later definition of Keçava Miçra it appears as a thing admitted because it is established by one of the means of proof, which is wider in extent, but not substantially different, since the tenets of schools all rest on some form of proof. But it seems, further, to have denoted a result in the nature of a corollary from admitted principles, and the proceeding by which a principle of the opponent is admitted in order to refute him by showing that some proposition which he sustains is inconsistent with that principle.

[1] i. 1. 26–30 with NBh. and NV.; TB., pp. 93, 94; ṢDST., pp. 74, 75; GSAI. xix. 331; TR., pp. 170–4.

Of the four divisions of this category the first is the *sarvatantra-siddhānta* which Gautama defines as a principle which is not contrary to the views of any school, and is accepted in one's own schools. Examples are the existence of the five senses and their objects, as given by Vātsyāyana, or of sound; even if we doubt its being eternal or non-eternal all admit that there is such a thing, to adopt Keçava Miçra's instance. The modern school give it a special sense as applicable to a principle which is conceded by two disputants engaged in a discussion for the purpose of that argument. The second class consists of the *pratitantra-siddhānta*, which is defined by Gautama as that which is accepted by similar schools but rejected by other schools. Vātsyāyana illustrates this from principles common to the Sāṁkhya and Yoga, while Keçava Miçra chooses instead the Nyāya and Vaiçeṣika for his example, a difference probably significant of the fact that in Vātsyāyana's time the similarity of the schools was not yet so far advanced as later. The modern school,[1] with Govardhana, take a different and improbable view: they mean by it a principle proper to one school and rejected by another, as the eternity of sound is asserted by the Mīmāṅsā and denied by the Nyāya and vice versa. The third class, *adhikaraṇa-siddhānta*, is a principle which follows from the establishment of another principle, rather than a hypothetical principle[2] which, if accepted, leads to the acceptance of some other, for it is illustrated by the suggestion that, if we recognize God as the creator, we must recognize as a corollary his omniscience.

On the fourth class, the *abhyupagama-siddhānta*, there is an acute divergence of opinion. According to

[1] So TR., p. 171, who gives the authoritativeness of God as a case.

As taken in SBH. viii. 9. NBh. makes it a principle, the establishment of which involves establishing other points.

Keçava Miçra the obscure text of Gautama means that one admits a view of the opponent without examination of its validity in order to follow out its consequences, and thus refute another view of the opponent.[1] Thus a Mīmāṅsā disputant may admit, in arguing with a follower of the Nyāya on the nature of sound, that sound is a quality: hence he deduces that, as sound is in the Nyāya view a quality of the ether which is omnipresent, it must be without parts, and so cannot grow in size. This confutes the Nyāya argument for the non-eternity of sound based on the fact that it grows and diminishes in intensity. The moderns, again with Viçvanātha and Govardhana, understand this form of principle to be one which, not explicitly stated in the text of a school, is implied in it, as in the case of mind in the Nyāya view, for, while it is not included by Gautama as a sense organ or means of proof but as an object of proof, it is interpreted by the school to be included in the class of sense organs. It is just possible to make either sense accord with the words of the definition.

The ninth category, determination (*nirṇaya*) or ascertainment, is defined by Gautama[2] as the ascertainment of a thing after reflection on the arguments for and against it. It is clearly nothing more than the definite result of a controversy (*kathā*), the different kinds of which are specified in the tenth, eleventh, and twelfth categories.[3] The discussion (*vāda*) is a serious debate carried on by those who seek to establish truth by means of thesis (*pakṣa*) and counter-thesis (*pratipakṣa*). It must not contravene the principles of the school, must, whether in demonstration or refutation, be based on the

[1] So NBh. i. 1. 30; otherwise NV. and NVT.

[2] i. 1. 41; TB., p. 97; TSD., § 81; NSāra, pp. 15, 149.

[3] NS. i. 2. 1-3; TB., pp. 97-100; TSD., § 81; ṢDST., pp. 77-9; GSAI. xix. 334-8; NSāra, pp. 15, 16, 151-61; TR., pp. 205-16.

rules of logic, and take place in syllogistic form. There are excluded, therefore, all the means which appertain to sophistry rather than to serious discourse: thus frauds (*chala*), futile objections (*jāti*), and cavilling (*vitaṇḍā*), wrangling (*jalpa*), and occasions for reproof (*nigraha-sthāna*) are all out of place. An exception is however, sometimes made of four kinds of occasions for reproof, namely fallacies, which in any case are to be attacked, and the three peculiar forms styled deficiency (*nyūna*), which means omitting a member of the syllogism, redundancy (*adhika*), which means adducing too many members, as by adducing more than one reason or example, and deviating from a tenet (*apasiddhānta*). These are clear cases which invalidate argument, and therefore are suitable for challenge. But the discussion must be conducted on the basis of the principles which the controversialist accepts: it is impossible to censure a Buddhist for not using the Nyāya syllogism, when his own school recognize two members only in lieu of five.

Quite opposed to the dispassionate argument (*vītarāgakathā*) is the passionate contest in which victory alone is the aim and in which frauds, futile objections, and occasions for reproof are the stock in trade. Such discussions are divided into two classes, the criterion being whether or not there are both thesis and antithesis. In the former case we have wrangling, in the latter mere cavilling.

B. METAPHYSICS

CHAPTER VII

ONTOLOGY

1. *The Categories of Kaṇāda and Gautama.*

IN the syncretist school it is an accepted doctrine that all things that can be known and named, that is all things which exist, fall under seven categories (*padārtha*, 'object (corresponding to) a name'). These are substance (*dravya*), quality (*guṇa*), motion or activity (*karman*), generality (*sāmānya*), particularity (*viçeṣa*)[1] and inherence (*samavāya*), which may be regarded as positive categories, and one category of non-existence (*abhāva*). It is, however, certain that this does not represent the ancient view of the Vaiçeṣika. We have the express statement of Praçastapāda that the categories numbered six, and this tradition prevailed long after other evidence shows that the last category had been recognized. Mādhava[2] thus expressly states that the number of categories in the system is six, as does Haribhadra,[3] though his commentator adds that others recognize non-existence. The exact period when the new category was added is unknown. It was anterior to Çrīdhara, for in his exposition of Praçastapāda[4] he insists

[1] Hence the name of the Vaiçeṣika system in Praçastapāda.
[2] SDS., p. 86.
[3] ṢDS. 60; GSAI. xx. 34, 35; so SSS. v. 19, 20.
[4] NK., p. 7.

M 2

that the category of non-existence is implied though unexpressed, explaining its omission as due to the relation in what it stands to existence generally, and in another work of the same century,[1] Udayana divides the categories into existence (*bhāva*) and non-existence (*abhāva*), and then subdivides the former head into the usual six. Thus by this date the recognition of non-existence as a separate category parallel in a sense to the six positive categories had come into being, but the full step of reckoning the categories at seven had not yet been definitely accepted. We find this process complete in the work of Çivāditya, which is styled *Saptapadārthī*, the sevenfold character of the categories thus appearing as definitely established.

It is less certain whether the six categories as such were recognized by Kaṇāda. The text of the Sūtra[2] in one place expressly enumerates the six, and, though Praçastapāda's[3] treatment of the topic may be invoked as proof that the Sūtra was not in this condition when he used it, this is not sufficient proof in view of the fact that Praçastapāda is not a commentator proper. What is much more important is the fact that Kaṇāda[4] evidently conceived the first three categories to stand apart from the others; he applies to them only the term object (*artha*), and in treating of the contemplation attained by Yoga he deals with the vision thus acquired of the first

[1] *Lakṣaṇāvalī*, p. 1; Kir., p. 6; so TR., pp. 130, 163, 164.

[2] i. 1. 4.

[3] pp. 6, 7; Bodas, TS., pp. 30-2. Vātsyāyana's use of the categories (NB. i. 1. 5 and 9) is conclusive for their priority to Praçastapāda. The Mīmāṅsā has the same set of four, or in Prabhākara's case five, to which he added capacity, number, and similarity, TR., p. 163; Kir., p. 26; PSPM., pp. 88-91. Raghunātha adds *çakti*, *saṁkhyā*, *svatva*, *vaiçiṣṭhya*.

[4] viii. 2. 3. For the distinction of *astitva* in all six categories, *sattāsambandha* in the first three, *svātmasattva* in the last three, see PBh. translation, p. 49; cf. NV., pp. 323 ff.

three categories only.[1] It is still more important that Kaṇâda specifically declares generality and particularity as relative to the intelligence,[2] which at once gives them a different place from that of the first three categories, while inherence appears only as the relation between cause and effect.[3] The conception of the categories as a complete division of the real universe is therefore to be ascribed either to Praçastapāda or to some predecessor in the school.

Gautama's categories, as we have seen, are rather divisions of a treatise on logic, and it is the second object of proof (*prameya*) which most nearly corresponds to the categories of Praçastapāda. The heads of that category are the soul or self, body, the senses, the objects of sense, cognition, mind, activity, error, transmigration, the effect of good and evil deeds, pain, and liberation. The list is completed by purpose (*prayojana*), which appears as the fourth of his categories. The confusion involved in such a division is obvious, and explains fully why the syncretist school, save Keçava Miçra, follow the Vaiçeṣika in their treatment of categories.

2. *Substance, Quality, and Activity.*

Substance is a distinct genus, but a positive definition can only ascribe to it either the possession of qualities[4] and action[5] or being the intimate cause of a product.[6]

[1] ix. 1. 14.

[2] i. 2. 3; hence the mysterious *buddhilakṣaṇam* of the last three categories in PBh.; cf. Kir., p. 30.

[3] vii. 2. 26; hence it is not very closely parallel to Plato's παρουσία (cf. Lutoslawski, *Plato's Logic*, p. 254).

[4] TB., p. 69; TK., p. 1; TS., § 3; TR., p. 132. For the Yoga view cf. Wood's *Yoga System*, pp. xv-xvii.

[5] VS. i. 1. 15 has all three. PBh., p. 21, uses the criterion of indestructibility by causes or effects; cf. Kir., pp. 32-4, 43, 44; VS. i. 1. 12.

[6] TB., p. 69; BP. 23; TR., p. 132.

The first suggestion, however, is contrary to the principle that at the moment of its coming into existence a substance has no quality, while the latter expresses a fundamental principle that only substance can give rise to a product. Quality again, as defined by Kaṇāda,[1] has substance as its substratum, is without quality, and is not a cause in conjunction and disjunction, a point which differentiates it from activity or motion, which is defined as abiding in substance, devoid of quality, and the immediate cause of conjunction and disjunction.[2] Motion again differs from quality in that the latter resides permanently in substance, the former temporarily. Beyond this definition does not go: the Vedānta recognized the impossibility of defining it, and called it inexpressible (*anirvacanīya*), while the Buddhists denied its existence *in toto*, a tenet which the Nyāya-Vaiçeṣika wholly rejected, as well as the Buddhist doctrine of activity or causal efficiency[3] as the one mark of reality.

To the Buddhist argument that all is non-eternal, the *Nyāya Sūtra*[4] replies that then non-eternity is eternal, nor can it be argued that what is non-eternal perishes utterly like a fire when its fuel is burnt out. There is a distinct divergence in our perception; what we can see produced and destroyed is non-eternal, the rest is eternal, and the counter argument that, if the atoms are eternal, then their products should be so is opposed to facts of

[1] VS. i. 1. 16; SP., § 68; TB., p. 78; TK., p. 1; TSD., § 4.

[2] VS. i. 1. 17; PBh., p. 290; SP., § 69; TB., p. 86; TK., p. 1; TSD., § 5.

[3] NB., p. 103; NBT., pp. 4, 5, 9, 16, 17; SDS., p. 7; cf. SBE. xxxiv. 410; SBNT., pp. 21 ff.; NK., p. 12; SDS., p. 20; NVT., pp. 387 ff.; TR., pp. 13 ff.

[4] iv. 1. 25–40. Cf. the Mīmāṅsā arguments, ÇV., pp. 119–82; Çaṅkara on BS. ii. 2. 31; NK., pp. 41, 42; SSS. i. 34 ff. For the Buddhist view see *Mahāyānasūtrālaṁkāra*, xviii. 82–103; Ratnakīrti, SBNT., pp. 20–77; SDS., p. 12, SSS. iv. 2. 9.

perception and the conception of time. Nor is it true to contend[1] that there is no substance apart from its qualities, or whole apart from its parts. The substance is marked out by its possession of parts or qualities as one: we recognize the jar we saw yesterday which we could not do, if there were nothing but sensations of touch and colour. If it is argued that nothing is really existent, because it is non-existent as regards any other thing, 'A horse is not a cow', the reply is that each thing has a true existence which necessarily excludes the other. If the same argument[2] is based on the necessary relativity of all things, the answer is that relations imply terms as much as terms relations.

Elsewhere[3] the question of whole and part is defended against the argument of unreality in connexion with the suggestion that perception is really inference, as we see only part of any object and not the whole. If there were no whole, it is pointed out there could be no perception, for without a unit everything would be liable to resolution into its ultimate atoms, which are not perceptible. Yet another attempt is made to meet this issue.[4] The Buddhist opponent asserts that the whole (*avayavin*) cannot exist, since the parts cannot reside in it either as a whole or partially, nor can it reside in them nor apart from them, nor is it identical with them. The answer given is that the attempt to treat the conception of a whole as a matter of spatial location is mistaken; a whole is something over and above the parts, which stand to it not in a spatial relation, but in a unique

[1] *Madhyamaka Vṛtti*, pp. 64, 71; Āryadeva in *M. Vṛtti*, p. 71.

[2] *M. Sūtra*, xv. 1, 6; *Āryaratnākara Sūtra* in *Vṛtti*, p. 90.

[3] ii. 1. 30-6; NB., pp.80-6; NV., pp. 219-52, insist on the argument that a whole is necessary to explain our conceptions of magnitude, conjunction, motion, and class; a curious argument as to weight as a criterion of a whole is found, NV., pp. 237 ff.

[4] iv. 2. 4-14; Cf. ÇV., pp. 329-47; SS. i. 42; PSPM., pp. 95-8

relation of inherence. The question stands, of course, in immediate relation to the kindred one of cause and effect; the Buddhists[1] deny that an effect before its production can be described as existent, non-existent, or both; the Nyāya[2] contends that a whole which is an effect is non-existent before its production from its causes, thus keeping in harmony with their doctrine that a whole is something entirely other than the parts from which it is made up.

There are nine substances, the four atomic, earth, water, fire, and air; ether; time and space; the self, or soul, and mind. The existence of yet another is postulated by the Mīmāṅsā of Kumārila[3] to explain darkness, whose claim to be a substance rests on its possession of blue colour and motion. These attributes are denied by Annam Bhaṭṭa,[4] who declares darkness to be no more than the absence of large illuminating light in general, a view akin to that of Prabhākara, who held that it was the absence of knowledge of light, while Çrīdhara[5] suggests that it the imposition on something else of blue colour. Darkness, therefore, is classed with non-existence pure and simple, as it is illegitimate to attempt to set up special categories of non-existence corresponding to each form of being.

The qualities enumerated by Kaṇāda[6] are seventeen: colour, taste, smell, and touch; numbers, dimensions, individuality, conjunction and disjunction, priority and posteriority, cognitions, pleasure and pain, desire and aversion, and volitions. The list has obvious imperfec-

[1] *M. Sūtra*, i. 6; vii. 20; Āryadeva in *M. Vṛtti*, p. 16; cf. Çaṅkara, BS. ii. 2. 26, 27.

[2] iv. 1. 48-54; below, § 4.

[3] ÇV., p. xliii; Ani. SS. i. 56; PSPM., p. 93.

[4] TSD., § 3; BM. on BP. 3; see VS. v. 2, 19, 20.

[5] NK., p. 9; cf. SP., §§ 55, 175; Kir., pp. 15-20.

[6] i. 1. 6.

tions, and the commentators from Praçastapāda[1] downwards are unanimous in interpreting the word 'and' used in connexion with the last member as implying others. The orthodox list is made up to twenty-four by adding gravity, fluidity, and viscidity; merit and demerit; sound and faculty; the last vague term being extended to cover velocity, elasticity, and mental impression. But some reduce the number by three, omitting priority and posteriority as depending directly on time and space, and individuality as the special form of non-existence styled mutual non-existence (*anyonyābhāva*). Others, however, increase the number by three or four, adding lightness, softness or hardness, and laziness, but these are rejected by Annam Bhaṭṭa[2] on the ground that lightness and laziness are the mere negatives of gravity and volition, while the other two depend on the degree of conjunction or disjunction.

Of these qualities[3] five belong to all substances—number, dimension, individuality, conjunction and disjunction, and may therefore rank as general[4] qualities. Time and space have no others; the ether has sound also. The four atomic substances have the five general qualities and priority and posteriority; air has also tangibility or rather temperature, and velocity; fire has temperature, colour, fluidity, and velocity; water has the qualities of fire with the addition of taste, gravity, and viscidity; earth has the same qualities as water, less viscidity, and smell. Mind which is regarded as corporeal (*mūrta*) has the seven qualities of the atomic substances

[1] p. 10.

[2] TSD., § 4; cf. for others NK., pp. 10 ff.

[3] BP. 25-34; elasticity also belongs to all tangible things.

[4] In the school terminology (PBh., p. 96) this class includes priority, posteriority, gravity, artificial fluidity, and velocity. But only the five belong to all substances. Comparison with primary qualities is misleading. All are real; NK., pp. 59, 96.

and velocity. The self has the five general qualities, and nine of its own, cognition, pleasure and pain, desire and aversion, volition, merit and demerit, and mental impression, while God has the five general qualities and cognition, desire and volition alone. While the qualities generally are attributes of one substratum only, conjunction and disjunction, number beginning with two, and individuality, in so far as resulting from reciprocal exclusion between two or more things, must have a multiple substrate.[1]

More important for the distinction of substance than any of these divisions is that between all pervading[2] (*gatatva*) substances which have extreme magnitude (*paramamahatpramāṇavattva*) and those which are corporeal (*mūrta*) and have limited magnitude (*paricchinnaparimāṇavattva*) or as is equivalent motion, since that implies the movement of the parts or whole from place to place, which is possible only if the substance is limited in space. Corporeal substances include the four atomic substances and their products together with mind. The other substances are unlimited, and enter into conjunction with all corporeal objects; they are the self, time and space, and the ether. The last and the four atomic substances constitute the elemental substances (*bhūta-dravya*), which singly or by combination among themselves become the material causes of all the products in the universe. Again, substances are divided as eternal and transient: the atoms, the ether, time and space, the self and mind are eternal; the products of aggregation are transient.

The special qualities fall to be considered together

[1] PBh., p. 95; BP. 86–8.

[2] TSD., § 14; NKoça, pp. 705, 706; PBh., p. 22; Kir., pp. 34, 35; cf. Raghunātha, PTN., pp. 25–7, who claims that *bhūta* and *mūrta* are true classes.

with the subjects to which they appertain, but the general qualities belong to all substances alike, and, though they are real, they are not necessarily so in the same way as the special qualities. This is most clearly seen in the case of number,[1] which is defined as the cause, precisely the proximate instrumental cause, of the use of the terms one, two, three, &c. Of numbers unity is eternal, and resides in the individual atoms and the other substances which are eternal: plurality exists only in products which are transient. But the Nyāya view is that duality, &c., are real like unity, and are only revealed by cognition; the Vaiçeṣika insists that all numbers above one are the creation of a relating cognition (*apekṣā-buddhi*), and not merely made known by it. The process is thus described: first, there is contact of the sense organ with each of two jars; then the knowledge of the genus unity; then cognition operates relating the objects, each recognized as 'This is one'; then duality is created; thence the knowledge of the genus of duality; thence the recognition of duality as a quality in the two things; and finally there is left only the impression of plurality, for, as the relating cognition is a form of consciousness, it can endure for no more than three moments: as soon as it has produced the knowledge of the quality two in the objects it disappears, and with it as cause must go its effect. Other numbers are arrived at in the same way, for, though some recognize indefinite multitude (*bahutva*) as distinct from definite numbers, this view is generally rejected. But, though

[1] First in PBh., pp. 111-13; SP., §§ 26, 87; TB., pp. 79, 80; TK., p. 5; TS., § 24; BP. 106-9; VSU. iv. 1. 11. Kaṇāda's doctrine of unity is given, VS. vii. 2. 1, 2-8. Cf. TR., p. 152; ibid., p. 164, Prabhākara's doctrine of a special category number is refuted. Cf. Cowell, SDS., pp. 151 ff. Raghunātha (p. 75) accepts it; cf. *Padārthāratnamālā*, pp. 29, 30.

the Vaiçeṣika thus accepts all numbers over one as a product of mental activity, it does not extend this view to unity itself.

On dimension (*parimāṇa*) [1] the school has little to say. It is the proximate instrumental cause of the use of measurement, and may be divided into four kinds minuteness (*aṇutva*), largeness (*mahattva*), length (*dīrghatva*) and shortness (*hrasvatva*), but this rough division between magnitudes or two or three dimensions, and those of one only is often dropped, and as in the Sāṁkhya only the first two recognized. Each class again may be subdivided as medium and extreme: the ether has extreme greatness, a product like a pot medium greatness; an atom extreme minuteness, a binary medium minuteness. Dimension is eternal in eternal substances, transient in others; in the latter the dimension is determined by the number, magnitude, and arrangement or aggregation of parts,[2] but in the former, as an essential part of the atomic theory, by number alone. But of the precise character of extension there is no investigation, though it is deemed to be absolutely real and not dependent on cognition.

Individuality (*pṛthaktva*) [3] is the proximate instrumental cause of the practice of separating one thing from another. As against the conception of reciprocal non-existence (*anyonyābhāva*), with which some seek to identify it, it is real, not notional in character: 'The pot is not a piece of cloth' is essentially different from 'The pot is separate from the cloth', which makes it

[1] PBh., pp. 130-2; SP., §§ 27, 88; TB., pp. 80, 81: TK., p. 5; TSD., § 25; BP. 109-13; TR., p. 144; SS. v. 90.

[2] VS. vii. 1. 8, 9 with commentary.

[3] PBh., p. 138; SP., §§ 28, 89; TB., p. 81; TK., p. 5; TSD., § 26; BP., 113, 114. Cf. VS. vii. 2. 2, 8; TR., pp. 144, 152. It is denied the rank of a quality, as are priority and posteriority by Raghunātha, PTN., pp. 28-30.

clear that the two things are positively distinguished. Again, we can say that a pot is not the quality of colour which resides in it, but not that the pot is separate from the colour. Individuality may be eternal or transient, according as the substance in which it resides, and by an adaptation of the theory of number a distinction, obviously of no value, is made between the individuality of a single thing and that of two or more objects, which is produced by the operation of a relating cognition. But individuality itself is not due to cognition, but absolutely real, and its relation to number is not examined, save in the unfortunate hypothesis of two kinds of individuality.

Conjunction and disjunction (*saṁyoga* and *vibhāga*)[1] also appear as real, being caused by motion. They are the proximate instrumental causes of our use of the expressions united and separate, and are artificial and transient, as they apply only to the contact of things which have been apart, and the separation of things which have been united. Contact is primarily and properly due to motion (*karmaja*) whether unilateral as of a bird to a tree, or bilateral as of two butting rams. Secondarily, it is due to another conjunction; thus the body is united with the tree through the conjunction of the hand and the tree, and an effect on its production thus becomes united with something already connected with its cause. Direct conjunction may be produced by a violent motion like sound, or by a gentle motion. Every kind of conjunction affects a part of the thing only and may be destroyed by separation or by the destruction of the things connected. Disjunction for its

[1] VS. vii. 2. 9-11 with commentary; PBh., pp. 139-41, 151-4; SP., §§ 29, 30, 90, 91, 137; TA., pp. 11, 12; TB., p. 81; TK., pp. 5, 6; TS., §§ 27, 28; BP. 115-20; TR., p. 144; PSPM., p. 93; *Padārtharatnamālā*, pp. 32, 33.

part is distinct from the act of separation, which is due to motion, and denotes the state of separation existing between two things formerly in contact. It is subdivided as is conjunction, but the Vaiçesika alone accepts the doctrine of disjunction by disjunction as in the case of the disjunction of the body from the tree by disjunction of the hand. This denial that the motion of part is the motion of the whole is repudiated by the Nyāya school.

The part played by the category motion[1] in the process of conjunction and disjunction is simple: it is the cause by means of separation of the conjunction of an object with another point of space after there has taken place the breaking up of its conjunction with an anterior point of space. Motion thus takes place in five stages: an object is in contact with a definite point of space; by the effect of motion it separates itself thence; thus there arises the destruction of its connexion with its first position in space; then there is conjunction with a new point of space; then the motion ceases. Motion may be vertical, throwing up or down, horizontal, expansion and contraction; or of any other kind, summed up in the generic term 'going'. The term used for it which signifies properly activity (*karman*, *kriyā*) is significant: it suggests that it originally[2] had a wider conception in which it applied both to volition and motion as the two great aspects of activity, and has come to be restricted to the latter by the designation of volition as a quality of the self. Motion as defined is in all its varieties transient, and is destroyed either by a subsequent conjunction or the destruction of its substrate, substance.

[1] VS. i. 1. 7, 14, 17; ii. 1. 23; PBh., pp. 290 ff.: TA., p. 14; TB., p. 86; TK., pp. 1, 20; TS., §§ 5, 76; BP. 6, 7; TR., p. 156; PSPM., p. 91; *Padārtharatnamālā*, pp. 40–2.

[2] So Kumārila, ÇV., p. 395. There is no trace of recognition of chemical action in Kaṇāda; he recognizes φορά only, not ἀλλοίωσις.

Unlike the other general qualities, priority and posteriority[1] are restricted to the four atomic substances and to mind, and in the latter which is eternal they are spatial only. They are the proximate instrumental causes of our conceptions of near and far in space and time alike. As such obviously their attributions as qualities to objects cannot be regarded as in any way ultimate: as we have seen this recognized by some members of the school who remove them from the list of qualities. An important admission as to their dependence on thought is made by Praçastapāda, when he recognizes that the judgement by which one object is assigned a position in time or space relative to each other is due to the operation of the relating power of cognition (*apekṣābuddhi*).[2]

While the ultimate atoms, air, the ether, time and space, the self and the mind, are inferable only in the Vaiçeṣika view, though the Nyāya permits the direct perception by the mind of the self, the qualities are for the most part the objects of perception if present in objects possessing magnitude. Thus the five qualities of temperature or touch, colour, smell, and savour and sound are perceived by one sense organ only,[3] that appropriate in each case; the five general qualities together with the illegitimate qualities of priority and posteriority, and with fluidity and viscidity, are apprehended by the two senses of sight and touch; cognition, pleasure and

[1] VS. vii. 2. 21-3 with commentary; PBh., pp. 164–7; SP., §§ 31, 92, 138; TA, p. 10; TB., pp. 81, 82; TK., p. 6; TS., § 29; BP. 121-5.

[2] p. 99; TR., p. 152.

[3] PBh., pp. 96 ff.; BP. 92, 93. VS. iv. 1. 6–12 requires colour for all visual perception which it alone recognizes as perception proper (*cākṣuṣa*); so NBh. iii. 1. 67; NV., pp. 232, 233; NSM., pp. 23–6; but the later view is in NSāra, pp. 2, 3. Cf. Kir., pp. 82–6; NK., pp. 44, 45. For magnitude see VS. iv. 1. 6; NS. iii. 1. 67 with NBh. and NV.; TB., p. 79.

pain, desire and aversion by the mind; and merit and demerit, mental impression, and gravity are supersensible and must be inferred alone. Motion also is perceptible through that in which it inheres.

Conjunction, disjunction, sound, and the specific qualities of the self agree in extending only to part of their substratum, unlike other qualities; when a man touches a part of a tree, he is held to be in conjunction with the tree, not merely with the part touched, for, if the latter view were pressed, we should be reduced to assert conjunction of the ultimate atom alone, and, as that is invisible, so its conjunction would be unseen.[1] Sound appears only in a part of the ether, and the qualities of the self are manifested only in connexion with mind, which, unlike the self, is not all pervading. Sound and the qualities of the self agree further in being of momentary or more precisely very brief duration, a view adapted from Buddhism by the Nyāya school as well as the Vaiçeṣika.[2] Qualities,[3] also, like substances, may be classified according to their causal potency in the various classes of cause: those of mind are efficient causes only, the others are non-inherent causes,[4] or both,[5] or neither.

3. *Generality, Particularity, and Inherence.*

From all that can be gathered from Kaṇāda it seems as if to him the conception of generality was a mental creation depending on the mode of cognition. From his assertion that generality and particularity depend on

[1] PBh., p. 102. [2] Below, § 5.

[3] PBh., pp. 99 ff.

[4] Viz., colour savour, odour, non-hot touch, number, dimension, individuality, viscidity, sound.

[5] Viz., conjunction, disjunction, hot touch, gravity, fluidity, and velocity.

cognition[1] it seems to follow that he conceived that if a property resides in many things, and if we use that property as means of grouping these things it becomes a general property (*sāmānya*), and that if it is regarded as distinguishing these objects from other objects it is a particularity (*viçeṣa*). But on this substructure Praçastapāda[2] and the whole school have built a rigid realism which regards generality as eternal, one, and residing in many things, but only in the categories of substance, quality, and motion. As eternal it is distinct from such things as conjunction and duality which though residing in many are transient; as one it differs from the dimension of an atom, and it resides in many by inherence (*samavāya*), thus differing from absolute non-existence, which is not so connected with things. Generality may be divided according to its degree into the major and the minor,[3] the former of which consists of existence alone, which is found in the three categories of substance, quality, and motion, while these categories themselves are minor generalities. But from another point of view a threefold[4] division may be preferred, that of most extensive (*vyāpaka*), which includes essence; that of intermediate (*vyāpya-vyāpaka*), which includes the three categories; and that of narrowest (*vyāpya*) which covers such generalities as the genus pot, where the term genus is to be understood as referring to the common characteristic and not to the individuals comprised under it. The latter division accentuates the fact

[1] i. 2. 3 ff. Badly explained away in Kir., p. 30, and in NK. as meaning that their existence is proved by intellect.

[2] pp. 11, 12, 311, 312; Kir., pp. 22–4; SP., §§ 7, 70, 111; TA., p. 14; TB., pp. 86, 87; TK., pp. 1, 20; TS., §§ 6, 77; BP. 8–10; TR., pp. 158, 159; *Padārtharatnamālā*, pp. 42–4.

[3] PBh. *l. c.*: VS. treats the lower generalities also as species relatively to being (*bhāva, sattā*).

[4] TA., *l. c.*; SP., § 111. For the *Daçapadārthī* see Ui, pp. 35–7, 68–71.

that the general characteristic is deemed to be something which actually exists, and in harmony with this view it is made the object of perception either by means of all the senses in each appropriate case, or of mind alone, in the latter case falling under the concept of extraordinary or supernormal perception.[1] The reality of generality lies also at the basis of all predication.

Generality as true is immediately connected with its substance, quality, or motion, and in this aspect can be styled a true class concept (*jāti*). On the other hand, there are common characteristics whose connexion with a number of things is only mediate, and which therefore rank only as mere generality (*upādhi*). The causes which prevent a common characteristic or mere generality becoming a true generality or class concept are given by Udayana[2] as six. If there is but one object such as ether, there can be no class. If the same object has different names such as pot and pitcher, there are not two separate classes. If there is cross-division a class concept is excluded: thus the four atomic substances and ether constitute the products (*bhūta-dravya*), the same four with mind the corporeal things (*mūrta-dravya*), and thus neither can be a true class. Nor can there be a class of a class, on pain of a *regressus ad infinitum*. Again, the notion of particularity absolutely refuses to allow of forming a class of it. Finally, as every class concept resides by inherence in its objects,

[1] Cf. Plato, *Soph.* 254 c–255 a, for the categories of *οὐσία*; *στάσις*, *κίνησις*; *ταὐτόν*, *θάτερον*; Plotinos, vi. 1–3. Generality is not dependent on the individuals, but does not exist apart from them; it is at once *ἓν παρὰ πολλά* and *ἓν κατὰ πολλῶν*. Cf. above, ch. ii, §§ 1, 3; Arist. *N. E.* i. 6. Raghunātha (PTN., pp. 49–54) denies a genus to existence (*sattā*) and quality as a whole (*guṇatva*).

[2] Kir., p. 88. Cited in TA., p. 14; SM. on BP. 8; ṢDST. 65; according to NS. ii. 2. 71 a *jāti* is *samānaprasavātmikā* and has a distinct form (*ākṛti*) as its sign. Cf. NM., pp. 297–310.

there cannot be a class of inherence, for else we would have the absurdity of inherence as a class residing by inherence in inherence. The distinction, therefore, is clearly that between real natural classes corresponding to facts in nature and classifications based on our thought only, and it is by no means unlikely that it was this distinction which made the younger school persist in, or even invent, the conception of generality as absolutely real. Such a conception afforded an answer to the apparent difficulty why we should frame such obviously conflicting ideas as those expressed in knowledge of true and arbitrary or shifting classes, and induced the school to adhere to their realism [1] despite the strong attacks directed against it by Buddhists and Jains alike.[2]

To particularity Kaṇāda refers only in its connexion with generality as dependent on cognition,[3] while he elsewhere distinguishes it from the ultimate particularities residing in the ultimate atoms of matter.[4] On this Praçastapāda [5] and the rest of the school of the Vaiçeṣikas found their theory of particularity as an independent reality residing in eternal substances, that is, the atoms and the other five substances, and distinguishing them from one another. The necessity for such a distinction is established thus. We can distinguish between any ordinary objects by enumerating their constituent parts, the empiric individual being that which has a bodily form and special qualities,[6] but when in the

[1] So Kumārila, ÇV., pp. 201-6, 216, 330-40, 464-8; cf. SS. v. 91-3, where also (94-6) similarity is rejected as a separate category, as by the Nyāya; PSPM., pp. 95 ff.

[2] Açoka, *Sāmānyadūṣaṇaprasārita*, SBNT., pp. 94-102; Candraprabha, *Prameyaratnakoça*, ch. xix; NB., p. 115; NBT., p. 84; SDS., p. 10.

[3] i. 2. 3 ff.

[4] i. 2. 6.

[5] pp. 18, 321, 322; SP., §§ 8, 71; TA., p. 14; TB., p. 87; TK., pp. 1, 20; TS., §§ 7, 78; BP. 10; TR., pp. 159, 160; Kir., pp. 24, 25.

[6] NS. ii. 2. 69.

ultimate analysis we reach simple substances like the atoms or selves we can find no parts to permit of distinction; yet, as we are assured of distinction, we must assume that there lies in each individual a quality *sui generis* which makes it distinct from all others, and serves this function alone. To this view the objection was taken before Praçastapāda, and is adopted by the modern school of Nyāya, that there must be something to differentiate the particularities, and the reply is made that this is a function which they perform for themselves as well as differentiating the substances in which they inhere. It is hardly surprising that this expedient should have proved unconvincing, and that the retort should be made that there is no good ground for not attributing to the atoms themselves the inherent power of self-discrimination instead of multiplying entities. Nor has the doctrine any acceptance [1] in other schools, being rejected by both the Prābhākara and Bhāṭṭa schools of Mīmāṅsā, the Vedānta, Buddhism, &c. In any case it is admitted that particularity cannot be the object of perception, but can only be inferred.

Of inherence Kaṇāda [2] tells us only that it is that through which it is said of cause and effect that the one abides in the other (literally 'that this is here'), but the principle is already developed in Praçastapāda [3] to the definition that it is a connexion which exists between things which cannot exist separately, and stand in the

[1] Species, of course, is accepted but not particularity; cf. TR., p. 163; PSPM., p. 90. The schools use *viçeṣa* indiscriminately in both senses. Raghunātha (PTN., pp. 30–32) denies particularity; cf. *Padārtharatnamālā*, pp. 44–8.

[2] vii. 2. 26; cf. x. 2. 1 ff.

[3] PBh., pp. 14, 324–9: SP., §§ 9, 72; TA., p. 14; TB., pp. 16, 17; TK., pp. 1, 20; TS., §§ 8, 79; BP. 11; cf. ṢDS. 66 with Guṇaratna; VSU. vii. 2. 26, 27; TR., pp. 160–3; Kir., pp. 25, 26; NV., pp. 55, 56, 226; KKK. ii. 82–4. Raghunātha (p. 76) denies its unity.

relation of substrate and that which exists in it, and which produces the concept expressed in the word 'Here'. There is no substantial difference in the modern definition of inherence as one, and consisting in an eternal relation between things which cannot exist separately (*ayuta-siddha*). The description as one and eternal is intended to refute the objections of the Prābhākaras and the modern Nyāya which reject both appellations. The unity of inherence is proved like the unity of existence by the fact that there is no difference in principle between the different cases in which we infer the relation of inherence. The eternity is proved by the simple argument that, since every cause is linked to the effect by inherence, assuming that inherence were an effect it would be based on itself, which would lead to a *regressus ad infinitum*, and therefore be absurd. But the eternity is relative, not absolute, like that of the atoms; it denotes only that the relation can only disappear with the disappearance of the things related. Such a relation differs entirely from conjunction, which can only exist between things normally separate, and it is confined to the five cases of the relation between the product and its parts, both of which must be substances; substance and quality; substance and motion; generality and the individual; and particularity and the eternal substances in which it resides. From the fact that it exists between things which are imperceptible such as sound and ether as well as between objects of sense the Vaiçeṣika[1] deduces that inherence is an object of inference only, but the Nyāya insists that it can be perceived by a special process of perception.

The difficulties of the doctrine have not failed to awake lively criticism, especially as the view of inherence

[1] PBh., pp. 328, 329; NKoça, p. 881; VSU. vii. 2. 28.

stands in indissoluble connexion with the doctrine of causation. The Bhāṭṭa Mīmāṅsā, Vedānta, Sāṁkhya, and Buddhist alike decline to accept it, and Çaṅkara in particular destroys the conception in his exposition of the *Vedānta Sūtra*.[1] He points out the impossibility of the argument which seeks to distinguish conjunction and inherence; the former is eternal as well as the latter, for instance, in the case of the relation between ether and the ultimate atoms; it is useless to assert that inherence can exist without a third thing to unite it with the things in which it exists, while conjunction needs inherence to hold it to the things which are in conjunction, and the difficulty is not removed by the verbal expedient of calling one a category and one a quality. Moreover, the argument that there must be this relation between cause and effect cannot be accepted. If cause and effect are inseparably connected as the Vaiçeṣika holds, then is it not far more simple to assume that there is identity of essence between the two? Moreover the conception of inseparable connexion contradicts point blank the idea that cause precedes effect, which is an essential part of the Nyāya-Vaiçeṣika doctrine of causality.

4. *Cause and Effect.*

The Nyāya-Vaiçeṣika doctrine of cause and effect stands in immediate relation to that of inherence, which as appears from Kaṇāda was first conceived as the relation between these two. But the development of the examination of cause did not adhere strictly to this

[1] ii. 2. 13–17. Cf. Açoka, *Avayavinirākaraṇa*, SBNT., pp. 78–86; *Sāṁkhya Sūtra*, v. 99, 100 with commentary; ÇV., p. 94; PSPM., pp. 89, 100, who regards it as many and both eternal and noneternal, perceptible and imperceptible.

dictum: the concept includes much beside the cause, which in the strict sense of the word is the inherent cause, though that always occupies an essential place in the theory.

In the final form[1] of the doctrine the cause is that which always precedes the effect, is necessary to it, and that not merely as an accessory cause (*anyathā-siddha*). The precise nature of accessory causes is not, however, very explicitly stated; they include matters which, though in relation of inherence with the cause proper, are not themselves directly instrumental in causation, like the colour of the threads in the production of a rug; those events prior to the cause which only remotely affect it, such as the father of the potter in relation to the pot; and generally all influences which, though in relation with the cause, are neither necessary nor sufficient to produce it, such as the ass who carries the clay for the fabrication of the plot. Viçvanātha subdivides the first two classes into two each, but the last class clearly covers the whole field, and its vagueness is obvious.

Causes are divided into three kinds.[2] The first is the inherent cause, in which case the relationship is that of inseparable connexion. It is illustrated by the relation of the threads to the rug, as opposed to the shuttle which aids in the production of the fabric, and the same relation exists between all products and the substances of which they are made. It holds also between sub-

[1] TA, p. 4; TB., p. 11; TK., p. 7; TSD., § 38; BP. 16, 19-22; cf. KKK. ii. 158-79. Raghunātha (PTN., pp. 71-4) claims for causation the rank of a category.

[2] The whole doctrine is implied in VS. x. 2. 1-7; i. 1. 18-ii. 1. 2, where the causal character of the substances, qualities, and motion is given; PBh., pp. 21, 24, 98-102; SP., §§ 62, 179; TA., p. 4; TB., pp. 15-25; TK., p. 8; TSD., § 40; BP. 17, 18; TR., pp. 152-4, 156, 157.

stance and quality and substance and motion: the rug is the inherent cause (*samavāyi-kāraṇa*) of its colour, and it is readily admitted that, as the cause must precede the effect at the moment of its coming into being, the rug must have no colour, and, since it can also have no dimension, cannot be perceptible at all, until these attributes have come after an infinitesimal delay into being. Secondly, there is the non-inherent cause (*asamavāyi-kāraṇa*), which inheres in the same substratum with the effect or with the inherent cause. The first is the relation of the arrangement of the threads of a rug to the rug; the arrangement or conjunction as a quality is inherent in the threads, which are the inherent cause of the rug. The relation may secondly be indirect: thus the colour of the threads of the rug stand in this relation to the colour of the rug; the colour of the threads inheres in them, they inhere in the rug, and the colour of the rug inheres in it. Thirdly, the category of instrumental cause (*nimitta-kāraṇa*) is the receptacle for every sort of cause which cannot be brought under the two preceding heads, including the agent; in it again there may be drawn a distinction between special and general causes, of which there are eight: God, his knowledge, desire, and action, antecedent non-existence, space and time, merit and demerit, to which some add absence of counteracting influence.[1] But in this view of the third category it seems that the term cause is too widely applied, and includes what is not necessary, and a better method is that followed by those who distinguish between primary (*mukhya*) and subordinate causes and

[1] Cf. Athalye, TS., pp. 207, 208. The idea is applied to the case of perception in NS. ii. 1. 22 as regards duration, space, time, and ether; as regards space and time see PBh., p. 25; Kir., pp. 38, 39; VS. vii. 1. 25; v. 2. 25, 26; Faddegon, *Vaiç. System*, p. 219.

subdivide the former only into the three classes, relegating the other matter to the inferior category.

A further effort to clarify the conception of cause is contained in the doctrine of efficient or proximate cause (*karaṇa*), which is explained as that cause which most materially contributes to attain the result,[1] in accordance with the grammatical definition of the term.[2] As we have seen, the older school[3] define it as a specific cause which produces the effect by an activity or function (*vyāpāra*), which intervenes between it and the result, while the modern school describe the function itself as the proximate cause, defining it as that which is not disjoined from its appropriate effect.[4] At the same time, however, the older school were precluded by the use of language from accepting as an instrumental cause an agent of any sort. So, in the case of perception, the dispute between the two schools centred itself in the question whether the organ with its functioning was to be deemed the cause, or whether the functioning in the contact of organ and object was the true cause, express words being used in the former case to exclude the agent from being deemed to be intended. The newer theory is accepted in the main by Keçava Miçra, Laugākṣi Bhāskara, and Viçvanātha, while Annam Bhaṭṭa shows a curious vacillation, especially obvious in his treatment of the allied questions of the proximate cause of perception and inference.[5]

The effect may, of course, be defined in terms of cause as that which follows on that which is necessary and not accessory merely,[6] but a more pregnant definition is

[1] TB., pp. 10, 25; TS., §§ 37, 41; NVT., p. 17; NVTP., pp. 187-95.

[2] Pāṇini, i. 4. 42.

[3] e. g. TK., p. 7; TB., p. 27.

[4] NKoça, p. 175.

[5] Athalye, TS., pp. 189-91.

[6] TB., p. 18.

that of Annam Bhaṭṭa,[1] who makes it the positive correlate of an anterior negation, thus emphasizing the fundamental feature of the doctrine of causality in the Nyāya-Vaiçeṣika, its denial that the effect always exists prefigured in the cause (*a-sat-kārya-vāda*). The doctrine is already expressly insisted upon by Kaṇāda:[2] without a cause there can be no effect, not, however, without an effect no cause. Thus the doctrine of the school is that the cause always precedes the effect, and the latter has no existence until it is brought into being. It has, therefore, some affinity with the Buddhist doctrine of the generation of being out of not being, and it stands in absolute contradiction with the Sāṁkhya[3] assertion of the pre-existence of the effect in the cause (*sat-kārya-vāda*), or the Vedānta[4] view which preserved the identity of the cause, while holding that the effect was ultimately illusory. The Sāṁkhya lays stress on such arguments as the fact that in experience we see that there can be no creation of anything new; the blue colour can never be converted into red; the sesamum can be traced in the oil pressed from it; no effect is ever produced from any cause as would be possible on the Nyāya view, but only from a specific cause; if the suggestion is made that the cause possesses some power to produce the effect, is this power connected with the effect? If so, that is as much as to say the effect is prefigured in the cause; if not, there is the fatal difficulty as to the concurrence of definite effects with definite causes. Finally, as cause and effect are correlative ideas, it is impossible to assert the existence of cause without its producing at once the effect. The Nyāya reply is not uningenious: the same

[1] TS., § 39.

[2] VS. i. 2. 1, 2.

[3] Garbe, *Sāṁkhya*, pp. 228 ff.; SS. i. 114–22; Keith, *Sāṁkhya System*, pp. 78, 93.

[4] Deussen, *Vedānta*, ch. xix, xxi; Çaṅkara on BS. ii. 1. 14–20.

atoms make a pot or a saucer; on the identity theory the atoms, pot, and saucer should all be the same which is not the case, an argument which the Vedānta meets by denying that things which are equal to the same thing are equal to one another. The shape of a pot again is not to be traced in its constituents and must be new. Or, if it is argued that the effect is latent but is made manifest, then the manifestation itself, being an effect, must have existed previously and so on indefinitely. This argument can only be met by resort to the Vedānta theory that the whole manifested work is but the play of illusion, and that one real alone remains. Hence Çañkara's onslaught on the conception of inherence in its relation to causality escapes the difficulty of the Sāṁkhya, which is compelled to ignore obvious facts by its insistence on the prefiguration of the real cause in a real effect. But it is difficult to hail Çañkara as the predecessor of Kant [1] in his treatment of cause, when it is remembered that it is not this category merely but everything in the universe which is projected by the cosmic power of illusion.

Apart, however, from the fundamental problem of causation, there are obvious weaknesses in the doctrine of the Nyāya-Vaiçeṣika. The ignoring of the agent is obvious and inexplicable, for on their own view the agency of God is an important feature in creation, and their doctrine of causality and non-existence adapts itself admirably to permit of the proof of the creative power of God. The distinction between inherent and non-inherent causes is untenable and inaccurate, as the latter are in indirect relations of inherence, while non-inherent applies properly to instrumental causes. Nor is there any recognition of the conjunction of inherent

[1] Athalye, TS., p. 205; *contra*, Deussen, *Allgem. Gesch.*, I. iii. 625.

causes to produce a result, despite the obvious problem presented in the familiar case of the pot in view of the presence of water in its materials,[1] and the argument against the Sāṁkhya theory which can be deduced thence is palpable. Needless to say, the more complex case of chemical compounds is ignored,[2] as are also the plain facts of the same effect produced by apparently different causes or the intermixture of effects. In no case does there more clearly appear the divorce of the system from practical scientific experience.

5. *Non-existence.*

In Kaṇāda non-existence, as we have seen, does not appear as a category. His own doctrine, misinterpreted by his commentators, amounts to this.[3] Absolute non-existence or negation is not a predicable at all; antecedent non-existence, the condition of the cause *qua* effect before it produces its result, subsequent non-existence, the condition of the effect when resolved into its elements, and mutual non-existence, the relation between things possessing identity of their own, all have definite relations to reality and do not form a special category. In the Nyāya[4] we find the germ of the idea of not-being as something knowable and existent in the

[1] VS. i. 1. 23 applies only to union of similar substances; combination of motions is denied, i. 1. 24, and causation of motion by motion, i. 1. 11.

[2] There is no trace of a recognition of chemical compounds or an organic whole, as suggested by Chatterji, *Hindu Realism*, pp. 27, 56, whose authorities (NVT., p. 280; Kir., pp. 114, 115) do not bear out his contention in any way. The refusal (VS. iv. 2. 1–4) to allow of a combination of heterogeneous atoms to form the body shows the real view of the schools. Contrast Seal, *Positive Sciences*, pp. 98–121.

[3] ix. 1. 1 ff.

[4] NS. ii. 2. 12 with NBh. and NV.; NBh., p. 2; NV., pp. 10, 33; NVT., p. 23; above, chap. ii, § 2.

same way as being, the knowledge being based in the Bhāṣya on inference, but later ascribed to direct perception in a peculiar form. Two forms of negation are recognized in the Sūtra, explained in the Bhāṣya as non-existence prior to being brought into being and non-existence after the destruction of the form of the thing brought into existence. Harmony between the Vaiçeṣika and Nyāya was established before Jayanta and Vācaspati,[1] the latter of whom gives the classical division of negation as based on identity or correlation, the latter comprising the three varieties of antecedent, consequent, and absolute non-existence.[2] The older Nyāya tradition, however, retained the Sūtra standpoint by explaining that absolute non-existence was merely antecedent non-existence without a determining limit, and negation of identity was similarly antecedent negation conceived of as in relation to a different thing which it never becomes. Antecedent negation explains also negation of requirement and of capacity not previously existing, while subsequent negation disposes of negation of prior capacity, if these further divisions of negation are adopted.

The syncretist school, while adopting non-existence as a separate category, always recognize its correlation to being; negation is knowledge dependent on knowledge of the positive counterpart (*pratiyogin*),[3] an idea familiar in rhetoric, where in 'Thy face is like the moon' the latter is the counterpart of the relationship of similarity abiding in the face. The pot is the counterpart of its

[1] NL., pp. 126–8; NVT., p. 307; Kir., p. 6; Lakṣ., p. 13; NK., p. 230; NM., pp. 53–61.

[2] *anyonyābhāva*; *prāg-*, *pradhvaṅsa-*, *atyanta-abhāva*; relation (*sambandha*) covers inherence and conjunction.

[3] SP., §§ 10, 58, 73, 112–15; TA., p. 15; TB., p. 38; TK., pp. 1, 21; TSD., §§ 9, 80; BP. 12, 13; TR., p. 168; NSM., pp. 34–58.

antecedent or subsequent non-existence; it is an effect of the one, and a cause of the other; in absolute negation the counterpart is determined by a relation of negation with its substrate, e.g. the ground on which the pot, once seen, is no longer present. From absolute negation mutual negation differs by resting on denial of identity not of relation. Beyond these four classes some Vaiçeṣikas[1] went by distinguishing from absolute negation temporary negation (*sāmayikābhāva*) as in the preposition 'The pot is not on the ground', while Annam Bhaṭṭa refutes this subdivision with the argument that the non-existence of the pot on the ground is permanent and only temporarily obscured by being covered up with the pot when it is present. Yet another teacher, Saudaṇḍa introduced the conception of the non-existence on the ground of a pot because there is there instead a cloth, but this futility did not win much support.

Needless to say this conception of non-existence as a reality received no support from the other schools, and the Mīmāṅsā in particular was ready to show that the position of the Nyāya-Vaiçeṣika involved them in a fatal *regressus ad infinitum* inasmuch as, if non-existence were a reality, then the negation of non-existence must be another reality and so on indefinitely. To meet this objection, the weight of which was of course decisive for the school, the ancient Nyāya developed the view that the negation of a negation was equivalent to the positive. The modern school, however, repudiate this view: a negation cannot, they hold, ever be equivalent to a positive, but they admit that the negation of the negation of the first negation is equivalent to the first negation.[2]

[1] NKoça, pp. 7, 75; Athalye, TS., pp. 371, 372; TC. ii. 53, 575; *Padārtharatnamālā*, pp. 24, 25.

[2] Cf. TSD., § 80, with Athalye's note; Raghunātha, PTN., pp. 55–7.

It is more interesting to note the sympathy which exists between the doctrine of the school and the Buddhist view of the momentariness of existence, which finds expression in the doctrine of causation also. Cognition in the Buddhist doctrine of momentariness developed in the Sautrāntika school[1] persists for a moment only: it is non-existent, existent, and gone, and in harmony with this we have the antecedent non-existence, existence, and subsequent non-existence of cognitions in the Nyāya-Vaiçeṣika, where, however, with characteristic adaptation to meet the view of the school[2] the length of existence of the cognition is conceived in three aspects, that of its coming into being, that of its disappearance, and the intervening space. Sound also is subjected to the same treatment possibly already in Kaṇāda, and certainly in the work of Praçastapāda.[3]

[1] SSS. iii. 3. 6, 7; SDS., p. 10; NB., p. 108; NBh. v. 1. 24; NVT., pp. 105, 380; NK., pp. 73, 74; *Madh. Vṛtti*, pp. 116, n. 1, 281, n. 1, 545, n. 6.

[2] The origin of this doctrine can be seen in the three stages of a *saṁskṛta*, 'confection', in *Añg. Nikāya*, i. 152; *Kathāv.* i. 61; *Madh. Vṛtti*, p. 145, as *utpāda, vyaya, sthityanyathātva*; the Vaibhāṣikas have four; cf. *jāti, jarā, sthiti, anityatā* (ibid. p. 545) in the *Abhidharma*, as occurring in *kṣaṇa*; the *Abhidharmakoçavyākhyā* applies the division to the series, not the *kṣaṇa*. Cf. the Yoga view of time as a series of *kṣaṇas*, YS. iii. 52 with commentary.

[3] p. 25; Kir., p. 38. Cf. for cognition, NS. iii. 2. 1 ff. To say that cognitions endure for three moments (Athalye, TS., p. 167: Suali, *Intr.*, p. 215, *utpatti, sthiti, nāça*) is the doctrine of the later texts, e.g. TK., p. 19; TB., pp. 83, 84, but it is a mere matter of terminology as the doctrine is in effect in PBh., p. 287. But the exact form of the doctrine is not proved for either Sūtra. On the *kṣaṇa* cf. PTN., pp. 58-61; *Padārtharatnamālā*, p. 85. Contrast the view of duration as real, James, *Psych.* i. 609 ff.; Pringle Pattison, *The Idea of God*, pp. 350 ff.

CHAPTER VIII

THE PHILOSOPHY OF NATURE

1. *The Atomic Theory.*

THE doctrine of the existence of real things in the universe had to face when it was first expounded in definitive form the presence of the powerful influence of the doctrine of vacuity (*çūnya-vāda*) or philosophic nihilism of the Mādhyamika school of Buddhism which owes its establishment to Nāgārjuna.[1] The essential principle of this school, whose views may be compared usefully with the dialectic of Zeno, asserted that on analysis our ideas present such inconsistencies and incompatibilities that there can be nothing real underlying them; they deny therefore not only the true existence of external reality, but they do not admit that thought itself is real, so incoherent and contradictory is it. Thus, against the claim of realism that there is both truth and reality, it is argued that on investigation the true essence of things is not revealed: we form the notion of a cloth, but when we examine it we find only a mass of threads, whence it follows that our notion was an error. Again it is urged, just as the objects seen in a dream, magic, *fata Morgana*, and mirage, are not real though we believe in them, so also neither is our knowledge nor its object real.[2] The response of the *Nyāya*

[1] *Mādhyamika Sūtra*, i. 1 ff.; iv. 8; xiii. 2, 8; cf. SDS., p. 11; SSS. iii. 1; above, ch. ii, § 2.

[2] *Mādh. S.* vii. 34; *Vṛtti*, pp. 178, 445; cf. Gauḍapāda, ii. 5 ff.

Sūtra[1] as expounded by Vātsyāyana is effective. If there is proof, it is urged, that nothing exists, then this proof sublates its own existence. If there is no proof, how can it be established that nothing exists? If it is to be assumed without proof, then the opposite contention is at least as legitimate. The fact of our ability to analyse our notions confutes the belief in their unreality and that of their objects; it cannot be expected that we should have a separate perception of the whole and its parts, or of the cause and its effect. As regards the argument from the dream state, it is pointed out that no argument is adduced by the nihilists to show that the knowledge we have is really comparable to that of a dream in place of that of our waking experience, nor again is it shown that our dream experience is of non-existing things. To these retorts Vātsyāyana adds the telling argument that the only ground on which it can be taken that things seen in a dream do not really exist is that they are seen no more in the waking state, which implies that our waking experience is real.

Probably at a time after the production of Vātsyāyana's Bhāṣya the need was felt in the school to combat the further development of the nihilism of Nāgārjuna, which in the hands of Asaṅga[2] and Vasubandhu led to the doctrine of idealism (*vijñāna-vāda*) which denied absolutely the reality of external things, and accepted as the only reality our ideas or mental acts, including perception; in their view therefore external things were merely products in our consciousness due to ideas

[1] iv. 2. 26-37. Cf. Çaṅkara on BS. ii. 2. 18-27; Kumārila, ÇV., pp. 148-82; PSPM., pp. 24, 25, 88; SS. i. 43 ff.

[2] *Mahāyānasūtrālaṅkāra*, i. 18; xi. 53 ff.; cf. SDS., p. 12; SSS. iii. 2; Stcherbatskoi, *Muséon*, vi. 144 ff. Gauḍapāda in his attitude to the Vaiçeṣika shows both Mādhyamika and Vijñānavāda influence; see JRAS. 1910, pp. 129-40; JAOS. xxxiii. 51-4.

existing independently of objects, a modified form of which doctrine we have already seen in Dignāga. It was, therefore, found necessary to reinterpret the Sūtra[1] to make it cover a refutation of the denial by the new school of realism, and this was the more easy in that such a refutation was necessarily in part implicit in the refutation of a nihilism which denied reality to thought and external being alike.

The essence of the argument against pure idealism is, therefore, that it contradicts the nature of our distinction between waking and dream experience. We believe that dream objects have no existence apart from our experience, simply because when awake we do not perceive them as objects, and this is explicable only on the theory that an external reality does exist. But if there were not a sensible world of experience the dreams themselves could not exist, for ultimately dreams are based on a real experience. Moreover, only on such a hypothesis as that of an external reality can we explain the distinction between truth and error as seen in hallucination or a mistake, and the conviction of such a reality is also forced upon us by the fact that we do not, as should be the case if the objects are only our ideas, have them continuously and at our pleasure before us, as is the case with our own ideas, while our perceptions depend on things beyond our power to affect.[2]

It remains, therefore, to discover what is the ultimate reality which is thus necessary to explain our experience. Things in the universe are made up of parts which are combined into wholes by the relation of inherence, and this conception serves to refute the objections directed against the conception of whole and part on the ground

[1] iv. 2. 26–30 as taken by Vācaspati. The rendering of iv. 2. 26 in SBH. viii. 188 is clearly erroneous, *buddhyā* being instr. not abl.

[2] Cf. Çañkara on BS. ii. 2. 28; Kumārila, ÇV., pp. 119–48.

that the whole cannot reside in the parts, since it is greater than any one or more of them apart, nor can the parts reside in the whole since they are less than it, objections founded on a false application of spatial conceptions outside their sphere.[1] Now the process of division of a whole can be carried beyond the limits of perception, but not indefinitely; there must on pain of a *regressus ad infinitum*, which is inconceivable (*anavasthānupapatti*), be a point at which division stops, and there remains a permanent substance, which is never destroyed and which cannot be subdivided. To this assumption there is obvious an immediate objection in shape of the existence of the all-pervading ether, which therefore must compel the atom to have parts. The reply is that the conception of within or without thus implied is inapplicable to an eternal thing which is not a product; the omnipresence of ether is admitted, but it neither repels nor is obstructed, and therefore in no wise implies the existence of parts in the atom, for it has no form and is intangible. There are the further objections that anything which has magnitude must have form and therefore parts, and that the possibility of conjunction with another atom is only possible, if the atom has parts, but these are rejected without detailed refutation on the strength of the overwhelming weight of the argument that there must be an end to divisibility. Nor does the *Vaiçeṣika Sūtra*[2] add any further argument of weight; it seems to conceive the grounds for accepting atoms to be the fact that there must be something uncaused, and that the existence of non-eternal things implies the existence of the opposed conception of eternal things, which can be found only in the atoms, though

[1] NS. iv. 2. 4 ff. Cf. Çañkara on BS. ii. 1. 26–31.

[2] vii. 1. 9, 10; PBh., p. 28; TB., pp. 73, 74; TK., pp. 3, 5; TSD., p. 10; BP. 36.

these save in an aggregate cannot be an object of perception. Aggregates differ by reason of the number of the atoms which produce them and thus create magnitude (*mahattva*), which is different from minuteness (*aṇutva*). In the atoms which are infinite in number we can distinguish classes according to their possession of qualities, air atoms possessing tangibility, fire that and colour, water these and savour, and earth these and odour.

The conception thus presented is simple and intelligible; it is possibly a development from the earlier position, which is represented in the Jain philosophy and which regards matter, understood as eternal and undifferentiated as the product of atoms each of which occupies a point in space, while they are all equal and not differentiated according to the four elements which are later evolved by a process of differentiation.[1] In the Sūtra as in the form of atomism found in Buddhism[2] the atoms are definitely brought into relation with the four elements by assigning to them specific qualities, and possibly also the element of peculiarity (*viçeṣa*) which enables them to remain distinct despite what otherwise must be their entire identity. In the hands of Praçastapāda, however, there appears already a characteristic development of the theory, which renders it far less simple and easy. The magnitude of an aggregate, which seemingly was in the view of Kaṇāda due to the number of the atoms constituting it, is held to arise not from these causes alone, but also from the magnitude of the constituent parts and their aggregation,[3]

[1] Above, Pt. I, ch. i. § 1.

[2] Cf. Çañkara on BS. ii. 2. 18; SSS. iii. 4. 13–15; SDS., p. 13; NV., p. 246.

[3] *mahattvapracayau* being supplied in VS. vii. 1. 9, which refers to number of parts only. Cf. Kir., pp. 50–3, 63–6.

these terms being read into Kaṇāda's aphorism wholly without warrant, and with a remarkable tendency to ignore the plain fact that the two new factors are on the ultimate analysis, as they are explained, nothing more than the results of the number of parts. On the other hand, below the stage at which magnitude is reached, number alone seems to act as a factor, a distinction wholly indefensible in theory, since if the atoms are really the source of all products there can be nothing save number to account for the diverse sizes of things. The impulse to this view may have been given by the aphorism of Kaṇāda, which makes the minute the reverse of the thing which has magnitude, and which seems to have been interpreted to set an impassable gulf between them, and to require that magnitude should be produced from magnitude only. If this were correct, it would follow that combination of minute with minute would produce still more minute results, but this conclusion would obviously have been contradicted by the fact that the atom was the *minimum divisible,* and therefore the rule that number gave increase in size was admitted. Two primary atoms produce the binary (*dvyaṇuka*), which still is minute (*aṇu*) for it is without magnitude in the technical sense; three binaries, however, produce the triad (*tryaṇuka*), which is later asserted to be the mote in the sunbeam and equated with the *truṭi*, the phrase used by the *Nyāya Sūtra*[1] in expressing the furthest length of division, and which there must be deemed to denote a dimension not too small for apprehension.[2] Possibly[3] there may have also contributed to

[1] iv. 2. 17. The phrase, however, is uncertain in sense; it may mean only that there is an end to division, NBh. *l. c.*; cf. NV., pp. 233 ff.

[2] SM. on BP. 15, 37; TB., pp. 73, 74; NKoça, p. 433. Some stopped here as the ultimate unit, Kir., p. 51; Raghunātha, PTN., p. 11.

[3] Jacobi, ERE. i. 202.

this result the fact that there was a division in things possessing magnitude between those which were eternal like space, and those which were non-eternal: the desire to emphasize this contrast also may have led to the setting up of the class of the eternal atom and the perishing binary, but the excrescence on the theory is palpable. The insistence on number, however, gives rise to an effective argument for the impossibility of infinite division, since, if this were possible, it would be necessary to admit the equality of the size of the largest mountain and the smallest heap, on the ground of the equality of infinities.[1] A further argument, which is probably late in origin, deduces that there must be a definite limit to subdivision just as there is a definite limit to extension in the sky.[2]

In Praçastapāda[3] appears also a clear statement of the mode in which the universe comes to rest, and is created again from time to time in an eternal cycle. When a hundred years, by the measure of Brahman, are at an end, there comes the time for the deliverance of the Brahman then existing. Then to secure rest for living beings wearied by their wanderings, the Supreme Lord desires to reabsorb all creation; simultaneously with this desire there arises a cessation of the operations of the unseen tendencies (*adṛṣṭa*) of all souls that are the causes of their bodies, sense organs, and gross elements. Then out of the Lord's desire, and from the conjunction of the souls and the material atoms, there come about certain disruptions of the atoms constituting the bodies and sense organs. The combination of the atoms is thus destroyed, and thus brings about the destruction of all things down to the atoms. There

[1] TSD., § 10; Kir., p. 51; NVT. iv. 2. 17.
[2] SM. on BP. 37; cf. NV., p. 251.
[3] pp. 48 ff.; Kir., pp. 89 ff.

ensues a successive disruption or reabsorption of the ultimate material substances—earth, water, fire, and air, one after the other. Thereafter the atoms remain isolated, and with them the selves permeated with the potencies of their past virtue and vices. Then, again, for the sake of the experience to be gained by living beings, there arises in the mind of the Supreme Lord a desire for creation, and there are produced in the atoms of air certain actions or motions, due to their conjunction under the influence of the unseen potential tendencies that begin to operate in all souls. These motions bring about the mutual contact of the air atoms, and there appears through diad and triad, &c., finally the great air which exists vibrating in the sky; from this springs the great reservoir of water, in which appear the great earth and the great fire. By the thought of the Supreme Lord there is produced from earth and fire atoms the cosmic egg, in it the Lord produces the worlds and the creator Brahman, to whom he assigns the further work of creation. Brahman then, endowed with extreme degrees of knowledge, dispassion, and power, recognizing the ripeness for fruition of the tendencies of living beings, creates his mind-born sons, the Prajāpatis, the Manus, gods, fathers, and seers, and from his mouth, arms, thighs, and feet the four castes and all other living beings, all having their knowledge and experience in harmony with their previous deeds, and then endows them with knowledge, virtue, dispassion, and powers in accord with their respective impressional potencies.

As to the exact mode of the process of destruction a difference exists between the old and the modern schools.[1] In the former view the process is from cause

[1] TSD., pp. 9, 10; TB., pp. 71-3.

to effect; the union of primary atoms in the binaries is broken, and with it the triads are destroyed and so on. The modern view is intended to meet the criticism made by the Vedānta,[1] which insists that the process of destruction must be the reverse of that of creation; if the cause is destroyed before the effect, there must be a period when the effect remains in the absence of its parts. It holds, therefore, that there is in every case one cause, the dissolution of the union which is the non-intimate cause of the effect, which permits the adoption of the view that the destruction of the universe proceeds from the final effect backwards to the dissolution of the union between the atoms. The conception of cosmic destruction also appears in the later school in two forms: in the one the intermediate dissolution (*avāntara-pralaya*) only tangible products are destroyed; in a universal destruction (*mahāpralaya*) all these things, material and immaterial, are dissolved in the atoms, and the repetition of creation is established by the authority of scripture, 'As before, the Lord placed all in order'.[2]

The whole theory is exposed to a very elaborate refutation by Çañkara in his exposition of the *Brahma Sūtra*.[3] The possibility of the beginning of motion in the state of dissolution (*pralaya*) is denied; it is then impossible to conceive human effort or impact as operative, since *ex hypothesi* they do not yet exist. If the unseen principle (*adṛṣṭa*) is deemed to be the source, it must either inhere in the soul, in which case it cannot affect the atoms, or in the atoms, in which case as unintelligent it cannot set motion on foot. If, again, the soul is supposed to inhere in the atoms and the unseen

[1] BS. ii. 3. 14 with Çañkara.

[2] *Mahānārāyaṇa Upaniṣad*, v. 7. For a *mahāpralaya* cf. NVTP., p. 381.

[3] ii. 2. 13–17. Cf. SS. i. 110 ff. with commentary; v. 87, 88; NV., p. 252.

principle to be combined with it, there would be eternal activity, which contradicts the existence of the state of dissolution. Again the unseen principle operates to secure reward and punishment for souls, not to produce dissolution which is equally uncaused with the origin of the universe. How also can two atoms combine? If in whole, then, as there is complete interpenetration, there is no increase of bulk, and no production is possible; if in part, then the atom has parts, just as it must have if soul, internal organ, and atoms, are to combine. Again, either the atoms must be ever active, or ever inactive, or both or neither. If ever active, dissolution is impossible; if ever inactive, creation is impossible; they cannot be both, as that is self-contradictory; if neither, then activity and inactivity would require operative causes, and these causes, the unseen principle, &c., being in permanent connexion with the atoms, would create permanent activity, or, if not, permanent inactivity. The possibility of connexion (*saṁçleṣa*) between the ether or the binary atoms is denied, and the argument again adduced that, if an atom has form, it must have parts. The presence of qualities in the atoms suggests that they are not simple entities, but compounds; moreover, the idea that one atom, though of the same size as another, has more qualities is untenable; yet it is a necessary part of the theory,[1] for, if the atoms all had one quality, there would be no variety of qualities; if they all had all, there would be no single qualities. The whole conception of inherence is proved, as we have seen, to involve a *regressus ad infinitum* as deadly as the infinite regress objected to by the school, while the idea of cause as distinct from the effect is strongly dis-

[1] In NS. iii. 1. 65-9 it is established by the argument that earth and water are visible, and therefore must contain colour, for, if mixture sufficed, why is air invisible? See NBh. iii. i. 67

approved. It is of importance to note that in this effective criticism there is no reference to the conception—which Çañkara knew—of the activity of the Lord as a source of motion of the atoms. The soul mentioned is that of the individual which in the dissolution is inactive, and therefore cannot prove the cause of motion.

The criticism of Çañkara is of special value by reason of its date and authoritativeness, for it shows that in his time the theory had assumed the form in which it appears in Praçastapāda [1] though its theistic tinge was evidently not regarded as a necessary part of it. The history of the development of the system is the more important in that it serves to dispose of the suggestion that in the atoms we are to recognize not material things, but real and self-subsisting stimuli without any magnitude whatever and non-spatial, not unlike the qualitative atoms of the Herbartian school.[2] This theory is supported on the assumption that the atoms being force-points, two, the binary atom, constitute a length, and three lines thus make up a solid body with magnitude. It is sufficient to observe that the binary atom is not a primitive concept in the school, and that thus the whole basis of the theory is removed. Nor are atoms absolutely without magnitude; the minute is opposed to magnitude, but in the same genus; it is not true that the measures of the atoms being added cannot create any magnitude, for in fact three triads consisting of binary atoms makes up a thing with magnitude; the atoms are not non-spatial,[3] but devoid of parts, and for the same reason, not because they are non-spatial, they

[1] Kumārila tentatively accepts the theory; cf. ÇV., p. 207; PSPM., p. 92. So the Yoga, YS. i. 40.

[2] J. C. Chatterji, *Hindu Realism*, pp. 19–84, 149–58, 164.

[3] NV., p, 522; Çañkara on BS. ii. 2. 12; the correct rendering is given in SBE. xxxiv. 388.

have no within or without. It is further entirely inconsistent with the theory that the size of a binary is declared to be minute,[1] if it differs from a primary atom as a line from a point, and that the dimension of an atom is declared to be spherical, the atom evidently being conceived as a very minute sphere (*pārimāṇḍalya*), a shape which is naturally denied[2] of a binary. Nor is it explicable how, if three lines can produce a visible magnitude, two lines cannot produce a visible superficies. The atoms are indeed super-sensible;[3] but that is admittedly due to their small size as is stated in the *Nyāya Sūtra*, which recognizes also, and seeks in its own way to solve, the question of their relation to the ether.

2. *The Atoms, their Qualities, Motion, and Products.*

The number of kinds of atoms is given at four: it represents the popular tradition of the different kinds of sense, sound being referred to ether, and therefore requiring no atomic substance to produce it. The qualities of all products, like the products themselves, arise from the atoms of which they are composed, and the magnitude of the products depends on the manner, size, and aggregation of its constituents, the latter conditions being ultimately reducible to the former. But there is no attempt at a development of the consideration of the material structure of the universe. The four classes of earth, water, and air may be roughly compared with the triple division of matter in the solid, fluid, and gaseous states, while fire is a quasi-embodiment of the energy of heat. It is characteristic of the quite elementary physics of the school that the connexion of heat and luminosity

[1] VSU. and VSV. vii. 1. 10.
[2] PBh., p. 130.
[3] NV., p. 288; NVT., p. 271.

is not suspected, and that luminosity is regarded as a particular variety of colour.[1]

As we have seen, all the atoms possess the five general qualities of all substances, and also the two of priority and posteriority. It has also the qualities of odour which is its special mark, savour, colour, and touch or temperature, gravity, velocity, and fluidity. Water has the special quality viscidity, and the other qualities of earth save odour. Fire has the usual seven, temperature, colour, fluidity, and velocity, while air has besides the seven, only touch and velocity. The qualities are eternal in the atoms, but transient in the products. The products again fall into three classes in each case, body, the sense organ, and object which is a loosely used phrase intended to exclude the other two classes, of which the first is plainly an object of sense, though the second, while possessing the qualities of its substance, possesses them in latent form. The atoms themselves are never objects of normal sense: they are only inferable by the process given above; the apparent inclusion of atoms in that category by Annam Bhaṭṭa must be attributed to inadvertence.[2] The qualities also of the atoms can be discerned only in aggregates. There is an obvious difficulty in the question of the relation of the further qualities recognized by the texts with the primitive four attributed to the atoms in the theory of the atoms. Praçastapāda and the Sūtra stand close to the later view in their enumeration of qualities, but, while the addition of the seven qualities common to all matter is natural, it is less easy to account for the relation of the special qualities of gravity, fluidity, elasticity, and velocity, the

[1] Athalye, TS., p. 118. The reference of *auṣṇya*, 'heat', to touch is explicable, as touch includes the temperature sense.

[2] Cf., however, NV., p. 233, where an early view to this effect appears.

last two of which are classed under the general head of impression (*saṁskāra*); the solution seems to rest in their being held to be intimately connected with the category of motion.[1]

Thus already in the *Vaiçeṣika Sūtra*[2] gravity is defined as the non-inherent cause of the first movement of a falling body. The movement created by gravity produces velocity, which produces a second movement, of which the non-inherent cause is the first. Gravity is possessed by earth and water, and is super-sensible, and thus must be inferred. Fluidity[3] in its turn is the non-inherent cause of the first movement in a thing which becomes fluid, and it gives rise to velocity in the same manner as gravity. It is natural (*sāṁsiddhika*) in objects which are liquid at a normal state of temperature, but artificial (*naimittika*) in those which require heat to produce liquefaction, as in the case of butter among objects derived from earth, and of metal among objects connected with fire, and it resides, therefore, in water, earth, and fire. Unlike gravity, fluidity is assumed in the metals, the gravity in them being attributed to portions of earth mingled with them. The obvious suggestion, that in the same way the fluidity of the metals should be attributed to the water element in them, is rebutted by the fact that in that case the fluidity of metals would be natural, not, as it is, artificial; the

[1] All qualities, general and special, are equally real, the former depending on peculiarities of their substratum, the latter differentiating substances, NK., p. 96. The attempt to distinguish primary qualities revealed by touch from other qualities, found in the *Dhammasaṅgaṇi* (Walleser, *Buddh. Phil.* i. 107; Rhys Davids, *Buddh. Psych.*, p. 43) is philosophically unsound; cf. Bosanquet, *Logic*², ii. 308; Pringle Pattison, *The Idea of God*, pp. 115 ff.

[2] VS. v. 1. 7, 18; PBh., p. 263; SP., §§ 44, 99; TB., p. 82; TK., p. 19; TS., § 30; BP. 153, 154; TR., p. 146.

[3] VS. i. 1. 29; v. 2. 4; PBh., pp. 264, 265; SP., §§ 45, 100; TB., p. 82; TK., p. 19; TS., § 31; BP. 154-6; TR., p. 146.

further suggestion that the fluidity of metals can be traced to the fluidity of their earth portions is rejected because the fluidity of metals is indestructible, while that of earth is destructible by intense heat. No trace is to be seen of any recognition of the general similarity of gravity and fluidity, while the restriction of both to the production of the first movement has to be supplemented by assigning a new quality, velocity, which then comes into operation. Velocity[1] is found in the four atomic substances and mind, for there can be no motion save in things of limited dimension, and, therefore, these five make up the class of corporeal substances (*mūrta-dravya*), while together with ether the four atomic substances constitute the elemental substances (*bhūta-dravya*). With velocity is included under the generic term 'impression' (*saṁskāra*), the quality of elasticity,[2] which is the power possessed by a thing of reverting to its normal condition after tension; it is declared to reside in all the atomic substances. Like velocity it results from motion, and it ends by the effect of the motion which it produces. The term 'impression' applied to these two has obviously been derived from the more primitive use of that word to refer to mental impression, which in the later classification forms the first of the divisions of the class impression; the analogy is obvious, since velocity and elasticity manifest the motion which creates them, and so in a sense survives as an impression in the substratum. The classification is suggestive of the late development of the conception; in fact in the list of qualities attributed to the various

[1] VS. i. 1. 29; v. 1. 17; PBh., pp. 266, 267; SP., §§ 47, 102; TB., p. 13; TB., pp. 85, 86; TK., pp. 19, 20; TS., § 75; BP. 158–61; TR., p. 146.

[2] Velocity on one view is a separate quality; cf. ṢDST. 68; GSAI. xx. 49.

substances elasticity is passed tacitly over, when velocity is mentioned, and it may represent a still further advance on the primitive idea.

Motion itself as a category is analysed into the five kinds of throwing up, throwing down, expansion, contraction, and going, which is intended to cover any other form of motion.[1] Motion resides in substance only, and perishes with it; it is essentially evanescent; it operates by conjunction and disjunction in as much as it is the cause of the separation of an object from the place where it is, which destroys the conjunction between the object and the place on which it resides, and leads to the formation of a new conjunction which terminates the motion. Thus there can be no generation of motion by motion, for, each motion requiring a disjunction after the first disjunction, there must be a conjunction to permit of fresh movement. It is for this reason that velocity is necessary to explain the subsequent movements of an arrow shot from a bow, but the later doctrine that gravity operates through generating velocity is contrary to the view of Kaṇāda, who distinguishes between the velocity (*saṁskāra*) in an arrow discharged, and the gravity which produces its fall when there is no counteracting impulse or velocity. Action, again, is also due either to volition (*prayatna*), which involves contact with the self, or without volition, as in the case of throwing a pestle into a mortar, which is due to volition, while its rebound is the result of conjunction (*saṁyoga*), which is otherwise described as impulse or impact (*nodana*, *abhighāta*). The movements of the body in sleep are also without volition. The evaporation of water arises from the conjunction of the rays of the sun with air, and the condensation and dissolution of water

[1] VS. i. 1. 7; see also i. 1. 11, 14, 20–2, 24, 26, 29–31; ii. 1. 21, 23; 2. 25; v. 1 and 2, and references above, ch. vii, § 2.

are due to conjunction with air, while fluidity causes the flowing of waters on the surface of the earth, and gravity the fall of rain. Other forms of action, however, exist which cannot be reduced to the operation of volition or conjunction. They comprise in Kaṇāda[1] a variegated list, including the initial upward flaring of fire, sideward blowing of wind, and actions of atoms and mind; the entry and egress from bodies by the self; the assimilation of food and drink; the conjunction of other products, apparently the production of the embryo; the circulation of water in trees; the occurrence of earthquakes and similar terrestrial disturbances; the attraction of the magnet; and the motion of the jewel towards the thief. All are accounted for, not by the action of the Lord, in the Sūtra, but by the unseen principle which represents the fruits of previous deeds. But it is clear that there is no serious effort to consider the question of the mode in which effort of the unseen principle can affect matter so as to produce motion. It is clear that, if volition involves the activity of the atomic sized mind, and therefore has some vague degree of mediation with the actual atoms, the unseen principle is conceived as operating directly both on the atoms and on mind.

Apart from the qualities which are closely connected with motion and the general qualities of all material objects are the old four qualities, to which must be added viscidity,[2] which is apparently a development of fluidity from which it is distinguished on the ground that its peculiar capacity of agglutination (*piṇḍībhāva*) is not resident in melted gold, that is fluid. It resides in water only; the viscidity of oil, milk, &c., is due to

[1] VS. v. 1. 15; 2. 2, 7, 13, 17. Candrakānta's effort (v. 2. 2) to explain *adṛṣṭa* as referring to unseen natural forces is unavailing.

[2] PBh., p. 266; SP., §§ 46, 101; TB., p. 82; TK., p. 32; TS., § 32; BP. 157; TR., p. 147; see VS. ii. 1. 2.

the presence in them of water, though no clear explanation is offered of the reason why oil inflames fire while water extinguishes it, for the stock answer that it has more viscidity leaves the question unsolved.

Of the traditional four qualities colour[1] is that special quality which is cognized by the eye alone, thus excluding substances like light, qualities like number which are also perceived by touch, and reflected colour which does not reside directly in the object. The classification of colours is not attempted by Praçastapāda or Çrīdhara, and is late; they are enumerated either as six—white, blue, yellow, red, green, and brown, or with the addition of variegated (*citra*) as seven. The addition of this last is due to the doctrine of the difference of the whole from its parts: acceptance of this forbids us to admit that a carpet made up of pieces of different colour can be seen as having the colour of its parts, which would involve the theory that the parts can be discriminated in the result, a view which, of course, is contrary to the doctrine that the cause perishes in obtaining the effect. The carpet must, therefore, have no colour, which would render it invisible, or it must have, as the school holds, a special variety of colour styled variegated. But it is in earth only that colour can appear in all these shades: in water it is transparent white alone, in fire resplendent white. Savour[2] again is that specific quality perceptible only by the taste organ; it is of six kinds—sweet, sour, saline, pungent, astringent, and bitter; earth has all these varieties; water is sweet only, the dissolution in it of earthy matter accounting for its sour or salt taste.

[1] VS. viii. 1. 1 ff.; PBh., p. 104; SP., §§ 22, 83; TB., p. 78; TK., p. 4; TS., § 19; BP. 100, 101; TR., p. 142.

[2] VS., *l. c.*; PBh., p. 105; TB., p. 79; SP., §§ 23, 84; TK., p. 4; TS., § 20; BP. 101, 102; TR., p. 142.

Odour[1] is the specific quality whose characteristic is perceptibility by the organ of smell alone; it is fragrant or the reverse, and resides in earth alone. Touch[2] (*sparça*) is the specific quality whose characteristic is perceptibility by the skin only; it is cold in water, hot in fire, and temperate in earth and air, and therefore is really the temperature sense rather than touch in the wider connotation or in its specific sense. Another view, however, suggests the addition of a variegated sensation of touch analogous to the variegated colour in sight, and this accords better with the wider view, which is not accepted, however, by the school, and in which touch is extended to include such qualities as roughness, hardness, smoothness, softness.[3] On yet another view smoothness and hardness are ranked as separate qualities apart from touch, but this is rejected by Annam Bhaṭṭa, who refers these qualities to degrees of conjunction.

It would appear natural to assume that all these four qualities are eternal in the atoms and non-eternal in products, since they admittedly rest in the atoms. But by a peculiar doctrine[4] the principle is laid down that in earth even in the atoms the qualities are all non-eternal and are produced by fire, although as regards the atoms this is plainly contradictory. The truth of the theory, so far as it has validity, must rest on the fact that the qualities of earth can be changed by the

[1] VS., *l. c.*; PBh., *l. c.*; SP., §§ 24, 85; TK., *l. c.*; TS., § 21; BP. 102, 103. The assignment of one quality only to each atom is rejected in NS. iii. 1. 64–9.

[2] VS., *l. c.*; PBh., p. 106; SP., §§ 25, 86; TB., p. 79; TK., p. 4; TS., § 22; BP. 103, 104; TR., p. 142; NBh. iii. 1. 56, 57; NVT., p. 150.

[3] Athalye, TS., p. 156; cf. *Hindu Realism*, p. 164. Raghunātha (PTN., pp. 85, 86) holds that touch, odour, and flavour adhere only to parts of substance.

[4] PBh., pp. 106, 107; TK., pp. 4, 5; TS., § 23; BP. 105, 106; TR., pp. 155, 156; NSāra, pp. 11, 131, 132; NSM., pp. 154 ff.; NM., p. 488.

application of heat, while in the view of the school water, air, and fire are not so affected: when water or air is heated, the result is due to the presence in them of fire elements, not to change of their fundamental qualities. But the mode of operation of the heating process is the source of one of the profound differences between the Vaiçeṣika and the Nyāya in their later developments. When the black pot is burned, the Vaiçeṣika hold, the pot is destroyed, its binaries even being dissolved; the action of fire produces in the individual atoms a red colour, and then joins the atoms to form a new compound which ultimately results in the new red pot. If this were not so, there would not be the possibility of baking the internal atoms of the pot, and the reason why we cannot see the process of dissolution and reassembling is its extreme rapidity, the whole occupying a time variously put at five, nine, ten, or eleven moments. This view of atom baking (*pīlu-pāka*), which gives the Vaiçeṣika school a nickname, is clearly incompatible with original colour even in the atoms. The Nyāya view is the sensible one that the pot remains identical, as it seems to do, and as is shown by the fact that pots above it do not fall down, while the difficulty of the penetration of heat is answered by the common instance of the boiling of water in a pot. This view of pot baking (*piṭhara-pāka*) is not inconsistent with original odour in the atoms.

All these four qualities are perceptible only under certain conditions as we have seen, and, while aggregates of earth, water, and fire are directly perceptible, air according to the older view of the schools is inferable only, though the modern Nyāya holds it to be perceived by touch, disagreeing with the view that perception implies manifest colour. The inference rests on the temperature of air as neither hot nor cold which differentiates it from fire or water, while lack of colour negatives its being earth. Nor is it all-pervading like the other four substances, and mind is excluded by its atomic size which would prevent any quality in it being known. Hence we infer a distinct substance, air.[1]

Of the products of atoms the sense organs, the tip of the tongue, the extremity of the nose, that of the pupil of the éye, and the epidermis, composed of atoms of water, earth, fire, and air respectively, are imperceptible as a condition of their functioning; they all act by contact.[2] There are bodies[3] of earth, fire, water, and air in this world and in those of the deities of fire, water, and air respectively, an adaptation to popular mythology of the more primitive hylozoism of Jainism which ascribes souls to the minute particles of the elements. Body is the seat of the enjoyment of pleasure and pain by the self; it is a final compound as opposed to a compound which is part of a greater whole, and it possesses motion. The Vedānta view of the human body as composed of three or five elements, and Prabhākara's preference for four are rejected; bodies in this world are of earth only, either womb-born, like viviparous and oviparous animals, or not so born, including on one view plants,[4] as well as insects and such sages as acquire by their merit bodies without physical birth.[5]

[1] PBh., p. 46; Kir., pp. 82–6; NBh., pp. 155, 156; NV., p. 71; TSD., p. 9; SM. on BP. 42; PSPM., p. 92; SS. v. 89 allows perception; so the Mīmāṅsā according to NSM., p. 28; Raghunātha, PTN., pp. 41–7.

[2] Above, ch. ii, § 2; ch. vii. § 2; NSM., pp. 59, 60. The Sāṁkhya derives the organs from egoism, SS. i. 61.

[3] VS. iv. 21–3; PBh., p. 27; Kir., pp. 56 ff.; Lakṣ., pp. 1 ff.; SP., §§ 122–4; TB., pp. 65–7; TK., p. 3; TSD., § 10; TR., p. 121; NS. iii. 1. 28. Cf. SS. iii. 17–19.

[4] Plants are denied bodies by PBh., p. 28; TK., p. 2; *Padārtharatnamālā*, p. 21.

[5] VS. iv. 2. 5–10.

As objects[1] (*viṣaya*) other than bodies, earth appears as the whole of inorganic nature; water as the sea, rivers, hail, &c. Fire products are terrestrial, the fuel being earthy in character; celestial, such as lightning; gastric, the fire of digestion; and mineral. Gold cannot be earth because it remains fluid under extreme heat; nor water, for its fluidity is artificial; nor air, because it has colour. It must therefore be fire, earth particles accounting for its absence of light and heat. Another division[2] rests on the degree of manifestation of colour and temperature; both are fully present in the rays of the sun, colour in the moon beams, temperature in a red-hot potsherd, and neither in the lustre of the eye. Aerial products include wind, and in the Nyāya view the vital air (*prāṇa*), which the Vaiçeṣika view illogically makes a separate division beside body, sense, and object. It covers the five *prāṇa*, *apāna*, *samāna*, *udāna*, *vyāna*, noted in the Upaniṣads and in the Vedānta, but made of little account by the other schools. One doctrine assigns the five in order to the lungs, rectum, navel, throat, and the body generally.[3]

3. *Ether and Sound.*

Ether[4] has sound as its specific quality, and is the inherent cause of sound. The two stand in a unique relation; the reference of sound to ether is established

[1] VS. ii. 1. 1–4; 2. 1–5; NS. iii. 1. 64; PBh., pp. 27, 28, 35, 36, 38, 39, 44; SP., §§ 11–14, 74–7; Kir., pp. 41–88; TB., pp. 69–71; TK., p. 12; TS., §§ 10–13; BP. 35–44; TR., pp. 134–7. One Mīmāṅsā view makes gold a separate substance, PSPM., p. 94.

[2] VSU. ii. 1. 3.

[3] Cf. Oltramare, i. 322–9; Deussen, *Allgem. Gesch.* I. ii. 248–52; *Vedānta*, ch. xxvii; Keith, *Sāṁkhya System*, p. 80.

[4] PBh., pp. 58, 59; SP., §§ 15, 78; TB., pp. 74–6; TK., p. 3; TS., § 14; BP. 44, 45; NSāra, p. 30; TR., p. 137; Kir., pp. 105–14.

by a process of exhaustion which establishes that sound is not connected with any of the four atomic substances. But as a quality it must inhere in some substance, and experience shows it is not the self. It is necessary, therefore, to infer a substance ether (*ākāça*) to be the substratum of sound. The Sāṁkhya argument that ether serves as the place of the coming in and going out of products, presumably as medium for the movement of sensible things, is decisively rejected by the *Vaiçeṣika Sūtra*,[1] and the argument for its existence both there and in the Nyāya is based on its relation to sound alone. It is one, motionless, and omnipresent, the Nyāya[2] expressly arguing that this is not contrary to the existence of atoms, as the ether is unrepelled and does not obstruct. It is eternal, and possesses the qualities also of number, as a unity, and dimension as omnipresent, of individuality, conjunction, and disjunction. These are manifested in the propagation of sound. As the atoms constitute the sense organs for the apprehension of the qualities which are present in atomic products, so ether provides the sense organ for the apprehension of sound. The ether enclosed in the cavity of the ear in contact with the ether without affords the organ, but it differs from other sense organs in that it possesses its quality sound in normal, not in latent form.[3]

Sound is divided into articulate and inarticulate according to its character, and according to its mode of

[1] ii. 1. 20–31; NV. iii. 1. 72; the effort (Candrakānta on ii. 1. 20; Chatterji, *Hindu Realism*, pp. 165, 166) to controvert the clear sense of the Sūtra is needless; Gaṅgādhara's reading of ii. 1. 5 is clearly wrong, and PB., *l. c.*; NK., p. 22; Kir., p. 85, only refer to ether as all-pervading. One Mīmāṅsā view makes sound a substance, PSPM., p. 94. Ether is denied by Raghunātha, PTN., pp. 3–10. Cf. Çaṅkara, ii. 2. 24.

[2] iv. 2. 21, 22; VS. vii. 1. 22; iv. 1. 6.

[3] NS. iii. 1. 74, 75. For the Jain, Sāṁkhya, and Mīmāṅsā view see ÇV., pp. 420 ff.; NV., pp. 292 ff.; *Padārtharatnamālā*, p. 26.

production into that produced by conjunction, as when a drum is struck by the hand; that produced by disjunction, as when a reed is split, and that due to sound. The last variety is requisite to account for the hearing by us of sound The organ of hearing is the ether in the cavity of the ear; it cannot, without loss of identity, go out to its object, and sound therefore must be propagated from its original source in a series of sounds in a manner likened either to wave motion (*vīcitarañganyāya*)[1], or to the filaments of the Kadamba[2] which shoot out in all directions from the plant. When a drum is beaten by the hand, the inherent cause of the sound produced is the ether; the non-inherent cause is the conjunction of the drum and the ether; the instrumental cause the conjunction of the hand and the drum. When a reed is split the separation of the ether and the parts of the reed is the non-inherent, the separation of the parts the instrumental cause. The sound heard and those intervening between the first and last have the sound as the non-inherent and the wind as the instrumental cause.[3] On the destruction of sound views differ[4]; Vātsyāyana attributes it to contact between sound and an obstructing substance, a view which conflicts with the Vaiçeṣika tenet that a quality like sound cannot have another quality like conjunction; Vācaspati, therefore, makes the contact one between ether and an obstacle, and Çrīdhara one between air as the instrumental cause and the obstacle. A later doctrine holds that the penultimate and the ultimate sounds mutually destroy each other, but this is rejected by

[1] VSV. ii. 2. 37; ÇV., pp. 424, 425.

[2] NV., p. 289; VSV., *l. c.*

[3] VS. ii. 2. 31; PBh., pp. 287, 288; SP., §§ 49, 105; TA., p. 13; TB., pp. 82-5; TK., p. 13; TS., § 33; BP. 164-7.

[4] NBh. ii. 2. 34; NVT. and NVTP., *ad loc.*; NK., p. 289; TB., p. 84.

Keçava Miçra on the sound ground that they cannot be contemporaneous at the last, and the destruction is, therefore, attributed to the destruction of the penultimate, obviously an unconvincing result.

These speculations, which are stoutly maintained against the Sāṁkhya view that the organ goes to the sound, or the Jain that sound travels bodily to the organ, or the Mīmāṅsā which holds that air vibrations affecting the air in the ear manifest the eternal sound, are not supported by any experimental evidence, a striking proof of the *a priori* character of the speculations of either school. They stand, however, in essential relation to the doctrine of the momentary existence[1] of certain qualities and of motion which, as has been seen, the schools adapt from Buddhism; in the new form of the doctrine the lack of connexion between the moments is removed by the view that each sound comes into being in one moment, exists in the next during which period the second sound comes into being, and is destroyed in the third moment, a conception which renders it possible to conceive of a real series of sounds and, applied to the qualities of the self and motion, renders continuity effectively possible.

4. *Time and Space.*

Time[2] is defined in the syncretist school as either the cause of our use of temporal expressions or of our knowledge of the ideas of priority and posteriority, simultaneity and non-simultaneity, soon and late, &c. It is one in number, omnipresent in dimension, individual in character, and possesses the qualities of conjunction and

[1] Abo ch. vii, § 5.

[2] PBh pp. 63, 64, 164 ff.; SP., §§ 16, 79; TA., p. 5; TB., pp. 76, 77; TK., p. 3; TS., § 15; BP. 45, 46; Kir., pp. 114–21; TR., pp. 138, 139; KKK. ii. 179–86. Raghunātha (PTN., pp. 1–3) refers both to God.

disjunction. The past of an individual is the time characterized by its destruction, the future that characterized by its precedent non-existence, the present is the time whose future existence is destroyed and whose own destruction is about to come.

In the *Nyāya Sūtra*[1] the question of the existence of the present time is discussed in answer to the objection that, when an object falls, we know only the time through which it has fallen and the time through which it still will fall. The reply is that without a present there can be no perception and no knowledge, and past and future would have no meaning or existence. In the *Vaiçeṣika Sūtra*,[2] whence as usual the syncretists borrow their definitions, there is further the pregnant doctrine that time is a cause for transient things in which it exists, but not for eternal things in which it is not found. This is a clear recognition of the fact that the eternal substances do not exist in time, while their qualities and motions have only existence there with all the products. But the term cause must not be understood in the sense that the Vaiçeṣika adopted the popular view that time was a great cosmic power which caused movement of things[3]; this is wholly contradictory to the view of the Sūtra, which never attributes the origin of motion to time, as well as to the harmonious tradition of the school. Time is a cause only in the loose sense of that term, which is affected in the school, namely as one of the many conditions which are necessary to the existence of a thing; it belongs to the category of general instrumental cause,[4] as opposed either to the

[1] ii 1. 39-43; NBh., pp. 87-90; NV., pp. 255-8; NM., p. 136.

[2] ii. 2. 6-9; v. 2. 26; vii. 1. 25; 2. 22.

[3] Chatterji, *Hindu Realism*, pp. 54-8, 167; *contra*, M. Walleser, *Buddh. Phil.*, i. 128-33.

[4] PBh., p. 25; Kir., p. 38; above, ch. vii, § 4.

specific instrumental cause (*karaṇa*) or the inherent or non-inherent causes.

The nature of the conjunction which results in the conceptions of priority and posteriority is made clear by the stock example of the school. If we say, 'Here now is a jar' we operate with a conjunction of a special character, that of the sun and the jar; this conjunction is not like that of material objects or their parts, and it is due to some reality which must be inferred, and is inferred as time. So, again, if we make a youth our starting-point, the cognition of priority is produced in the case of an old man whose birth precedes that of the youth by many revolutions of the sun.[1] These motions of the sun are the conditions which mark the divisions of time, such as moments, months, and days. It is these conditions which render time apparently manifold instead of one as it really is, and help to create the impression held by some of the Nyāya school that time was, as claimed by the Buddhists, merely a series of moments, a view, which, as we have seen, the Nyāya and Vaiçeṣika repudiated as a general principle, but adapted with modifications in their theory of the character of all non-eternal existence, in the shape of the theory that every quality and action lasts for three moments only. There remains one obvious difficulty in regarding time itself as eternal, when its presence in eternal substances is denied. But in both cases the term 'eternal' denotes that which has no cause save itself and really exists, and which in the temporal terms which we cannot avoid in use can

[1] The process is a conjunction (*pratyāsatti*) through inherence of the motion in the sun, which is conjoined with what is conjoined, viz. the youth; Kir., p. 115; VSU. ii. 2. 6; NK., p. 84, negates this, and (p. 65) uses bodily conditions as different to give inference of time. The number of conjunctions with parts of space and time is given as the basis of proximity and distance, TB., p. 42; PBh., p. 164; NK., p. 168.

only be described as eternal, unless we frame the concept —though it can have no concrete meaning for us—of that which is not in time at all.

Time, therefore, is regarded as a fundamental reality which is the basis of our time knowledge with which all transient existence is bound up. Thus time is absolutely *a priori* for the school as much as for Kant, but as consistent realists they do not ascribe time to the product of mental activity in any form, but hold that it imposes its nature on mind.

Space,[1] Kaṇāda tells us, is that which gives rise in respect to two coexisting objects of the recognition that one is distant from the other; in more technical language it is the proximate instrumental cause of our use of terms such as, or of our conceptions of, far and near, according as we view the matter from the point of view of our speech or of the thoughts which it embodies. Like air, space is a substance which is independent and eternal in the sense in which all substances possess that characteristic; like existence, it is one and possesses individuality. Like time, it is all pervading, and possesses conjunction and disjunction, and its multiplicity is also due not to its own nature, but to the divergence of effects. Our conception of direction as east is derived from the conjunction of the sun as past, future, and present, and similarly with other directions; they are given their character by reference to the sun which thus plays with regard to space an analogous part to its action in regard to time. Similarly, like time, space is inferred on the ground that without some such reality it would be impossible to explain our ideas and language. Space also is a cause, but only in the general sense of

[1] VS. ii. 2. 10-16; PBh., pp. 66, 67, 164 ff.; SP., §§ 17, 60; TA., p. 6; TB., p. 77; TK., p. 3; TSD., § 16; BP. 43, 44; Kir., pp. 121-6; TR., pp. 138, 139; Lakṣ., p. 7.

a part of the conditions necessary for any existence as is time with which it therefore is classed as part of the eight or nine general causes.[1] That space is a reality[2] which holds things in their place, comparable to the power of gravitation, regarded as an independent reality and not merely as an attribute of things, is certainly not the conception of any period of the Vaiçeṣika school.

The distinction between space and time is made clear in the texts which expressly counter the suggestion that priority and posteriority in time and space should be attributed to one and the same cause.[3] The condition (*upādhi*) which diversifies time is production or action; that which diversifies space is contact with objects occupying space (*mūrta*). The old man may be near the young man in space but prior in time. Or, again, the relations of time have a certain degree of constancy (*niyata*), which is denied to those of space; the true explanation of this doctrine can be seen from one of the examples which illustrate it; when one thing is present in time with reference to another thing, the latter is also present in time with reference to the former, while a mountain which is at one time to the east of us may later be to the west. The idea thus somewhat crudely expressed is clearly that there is a generic distinction between simultaneity in time and side by side relations in space, though the example cannot be taken as happily framed or accurate.

From ether space is clearly distinguished in the

[1] Above, ch. vii, § 4.

[2] Chatterji, *Hindu Realism*, pp. 57–61, 167, 168. The real view of the schools has more affinity with the modern doctrine of space and time as *principia individuationis*, Pringle Pattison, *The Idea of God*, pp. 267, 364.

[3] VSU. ii. 2. 10.

system by the fact that the former has the specific quality of sound, while the latter has no specific quality at all; ether produces one effect only, sound, space is a general cause; ether has affinities to the atomic substances with which it forms the class of elemental substances (*bhūta-dravya*). What, however, is the precise ground on which this distinction is set up? The answer is not obvious, and it has been suggested [1] that in fact Kaṇāda accepted only one reality variously called, according to the difference of its effects and conditions, ether, time, and space, a view supported by the fact that, though he establishes the difference of ether from the atomic substances, self and mind, he does not explain the difference between ether, time, and space, nor differentiate the two from other substances. But this is to ignore the clear meaning of the Sūtra. It is equally unavailing to assert that space is really a force holding things in place in ether, which is really space, against the driving power of time. The true explanation of the distinction, doubtless lies in the inherited differentiation of ether as the substratum of sound, and the necessity of expressing by a new term the idea of space,[2] which ether was not well fitted to convey in view of its connexion with the concrete quality sound, which brought it into analogy with the atomic substances.

[1] Candrakānta on VS. ii. 2. 12. This is the Sāṁkhya view, SS. ii. 12.

[2] In NS. ii. 1. 22 *dikdeça* are found with time and ether as general causes. On the perceptibility or inferability of time and space see NM., pp. 136–41. Çañkara Miçra (v. 2. 25) calls space a non-inherent cause, against PBh., p. 25.

CHAPTER IX

THE PHILOSOPHY OF SPIRIT

1. *Soul, Mind, and Body.*

The arguments for the existence of the self or soul (*ātman*) are presented in the *Vaiçeṣika Sūtra* [1] in a form to which nothing in substance is added later. The experience of the objects of sense, he argues, proves the existence of something other than the senses and their objects, and expiration, inspiration, the closing and opening of the eyelids, life, the movement of the mind, the affection of the other senses—pleasure, pain, desire, aversion, and volition are the evidential signs of the self. The necessity of resort to proof by a sign is due to the fact that in the Vaiçeṣika view, as opposed to that of the Nyāya, there is no possibility of direct perception of the self, which must therefore be determined by inference in the form of exclusion of other possibilities, such as the attribution of consciousness to the body, or the senses, or the vital spirit, or the mind, or even the objects themselves.

The claim that consciousness is a mere function of the body which was the Cārvāka view, and must have been

[1] iii. 1. 1-6. 18, 19; 2. 4-21; vi. 1. 5; vii. 1. 22, with commentary; NS. i. 1. 10; iii. 1. 1-27; 2. 1-78; NV., pp. 338-49; cf. PB., pp. 69, 70, 99, with NK.; TA., pp. 6, 7; TB., pp. 62-5, 77; TK., pp. 3, 4; TS., § 17; BP. 47-50; SP., §§ 19, 81, 134, 135; NSāra, pp. 36-8; TR., pp. 119, 120. Cf. a summary of the Vaiçeṣika case in ÇV., pp. 398-400, and the Mīmāṅsā case, pp. 401-7; Çañkara on BS. iii. 3. 54; commentary on SS. iii. 20-2; v. 129 (130). See also NM., pp. 429-73.

popular, to judge from the anxiety of the schools to refute it, is met in a variety of ways. Consciousness must exist then in the elements which make up the body, but this is contrary to fact; if each part has consciousness, the result would be confusion, for there could be no agreement among the several consciousnesses to produce a united effect such as is actually seen in our consciousness. Moreover, if body had consciousness, why not the water-pot since it is composed of the same elements as body, and should equally well be conscious? If, again, consciousness were a property of matter, it, like colour, would endure, but we find none in a dead body even immediately after death, and even in life cases of unconsciousness occur. How, again, can a man on this supposition recollect in age what he saw in youth, for his body is completely changed? If it be answered by the fact of causal continuity, it is replied that in that case the son should know the experiences of his father. Without memory too existing in something else than the body, how could a child perform such instinctive acts as that of sucking? Moreover, consciousness is essentially of an object which is not itself; the body is recognized as that which is used by, that which belongs to, something not itself. It would be absurd that it should be an object of its own property. Moreover, the whole moral order rests on the difference of the self from the body and its persistence through many different bodies, and the denial of it would be direct impulse to immoral deeds.

The same organs as little are adapted to be the seat of consciousness. Apart from the fact that they are in the ultimate issue matter and, therefore, open to the same objections as are raised to the body, their essence is to be instruments, and an instrument implies an agent who uses it, a fact necessary to explain vision with two eyes. Again, if a sense organ be destroyed, we still have the recollection of the thing experienced by its aid. We remember objects also, though contact between them and the organs has ceased. We have also cooperation of senses which *ex hypothesi* would be impossible, as when on seeing a fruit we remember its flavour. Still less is the vital spirit the self, for it is no more than the relation of the self to its material environment, the body. More generally, consciousness cannot belong to an object, else there would be no memory after consciousness had been destroyed by the destruction of the object. Nor has an object any sense of its own position or of the pleasure it causes, nor does it move with intelligent purpose. Nor could there then be the consciousness which is admittedly experienced, 'I have seen the colour, perceived the taste, and am feeling the touch', which presumes a power of synthesis impossible in varied objects or in the sense organs.

But consciousness cannot reside in the mind, unless that term be used to mean some reality which has cognition by using some instrument other than the senses, in which case it amounts to what is in the Nyāya-Vaiçeṣika called the self, and the instrument is what is known in that system as the mind. The existence of an intermediary between self and the senses is proved by the fact that, if there were direct relation, we should have simultaneous cognition of all kinds, and equally simultaneous memory, and further both would always be present, which is contrary to fact, and drives us to accept some atomic substance to mediate, and secure successive perception and recollection. Further, the objects of inner sense, our cognitions, feelings, and volitions, must be perceived by the self by means of an instrument which is mind.

Nor, again, can there be accepted the doctrine that

cognition is a momentary self-cognizing existence as held by the Buddhists[1]; this is contradicted by memory, and the idea that of two ideas related as cause and effect each has the power, though unconnected, of conceiving itself as effect or cause as the case may be is purely absurd.

Positively, then, we can infer from cognition as a property that it resides in the substance self. Moreover, as from the motion of the chariot we infer the existence of an intelligent agent, so we infer such an agent for the body from its activity and cessation of activity, which serve to attain the desirable and avoid the undesirable. Breathing and winking lead us to infer an agent; from the healing of bodily wounds we infer an agent like the master who repairs his house; from the action of the mind towards contact with sense organs apprehending desirable objects, an agent must also be inferred; the same result follows from combined perceptions and recollections; the qualities of pleasure and pain, desire and aversion, and effort must belong to a subject; these qualities cannot belong either to the body or the sense organs, for the following reasons. They are always experienced along with the feeling of the self: pleasure means nothing save for a self, and so with volition; they do not extend to the whole of the body or the organs; pleasure or pain may be felt in one part only; they do not last as long as their substratum: all these states are evanescent; they are not perceptible by external senses like corporal qualities. The existence of the self as a distinct substance is also established by the fact that it is spoken of as 'I', which is quite different from any

[1] NV., *l. c.*, contains an interesting refutation of the Buddhist suggestion of *nairātmya*, adducing against that view the Sūtra of the burden bearer. Cf. Çañkara, BS. ii. 2. 25, 28; SS. i. 27-41; NVT., p. 55; NVTP., pp. 398-405.

other object; one man's body another can see, but not his self. No scriptural proof is therefore essential for the demonstration of the existence of the self.

But there is not one self only which by differentiation becomes many as on the Vedānta theory where ignorance causes the one Brahman to appear as many individuals.[1] This theory is guilty of the paralogism that it ascribes ignorance to that which is pure intelligence, or alternatively it assumes ignorance in the individual souls which come into being only through ignorance. The plurality of selves is proved by the variety of experience and condition; each self has its own series of experiences through which it remains one, while it has no knowledge of the experience of any other self. Nor is there any risk of the cessation of the world by the complete emancipation of all the selves, for their number is infinite. They possess also individuality as follows from their number, and they are in dimension all pervading, as is proved by the upward flaming of fire, and the horizontal blowing of air. These are contrary to the property of gravity, and can be explained only by the operation of the unseen principle (*adṛṣṭa*) inhering in the self, the latter being all pervading. Again, each self is unproduced and eternal; the argument that being so it can never be released is rejected on the ground that emancipation can be obtained through dispassion arising from recognition of the evils inseparable from the objects of enjoyment in one who recognizes the eternal self. The self also has the properties of conjunction and disjunction, since pleasure and other properties arise from the conjunction of the self and the mind, and destruction

[1] Candrakānta on VS. iii. 2. 19-21 thus interprets the Sūtra. Contrast SS. i. 149-64; PSPM., pp. 80-3. SSS. viii. 88, 89 makes Kumārila accept the Vedānta view, one of many signs of its late date.

of such experiences must be brought about by disjunction. Accounts later than Praçastapāda add little to his outline; the all-pervading character [1] of the soul is also established by the more empiric argument that, if atomic, it could not feel pleasure or pain simultaneously in different parts of the body; if of intermediate size, it must either be larger or smaller than the body, in which case it will be unable to occupy the body exactly as it does and should do; if of the same size, it will be too small for the body as it grows from birth onwards, not to mention the difficulty of it changing in dimension from birth to birth. The objection to its all-pervading character, that it should then have all experience, is answered by the fact that the self has experience only by contact with mind.

Mind [2] thus plays a most important part; it is through it that are mediated all the sense impressions from outer sense, which else would all be in immediate and eternal conjunction with every self, and it explains the recollection of these impressions; moreover, it is the direct means of cognition of the self's own qualities of cognition, feeling, and volition, and it explains our memory of them. It is the real ground of individuation, for, though each self like each mind is supposed to be distinguished by a peculiarity (*viçeṣa*), it is impossible to see any distinction other than that based on mind.[3] The mind must accompany the self in all its peregrinations through bodies as a condition of the identity of the latter, and of its power to exercise in a new body such functions as

[1] TSD., p. 13. Cf. Çañkara, BS. ii. 2. 34–6.

[2] VS. iii. 2. 1–3; vii. 1. 23; viii. 1. 2; NS. i. 1. 16; iii. 2. 20, 22, 26–34, 41, 60–3, with commentary; PBh., p. 89; NK., pp. 90–3; SP., §§ 20, 82; TA., p. 7; TB., pp. 77, 78; TK., p. 4; TSD., § 18; BP. 85; NSāra, p. 3; TR., pp. 124, 125; PSPM., pp. 75–8; NM., p. 497.

[3] Cowell, SDS., p. 148, n. 6, doubts if soul has particularity.

sucking. There is but one mind to each self; only thus can we explain the fact that there are not many simultaneous cognitions and volitions; the apparent simultaneity in such cases is always due to rapidity of motion of the mind, just as we see in the whirling of a firebrand a circle of light, not a series of separate points. The sight and taste perceptions of treacle are not simultaneous, but in extremely rapid succession. A final argument against this primitive suggestion of panpsychism is given to meet the case of the movements of the parts of a snake on its being killed. These are due to the impact of the chopper, the rapid motion of its mind, or the entry into some part of it of a soul which has been liberated from its body.

In dimension[1] mind must be all pervading according to one Mīmāṅsā view on the ground that it is a substance, like time, and has no special quality. This must, however, be denied; if it were so, it would have all sensations simultaneously and permanently, so that cognition would never cease, and sleep would be impossible. Moreover, mind would then never be in contact with the self, since two all-pervading substances can never come into contact, for if they did they would produce a twice all-pervading dimension which is absurd. There would, therefore, be no experience of cognition, feeling, and volition which depend on the contact of mind and self. If it is argued that contact between the self and the object would suffice, it must be pointed out that in this case the cognition would appear at the place of the object outside the body, while, if the contact were of the self and the organs, sound would be impossible since the self

[1] TC. i. 762 ff. Çañkara makes mind *aṇu* only as subtle and limited in size, but is inconsistent; see Deussen, *Vedānta*, ch. xxv; so SS. iii. 14; v. 69–71; Prabhākara thinks it atomic, PSPM., p. 77. Cf. NSM., pp. 59, 60; Raghunātha (PTN., pp. 10–15) denies its atomic size.

can never have contact with ether which is also all-pervading. Sleep also, it is argued, would be impossible if mind were all-pervading, but the reason given why it is possible on the Nyāya view is not convincing, since it involves the arbitrary assumption that mind can in sleep shut itself off from the self in the vein styled *purītat*. If not pervading, the mind must be of intermediate magnitude, which would mean that it consisted of parts and was perishable, or of atomic size; it must also possess motion and extreme velocity, and the qualities of conjunction and disjunction, which are seen in exercise at the leaving or entering a new body, and those of priority and posteriority common to all atomic substances. It is of course individual, and, as unproduced, eternal.

There are obvious difficulties in this strange atomic substance of corporeal (*mūrta*) character which is invoked to explain the activity of mind in the modern sense of the term. It is a minor point that Gautama[1] did not class it as an organ of sense (*indriya*), and that Vātsyāyana is compelled to read its inclusion in this class into the Sūtra, which in fact classes it only as an object of proof. The argument of Vātsyāyana, that the mind was accepted as an organ in other systems and, not being expressly stated not to be an organ by Gautama, must be taken as one, is sufficiently refuted by the retort of Dignaga[2] that the other organs which Vātsyāyana mentions should not have been referred to if that principle were valid, but the omission in Gautama is of no great importance for the conception of the mind, which, if an organ, is one of a very peculiar kind. A more

[1] i. 1. 9.

[2] *Med. Log.*, p. 87. According to NBh., p. 16, mind differs from the organs as being concerned with all objects, as without specific quality, and immaterial (*abhautika*), but NV., p. 40, accepts the first differentia only. To call it attention (*Six Systems*, p. 548) is rather misleading.

serious objection is suggested by the raising of the question whether an instrument is needed to perceive cognitions, feelings, and volitions, since they can be self-conscious.[1] This is answered by insistence on the fact that the agent, the instrument, and the object are three essentially different things which cannot be combined in one. The agent is something which is not urged on by something else; the instrument is a thing employed by an agent; the action does not exist when the instrument is already in readiness, a view supported by the doctrine of the posteriority of effect to cause. We must, therefore, have a self, an instrument, and the cognition, feeling, or volition, which is an action in one sense, in one sense an object. The Prābhākara view that on the occurrence of a cognition it becomes self-luminous like a lamp, and the soul becomes manifested as the substratum of, and the notion of 'I' in, the cognition, like the wick of the lamp, is rejected on the ground that in the visual cognition, 'This is a pot', there is no idea of cognizer or cognition, and that, when these do arise, there is a direct mental cognition of the object as qualified by the cognition and the cognizer, as 'I know the pot'. On the strength of this analysis, as it seems, is based the Nyāya[2] view that the self is directly apprehended by mind in such a cognition as well as inferable, while the strict Vaiçeṣika[3] view appears to be that in such a cognition we have no direct cognition of the self, but merely ground for an inference, though Çrīdhara[4] admits the

[1] NK., p. 96 ff.; NV., pp. 66–71.

[2] NVT. i. 1. 10; Lakṣ, pp. 7, 8; NSāra, p. 36, makes it inferable only; see NV., pp. 344–7; in NBh., p. 10, it is not perceptible.

[3] See Candrakānta's exposition of NS. iii. 2. 6–18; TR., p. 119, refers to inference only; so PBh., p. 70.

[4] NK., p. 91; perception is asserted, pp. 24, 91; so Kumārila, ÇD., p. 101, against PSPM., pp. 78–80. Cf. the Anpavarṣas, NM., p. 429.

possibility of the Vedānta view of the self as knowing itself, and like Cañkara Miçra[1] approximates to the Nyāya view. But both schools are agreed that mind is inferable only on the ground given above.

This unhappy conception of a material atomic[2] substance as an instrument in perception appears thus to have been largely due to the false desire to secure an instrumental cause as well as to the wish to explain the succession of impressions and memory, and the imperfect character of both. Mind is thus active in the whole field of our perception including the extraordinary perception which recognizes invariable connexion (*jñāna-lakṣaṇa*), and in perfected sages it reaches still higher uses, for by contact with their merit it enables them to see all reality, even the self, directly. It must be understood to be the instrument of thought, of the reflection (*parāmarça*) of inference, but this side of its activity is subordinated if not ignored in the schools. On the other hand, it serves obviously as a mode of connexion between matter and spirit, for it intervenes between the material if imperceptible sense organs and the self, and it may best be appreciated when compared with theories of psychophysical interaction which ascribe to the physical side much of the necessary conditions for remembrance.

With the body the self stands in a temporary relation only, for, as will be seen, the body serves only a passing purpose, and arises from merit or demerit of the self.[3] Unlike the Vedānta and Sāṁkhya, the Nyāya and Vaiçeṣika do not picture the self as ever accompanied

[1] VSU. iii. 2. 14, 16.

[2] The argument that it has no magnitude (*Hindu Realism*, p. 92) is untenable.

[3] NS. iii. 2. 64-78; iv. 2. 44, 45; NBh., NV., iii. 1. 19; VSU., VSV., v. 2. 17; vi. 2. 15; PBh., pp. 280, 281, 308, 309.

by a microcosm of the body in the shape of the subtle body;[1] it passes from one frame to another with only the aid of the mind which as atomic is beyond perception, and therefore cannot be seen leaving the body on death.

The self again is wholly different from the self of the Vedānta or Kumārila, for cognition is merely a quality, manifesting itself through mind transiently, and feeling and volition, which on the Vedānta theory have no place, are equally qualities. Of the qualities[2] of the self cognition has already been examined; pleasure is defined as that which is felt as agreeable by all, a definition amended to apply to individual tastes in its relation to the individual. A more fundamental doctrine asserts that it is what is desired for its own sake, as an ultimate aim, while pain is what is shunned for the same cause. Pain is positive, not merely absence of pleasure, and can co-exist in the same subject with regard to different objects, though it would appear that co-existence must really be swift succession. Pleasure, however, is always closely accompanied by pain. Desire, according to Praçastapāda, consists in seeking to obtain a thing, not yet acquired, for one's own sake or that of another; it[3] may be directed to the supreme good, freedom from pain or pleasure, or to some object as a means to something else; or it may aim at an action which can only be directed towards an object which is capable of attainment by human effort; no one desires an action if the end is unattainable by man. Aversion

[1] Rejected also by Kumārila, ÇV., p. 393. Cf. SS. v. 103. The Vindhyavāsin of Kumārila is clearly not Īçvarakṛṣṇa, nor any true Sāṁkhya writer.

[2] See PBh., pp. 259-63; SP., §§ 39-43, 94-8; TA., p. 13; TB., pp. 85, 91; TK., pp. 18, 19; TS., §§ 66-70; BP. 145-52; VS. x. 1. 1-7 proves pleasure and pain not to be cognition in any form; cf. NM., pp. 74-6.

[3] SM. on BP. 146.

which includes anger and similar emotions is directed either to pain itself, or to an object whence it can spring. As desire and aversion spring from pleasure and pain, so they find expression in volition (*prayatna*), effort (*utsāha*) or action (*kṛti*) which is the disposition of the self towards carrying out an object. It is of two kinds; on the one hand it is activity (*pravṛtti*) generated by the desire to obtain what is pleasant, on the other inactivity (*nivṛtti*) generated by the desire to avoid the painful, but in a different sense it is the vital force (*jīvana-yoni*), which is the cause of expiration and inspiration, but which, unlike volition, is not even perceived by mind.[1] The classification as akin to volition is instructive: it could not be admitted as physical without introducing an alien element into the self. The cycle is completed by merit and demerit which are produced by actions good or bad, and themselves generate pleasure and pain; they form together the unseen principle (*adṛṣṭa*) which mould man's body, but they are not merely positive and negative; demerit is produced not merely by omissions but by positive evil deeds (*pāpa*).[2]

The last quality of the self is impression (*saṁskāra*),[3] which is the result of original perceptions of every kind, and is the explanation of memory. It is impossible to refer the latter to the original impression as the cause, since the impression is transient; nor can the absence of the impression produce the result: if this were the case, as absence is one and the same, we should not find the difference which we do observe between the power of

[1] TK., *l. c.*; BP. 149, 150. Cf. on *jīvana* and mind, NM., p. 499.

[2] VS. vi. 2. 1-16; PBh., pp. 272, 273, 280-2; SP., §§ 48, 103, 104; TA., p. 13; TB., p. 85; TK., p. 19; TS., §§ 71, 72; BP. 161-4; NSāra, p. 35; TR., p. 148.

[3] PBh., p. 266; TA., p. 13; SP., §§ 47, 102; TB., p. 85; TK., p. 19; TS., § 75; BP. 158. See NS. iii. 1. 13 ff.; VS. ix. 2. 6; NM., p. 377.

remembrance based on the number of times an impression has taken place. If it be maintained that, despite its destruction, the cognition is sufficient to cause remembrance, it would follow that the performance of sacrifice would result in heaven without the intermediate working of merit which is not the case.[1] But the operation of the impression is not explained in principle: all that we learn[2] is that attention, context, repetition, marks, likeness, possession, the relation of substratum and contained, immediate subsequency, separation, similar employment, opposition, excess, receipt, intervention, pleasure, pain, desire, aversion, fear, entreaty, action, affection and merit and demerit are sources of the awakening of memory. The arrangement is not scientific; it expresses and illustrates in detail the different kinds of association, but without an examination of the nature of association, still less any effort to explain how memory is related to the self and the mind, which is operative in preventing all memories being simultaneous, and securing the succession of perceptions which is the basis of memory. With merit and demerit impression is connected in a vital way since it is thus that our deeds persist to bear fruition in other lives.

2. *The Purpose and Destiny of the Individual.*

What then is the end of man, and how is it to be obtained? The *Nyāya Sūtra*[3] replies that supreme felicity is produced by the knowledge of the sixteen categories which it enunciates; on the disappearance of false knowledge there disappears fault (*doṣa*), which consists of passion or desire, aversion, and confusion or error;

[1] On *apūrva* see PSPM., pp. 159 ff. [2] NS. iii. 2. 44; PBh., p. 267.

[3] i. 1. 1, 2; NBh. i. 1. 2. Faddegon's view (p. 46) of *doṣa* as a Pāli word meaning *dveṣa* is impossible.

with their disappearance action ends, and with it birth and the sorrow consequent thereon. In Kaṇāda[1] the system is less simple: the obtainment of supreme felicity is declared to be due to merit (*dharma*), but also to be due to the knowledge of the categories by means of similarity and dissimilarity, that knowledge being produced through special merit. Again[2] he declares final release (*mokṣa*) to lie in the separation of the self from the body without entering another body, in the absence of merit or demerit which would produce a subsequent embodiment. The process is more fully expressed by Praçastapāda[3]; the desire to obtain the release leads one to acquire knowledge of the categories from a master; this knowledge terminates ignorance; hence love, hate, &c., corresponding to the fault of the Nyāya, are extinguished: thus no further merit or demerit can arise, the old merit and demerit are extinguished as they have produced their effects: the subject remains free from desire or attachment to the body,[4] and finally his merit ceases having produced the joy of the contemplation of the self; he is done with the body and every result of past activity, and rebirth is impossible. The knowledge of the truth thus is the real cause, the merit only a contributory, but Kaṇāda's words rather ascribe the origin of knowledge to merit, and serve to remind us that the process is one of great complexity, for a man is never free so long as he is not released from the effects of his deeds.

Supreme felicity, however, is variously interpreted.[5] The Buddhist view finds it in the cessation of all know-

[1] i. 1. 2, 4; PBh. pp. 6, 7. [2] v. 2. 18.

[3] pp. 281, 282; NK., pp. 282, 283.

[4] Cf. VS. iii. 2. 63-5 on disappearance of *kleças*, a term of the Yoga: Tuxen, *Yoga*, pp. 109 ff.

[5] VSU. i. 1. 4; NK., pp. 3, 4; Kir., pp. 6 ff.; NM., pp. 507 ff.

ledge, feeling, and volition, but this cannot be as no man would seek to destroy the self which is the dearest of all things, and release means destruction of bondage, not destruction of existence. The Vedānta view, that it is the appearance of pure consciousness free from all objective character, is unsatisfactory, as it is impossible to explain the emergence of this consciousness without an extraneous cause. Nor is the Sāṁkhya view correct which holds that, on the recognition of the distinction of spirit and matter, the latter ceases to function and spirit rests in its own nature, for matter as active and unintelligent cannot be credited with such powers.[1] Nor is the Yoga view of release as everlasting and unsurpassed bliss more satisfactory. In truth release is the absolute cessation of pain, for pleasure is only obtained through pain, as Vātsyāyana[2] says; pleasure leads to action which merely involves man in the pain of birth, death, old age, sickness, the possession of what one does not wish, and the desire for what one cannot have. There is thus the germ of a doctrine that pleasure is essentially mere relief from pain, and has no positive value, or at least as much too little value, to counterbalance pain, but this is not systematically developed, even were it tenable.

Why, however, is it that man is not released from misery at death, and why must he pursue a series of unhappy births? The answer is that he is compelled to transmigrate, and so accepted is the idea that it receives no formal proof. But considerations are adduced which point to proofs of varying weight.[3] The self is eternal, as we have seen; it is also in fact known often to be

[1] NS. iii. 2. 73–8.

[2] NBh. iv. 1. 58. Cf. NS. iv. 1. 55–7; PBh., pp. 6, 7; Kir., p. 9; NSāra, p. 35; SS. vi. 7, 8; YS. ii. 15; iii. 18.

[3] Cf. Chatterji, *Hindu Realism*, pp. 114–23.

embodied. It is inconceivable that this should be uncaused,[1] for we realize the endless chain of cause and effect as in the series of seed and shoot; nor can there be a single cause whether the absolute Brahman as in the Vedānta or the nature of the Sāṁkhya, for the effects are various, and so must be their causes. Nor can the cause be something visible, for men universally offer sacrifice to attain heaven, and this must presume an intervening stage of merit so acquired, since plainly the sacrifice cannot produce its distant effect without an intermediary Nor does the desert reside in what is its fruit, for that is apportioned to each individual, and enjoyed by it. The body of man, therefore, must be the fruit of previous merit or demerit, and there is no ground on which we can conceive a break in the series of embodiments. Confirmation may be found for belief in previous embodiment from the fact of instinct as when a child sucks without teaching, or more generally from memory of past births,[2] which seers enjoy, and which exist in us as impulses and potentialities lying hid beneath our normal selves, and explaining the infinite possibilities of our nature.

Our deeds, therefore, leave ever their impressions behind, and merit and demerit, regarded as our actions when they are performed, and not in the more general sense in which they include impression,[3] spring from impressions, and give birth to impressions again in unending series. Man does not necessarily remain in the human state;[4] he may descend into lower bodies, be

[1] NS. iv. 1. 22 with commentary.

[2] VSU. v. 2. 18; vi. 2. 16; cf. YS. ii. 39.

[3] The distinction in *Hindu Realism*, pp. 108–9, between impressions and merit and demerit is ingenious but out of harmony with tradition.

[4] NBh. iv. 1. 55; cf. VS. iv. 2. 5 with commentary; NVT., p. 441. On transmigration (*pretyabhāva*) cf. NS. i. 1. 19 with NBh.; NV. iv. 1. 10.

a denizen of hell, or rise to divine rank, for the whole pantheon exists in name, though the gods are now mere office holders whose posts last no longer than the duration of their merit. The sentient universe then may justly be styled a society of selves in hierarchical order, remembering always that there are worlds beyond our knowledge peopled by other selves of higher and lower range, creatures of heavens and hells, whose reality the school neither can nor will deny. There is a strict régime of justice in this universe, for each man reaps what he has sown.

Can we carry the doctrine further, and claim that the environment of the selves is built up for the precise purpose of giving to each being its due meed of joy or suffering according to its deeds? There is no doubt as to the orthodox answer, for we have seen it given by Praçastapāda[1] in his theory of creation. The virtue, knowledge, dispassion, and powers of beings of all kinds are allotted to them by the god Brahman in strict accordance with their impressional potencies, but he is not credited with actual cosmic creation of other than living beings, for the creation of the worlds is assigned to the Supreme Lord himself. It is impossible then to regard the universe as the creation of the merit of him who appears in it as Brahman, and similarly the destruction of the universe is not due to the exhaustion of his merit,[2] but is the work of the Supreme Lord from period to period for the deliverance of the Brahman of the epoch and other wearied living creatures. Did Kaṇāda hold the view that the unseen principle alone produced the periodic creation and destruction of the world? The obscurity of his Sūtra leaves the matter open: it may,

[1] pp. 48, 49.

[2] Chatterji, *Hindu Realism*, pp. 125, 172.

however, be remembered that Çaṅkara[1] attacks the doctrine of atoms on the basis of their receiving their first motion from the unseen principle alone, but this may merely mean that he took advantage of the vagueness of the doctrine of the Vaiçeṣika. Nor, certainly, can it be deduced from the word Kalpa used of a cosmic age that it is an imagining[2] of Brahman.

The ceaseless process of creation and destruction carries with it important results. It negatives once and for all the idea of progress; there is nothing new under the sun, and, though sound is not eternal, the teaching of the Veda is eternal, and has been handed down from age to age and from teacher to pupil. The importance of this lies in the fact that the teachers of the Veda, as Gautama assures us, were persons of authority, like those who laid down the science of medicine and spells—hardly reassuring society—and Kaṇāda himself fully accepts the weight of the authoritativeness of the sacred tradition. Nor were the sages mere men of ability; they had a direct intuitive vision of the final truths, they desired to benefit men, they had the desire to communicate their valuable knowledge.[3] Thus all our knowledge is no more than the recognition of truths known long before us, and our conduct in like manner should accommodate itself to the rules which have been declared by the sages of old, the principles regulating castes and rules of life (*varṇāçrama-dharma*).

There can, therefore, be no real attempt to place morality on a reasoned basis; merit and demerit arise from observation of the rules laid down by sacred scripture, resting on the divine prompting according to

[1] BS. ii. 2. 11–17; on ii. 2. 37 in fact he admits that the Vaiçeṣikas have the idea of a creator.

[2] *Hindu Realism*, p. 172. It means 'arrangement'.

[3] VSU., p. 2; VSV., p. 2; v. 2. 16.

Praçastapāda,[1] and the later school, and possibly even in Kaṇāda's view. A considerable part of meritorious actions is made up of ceremonial ritual such as ablutions in the Ganges and the offering of sacrifices, and Kaṇāda's[2] rules of ceremonial have been twisted by his commentators to sanction monstrous conduct, which doubtless never entered his mind.[3] But the more serious defect in the whole scheme is its completely self-regarding character;[4] whatever value morality may have for others and for society at large, its true end is the profit of the individual whose advance in the scale of existence towards final liberation is thus furthered. But, more than this, morality in the sense of choice of any kind is imaginary; it is not open to a man to advance himself by seeking to follow the law even for selfish motives; his action is determined irrevocably by his former deeds, possibly in long anterior births, and his freedom, which is the requisite of morality is an idle dream, no less unreal because with singular inconsistency the thinkers of India resolutely shut their eyes to this fatal difficulty in the path of the legitimacy for human life of the doctrine of retribution. To enunciate the due reward of actions as explaining man's lot in life asserts a moral principle only to lose it again by denying man's power to choose his path of action.

Why, however, if the practice of good deeds raises us ever in the scale of existence, does not man by attaining the highest rank, that of Brahman, remain content in it for ever? Here, again, no obvious explanation can be given; how can he in the perfect wisdom he then has acquire demerit or lose his place? The only reply must be that the sin of some former birth comes to deprive

[1] p. 7.

[2] vi. 1 and 2.

[3] VSU. vi. 1. 12-16.

[4] *Hindu Realism*, pp. 177-81.

him of his high place, so that all may realize that in earthly or heavenly pleasure there is no satisfaction. Apparently even Brahman must be on the watch less others do better their work and win his place.[1]

To escape this unending[2] process of troubled striving, in which not even a god can find abiding joy, it is necessary to turn to the knowledge of the self, as enjoined in the scriptures which demand meditation and reflection on the self. It is egoism (*ahaṁkara*), which leads us to a false estimate of the things of life; we see the whole only in its beauty, and are moved to eager desire and action,[3] or we see its defects, and shrink from it; but, if we realized the parts which make up every whole, we would see that they are compounds all of the same elements which arouse no emotion in us. We would realize also the absolute sameness of the selves and their independence of the bodies in which at present they continue to transmigrate, and our empirical existence would come to an end with all our woe.

To attain this end we have the aid of the seers of old whose lore is handed down in the schools of the day. A necessary propaedeutic as Kaṇāda clearly lays down is the performance of meritorious conduct. Then only are we ripe to take up the first part of the course of instruction, hearing (*çravaṇa*) the enunciation of truths from teachers. From it we proceed to the examination in the light of reasons for and against of the truths thus accepted on authority. It is at this stage that the philosophical expositions of Gautama and Kaṇāda and the systems based on them must be subjected to

[1] NK., p. 6.

[2] An absolute first creation is assumed to be absurd; cf. NBh. i. 1. 19; iii. 1. 27; PBh., p. 49; for a proof see BS. ii. 1. 34–6 with Çañkara.

[3] NS. iv. 2. 3. Cf. NBh. iv. 2. 1.

examination. In an interesting passage Vātsyāyana[1] asserts the characteristic of the Nyāya philosophy which gives it a claim to be more than a mere doctrine of the self, like the Upaniṣads. It uses investigation (*anvīkṣā*) to examine all things which are known to us, whether based on the senses or on the sacred tradition. It must not be thought that it is meant that philosophy can override that tradition which Gautama and Kaṇāda constantly refer to. Philosophy is rather the reasoned exposition and demonstration of that which is known already from a source of eternal truth, the Veda. If Kaṇāda and his school deny a separate place to verbal testimony among the means of proof, that is only because it can be brought under inference, since we believe testimony either because of the worth of him who bears it or the truth of the facts it reveals.

But it is not enough thus to know the truths; they must be realized in experience,[2] which is produced by concentration (*yoga, samādhi*) of our mind on the object of knowledge.[3] Such an experience must have been prepared for by merit of an earlier existence or period of our life, and it may be helped by restraint (*yama*) and observance of rules calculated to secure a due state of body and mind, and the choice of a forest, cave, or sand-bank for a place of meditation. But it presupposes the mental preparation ensured by the study of the philosophy of the school and discussion with preceptors and others bent on truth. The result of this mental effort is the attainment of the actual perception by the adept (*yogin*) of the self by a special conjunction of the self and the mind in the self.[4] He has also perception

[1] NBh., p. 3. [2] Kir., p. 11.

[3] NS. iv. 2. 38–50; cf., for details of Yoga, NSāra, pp. 38, 39.

[4] VS. ix. 1. 11–15; NSāra, pp. 37, 271, 272; cf. VSV. v. 2. 16; PBh., pp. 281, 282; NK., p. 282; NVT., p. 50; NVTP., pp. 379–82.

of the other substances—the atoms, space, time, the ether, and mind—and he perceives their motion and their qualities as well as the qualities of the soul by their inherence in their substrates. He will also have the power to withdraw the mind from the body, and thus separate himself from his mortal frame, like a snake from its worn-out skin. All his former lives will come to him, and he will realize how his self passed from body to body on death and rebirth. He will realize also, it is later made clear, the merit and demerit accumulated by him through former deeds, and he will be able to construct bodies suitable for the embodiment of their experience. In this way, by actually experiencing the merit and demerit, he will exhaust it and reach the stage of liberation in which there will be complete cessation of pain as a cessation of activity and rebirth. There are, however, two stages of the vision of seers, one appertaining to those who are complete masters of concentration with whom vision is ever present, and the other which belongs to the less perfect visionary who needs to attain such insight the application of a definite act of concentration.[1]

And here we must leave the mystic, for the bounds of philosophy are clearly outpassed. It is a strange and incomprehensible vision which the seer has before him, in which the eternal structure of the world lies before him intermingled with the memory of the infinite detail of endless lives.[2] Its objective value, we may safely

[1] So VS. ix. 1. 13 may best be taken. Cf. PBh., p. 187; NK., p. 198; ȘDBT. 67 with VSU. and USV., *l. c.* NSāra, pp. 3, 4, 82–6, makes a division of Yogins according to having *samādhi* or not.

[2] According to Chatterji, *Hindu Realism*, p. 176, the Yogin has intuition of general truths, or ideas, as existing independently from concrete ideas. But this is not in the texts, and is only suggested in recent works like VSV. ix. 1. 14. NSāra, *l. c.*, gives to Yogins in the

deny, since other mystics of India and distant lands have presented us with a very different picture of the beatific visions attained by them, when the mind has been divested of all its normal trappings, in the hope that thus there will enter it truths which are denied to the strivings of intellect. And one further criticism is inevitable; the problem how man is to counteract the effects of former deeds which must bear fruit proves intractable to a reasonable solution. We are compelled in the normal theory of retribution to admit that no one life represents the whole of the potential merit or demerit of man; were it not so, there would not be a long round of varied lives in animals, man, gods, and denizens or hell, but there would be definite progress in one way or another. It is impossible then to admit that the one life in which enlightenment is attained can extinguish all the prior merit and demerit, and it is necessary to conjure up new lives of a magic sort in which the seer may experience in his proper self ere final emancipation the merit and demerit of his past. Thus room is made for the introduction at a moment which should be sublime of an element of vulgar thaumaturgy, which is in no wise excused by the fact that it can claim the august authority of the Upaniṣads and of the Vedānta itself.

When then life finally ceases, what is left? The schools reply, 'The utter annihilation of pain',[1] and the answer is true, but at the cost of the complete annihilation of all that we were or sought to be. What is the condition of a self which has ceased to be in relation with the transient, and therefore can have neither consciousness, feeling, or volition, is a problem which the

state of *samādhi* an indeterminate perception of the whole expanse of reality at one glance. Cf. NM., pp. 102–8.

[1] NS. i. 1. 22; NK., p. 6; TB., p. 91; *Padārtharatnamālā*, pp. 49–51.

schools make no effort to solve, nor is their wisdom in silence doubtful.[1]

The final severance of the self and the body is the aim also of the Sāṁkhya and Yoga schools, but there is a distinction in the conception which either school has regarding the severance of the self and the body. If, the Nyāya[2] argues, the body is connected with soul merely in order to enable the latter to realize its difference from matter, and then to obtain permanent separation from it, this end cannot be deemed to be accomplished, for the same relation might easily occur even after the release of the soul; mere knowledge of the distinction is not enough to produce final severance; there must be a complete exhaustion of desert with which the possibility of revival of the connexion between self and body for ever disappears. Nor can the Nyāya[3] permit any breach, through the intervention of God, in the series of fruition of mortal action. If we seem not to see the fruition of man's deeds, yet we cannot invoke the causality of God, for without action no fruition is ever possible, and we must assume that ultimately all fruition results from man's action alone.[4]

[1] NSāra, pp. 39–41, pronounces in favour of real happiness in release, but see NBh., pp. 30-4; NV., pp. 88–91; PSPM., p. 81. The Nyāya of SSS. vi. 41–8 protests against the Vaiçeṣika ideal (v. 36) of an existence without happiness, like a stone, and demands constant pleasure without objects of sense perception; cf. NVT., pp. 6, 7; NVTP., pp. 84–8, where the reference is to SSS. vi. 41 rather than as taken in the ed. Cf. NM., pp. 507 ff.

[2] NS. iii. 2. 73–8. The Sāṁkhya retorts by rejecting the Nyāya view, SS. v. 74, 75.

[3] NS. iv. 1. 19–21; the rendering in SBH. viii. 112 is quite impossible, in asserting God's intervention; cf. p. 266, n. 1.

[4] The means towards merit in PBh., pp. 272, 278 are commonplaces of Indian asceticism and need not be referred with Faddegon (p. 351) to YS. ii. 30 or the Buddhist *daçaçīla*.

CHAPTER X

THE EXISTENCE AND NATURE OF GOD

1. *The Theism of the System.*

THE Nyāya-Vaiçeṣika in the syncretist texts[1] is frankly theistic; those which follow the tradition of the Vaiçeṣika and adopt its order of exposition, find place for the conception of God under the category of substance, as one great subdivision of the self, with which on their theory God has eight qualities in common, the five common to all beings, number, as one, dimension, as all-pervading, individuality, conjunction and disjunction, which are necessary in creation, and cognition, desire and action. But they admit that his cognition differs essentially from that of man in that it is eternal, universal, and absolute, while that of man is transient, particular, and relative. On the other hand, the Nyāya tradition as seen in the *Tarkabhāṣā*, not being confined within the strict system of categories of the Vaiçeṣika, is free to treat God as a being of quite exceptional character, not to be regarded as in any sense on a par with the human soul.

It is of interest also that there is clear evidence in the fourteenth century of the very definitely religious tinge of the votaries who professed one or other of the systems. Rājaçekhara, in his *Ṣaḍdarçanasamuccaya*[2] expressly applies the term Yoga to the Nyāya and makes the followers of the Vaiçeṣika also in their religious aspect

[1] TK., p. 4; TS., § 17.
[2] vv. 94, 113, 129–31; Suali, *Intr.*, pp. 127 ff.

similar to those of the Nyāya; the only difference between the two on his view is that the adherents of the Nyāya are called, Çaivas, those of the Vaiçeṣika Pāçupatas. He described the ascetic practices of these sectarians, which equate them to the ordinary votaries of Çiva. His evidence is supported by that of Guṇaratna in his commentary on Haribhadra's *Saḍdarçanasamuccaya*[1] of slightly later date, though it is possible that he draws from the same source as Rājaçekhara; he gives four main divisions of the Nyāya-Vaiçeṣika sectaries, the Çaivas, Pāçupatas, Mahāvratadharas, and Kālamukhas, with various subdivisions, including the Bharaṭas, who are mentioned also by Rājaçekhara, and whose characteristic trait was the fact that they accepted a man of any caste, provided he was a devotee of Çiva. Jinadatta in his *Vivekavilāsa*,[2] about the middle of the thirteenth century, states that the texts of the Nyāya and Vaiçeṣika were used in the Çaiva system, and that these systems had Çiva for their deity. It is impossible to discredit the value of this testimony, which is the more valuable in that the normal source whence to seek the inspiration of the Çaiva systems is the Sāṁkhya which has admittedly close relations with the development of Çaiva philosophy. The antiquity of the connexion is attested by the tradition which is preserved by Praçastapāda[3] that it was Çiva in the shape of an owl who revealed to Kaṇāda the Vaiçeṣika system. Praçastapāda[4] also in his exposition of creation uses as the name of the creator Maheçvara, a choice in which we can hardly fail to see a deliberate preference for the view that the true God is Çiva. Of Uddyotakara we have the express evidence of the *Nyāyavārttika* that he

[1] pp. 49 ff.

[2] viii. 285–303. Cf. SSS. vi. 13, 19.

[3] p. 329.

[4] pp. 48, 49; at p. 7 *īçvara* is used.

was a Pāçupata, and it is interesting to note that in his *Nyāyavārttika* [1] he adopts theism and quotes a verse which is given by Mādhava in the *Sarvadarçanasaṁgraha* [2] as one in which the supporters of the Çaiva system maintain the existence of God. Theism in the Nyāya is shown to be recognized by Vātsyāyana [3] not so much because he declares that the self sees all, feels all, knows all, and perceives all, a description which would hardly be true if he did not in the term self include God as the self *par excellence* as because of his defence of the activity of God in the fruition of deeds. An express proof of the connexion of Nyāya with Çaivism is seen in Bhāsarvajña's *Nyāyasāra*,[4] which may date before Udayana and in which it is expressly said that final release is produced in the Çaiva system, and stress is laid on the necessity of the practice of the recognized kinds of mental concentration which at last will yield the direct vision of Maheçvara. Similarly Udayana,[5] who is the classical exponent of the theism of the two systems treats the God whom he demonstrates as equivalent to Çiva.

Can we therefore assert that the silence of Kaṇāda and Gautama, unless in the latter case we believe that the self for him included God, means that the authors of the *Nyāya* and *Vaiçeṣika Sūtras* were not believers in God? It has been contended not only that this is the case,[6] but that the atheism of the schools was borrowed from the Sāṁkhya, but for this theory there is no positive evidence forthcoming, and it must be judged merely on the probabilities of the case. On the whole there is so little sign of Sāṁkhya affinity that it would be as easy to attribute the atheism of the systems to the

[1] iv. 1. 21. [2] p. 67. [3] NBh. i. 1. 9; iv. 1. 21.
[4] p. 39. [5] Kus. ii. 4.
[6] Garbe, *Sāṁkhya*, p. 119; *Phil. of Anc. India*, p. 23. He ignores the early evidence entirely.

influence of the Pūrva Mīmāṅsā whose importance as discrediting the idea of God must not be underestimated. A different explanation is suggested by the later and modern Indian doctrine[1] that the systems are not to be deemed as fundamentally opposed, but as aspects or standpoints whence so much of truth is revealed as may be adapted to the minds which are to receive it. In this sense the doctrine is pressed too far; it is the result of a philosophic mind reviewing from the standpoint of wide knowledge of the systems their points of community and seeking to find a comprehensive formula to fuse them in one. This can be accomplished by treating the Sāṁkhya as a further advance in analysis on the Nyāya-Vaiçeṣika, and then finding in the Vedānta the final truth. But to convert a theory of reconciliation into sober history is unwise, and unconvincing.

On the other hand the actual condition of the two Sūtras provides ground for the belief that they cannot be deemed to cover the whole field. Neither gives the impression of a well-thought-out and ordered whole; Praçastapāda, indeed, had to restate the Vaiçeṣika before it could be deemed a systematic treatize in any sense, and the Nyāya is so predominantly dialectical in interest that its excursions into metaphysics have an air of divagation from the work in hand, which forbids us to assume that silence on any topic means its exclusion. One thing at least is certain; if we assume that Kaṇāda[2] or Gautama intended the theory to stand by itself without the introduction of a creator we fall into the difficulties pressed relentlessly by Çaṅkara who assumes

[1] Max Müller, *Six Systems*, p. xvii; Chatterji, *Hindu Realism*, pp. 5–17; Gaṅgānātha Jhā, NL., pp. 6–8. Müller's denial (pp. 276–81) of Jaimini's atheism is an error; PSPM., pp. 85–8.

[2] The comm. find references to God in VS. i. 1. 3 (= x. 2. 9); vi. 1. 1–4; ii. 1. 18, 19 as author of the Veda, of names, &c.; above, ch. v, § 2. Faddegon (p. 354) favours, without proving, atheism.

a Vaiçeṣika without a Supreme Lord, and establishes beyond a peradventure that on this theory there never could be any creation or destruction of the world or beginning of activity. It may be that early criticisms of the system in the period between Kaṇāda and Praçastapāda resulted in the recognition of this defect and that the creator was assumed to fill the lacuna; it may equally well be that Kaṇāda himself would have accepted this doctrine as part of his system; what is clear is that, given the Vaiçeṣika tenets, a creator becomes a necessity, as is assumed by Praçastapāda, demonstrated by Çrīdhara, and expounded in classical form by Udayana.[1]

2. *The Proof of the Existence of God.*

Udayana[2] divides his proof of the existence of God into five heads, but his exposition is far from simple; it is complicated by the desire to discuss more or less completely rival theories both of causation and knowledge whose inclusion in this place gives a somewhat artificial trend to his reasoning. The first proof adduced is based on the establishment of the unseen principle (*adṛṣṭa*) as that which governs the fates of men in their various lives. This principle is unintelligent in itself, and it must therefore act under the direction of an intelligent power, who does not create it or alter its inevitable action, but renders possible its operation.

The second proof rests on the fact that right knowledge requires an external source and thus the Veda presupposes a creator. This conception is defended against objections to the doctrine of creation and destruction

[1] Īçvara is denied to be a cause in fruition of action in NS. iv. 1. 19–21, interpreted otherwise by the commentary as implying theism; see Max Müller, *Six Systems*, p. 554.

[2] *Kusumāñjali*; cf. his *Ātmatattvaviveka* and *Kiraṇāvalī*, pp. 97 ff.

based on the regular alternation of day and night; the impossibility of the birth of a Brahman at the outset of creation without one of that caste to be his father; the impossibility of the inauguration of language or traditional arts; and the impossibility of cessation in the process of the ripening of the fruits of action. Merit, he replies, may produce miraculous birth, God may teach language and the arts assuming both the preceptor's and the pupil's forms,[1] in deep sleep the fruition of acts is suspended, and still more so at the destruction of the world, a view which removes the difficulty of the process of time. Positively too the decay of customs, morals, and learning show how the Veda gradually dies out, to be revived at a new creation.

Thirdly, it is shown that no means of proof yields results opposed to the reality of God. He is not perceived, but *ex hypothesi* he is not perceptible. He is inferred, and inference is trustworthy; its refutation always rests on inference, which shows that it cannot inherently be invalid. Comparison yields only knowledge of the significance of words, and tells nothing of existence, and thus cannot negate God. Verbal testimony declares his being; when it seems to negate it, it merely denies him attributes. The argument from presumption. 'If God were omniscient, would he not cause us to act without laying down injunctions?' whence the uselessness of the Veda and the non-existence, therefore, of its author are deduced, is invalid, for we must have directions for our actions, and in any case presumption and non-apprehension are not valid means of proof.

Fourthly, the Mīmāṅsā argument that, even if God exists, he cannot be the source of right knowledge for us, since his own knowledge lacks the essential characteristic of true knowledge, the apprehension of objects

[1] NSM., pp. 150 ff.

hitherto unknown, is met by a denial of this definition of knowledge; right knowledge is an independent impression in accord with reality, and its truth does not depend on novelty.

Finally, with some repetition, direct proofs for the existence of God are adduced. These are the nature of effects; the combinations of atoms in creation; the support and destruction of the world; the existence of traditional arts; the authoritativeness of the Veda which produces right knowledge in us and presupposes a being who imparted this virtue; its existence, which implies a maker; its consisting of sentences like books made by man; and last the peculiar nature of number: duality and subsequent numbers as we have seen have no absolute existence but depend on the relating power of the intellect and thus at creation it must have been God whose concept of duality produced the binary atom, which ultimately starts the formation of the world. The first five of these arguments, however, may be interpreted of scripture as referring to the purport of words, which is God; their explanation, due to God; their preservation through him: their significance in words denoting God; and the affix of the imperative which alludes in commands of scripture to the expression of the will of God.

Leaving aside these needless exercises of ingenuity, the argument for the existence of God rests on the fact that creation needs an agent. The argument runs, 'Every effect must have an intelligent agent; the universe is an effect; therefore it must have an intelligent agent.' This is the doctrine expressed by Çrīdhara[1] in commenting on Praçastapāda's account of creation, in

[1] NK., pp. 54–7; cf. SDS., ch. xv; NSāra, pp. 35, 36, 254 ff.; SSS. vi. 6 ff.; TC. ii. 2. 1 ff.; NBh., NV., NVT. on iv. 1. 21; ṢDS. 13; NM., pp. 190 ff.; GSAI. xix. 11–15; TR., pp. 171, 172; Kir., pp. 97–104.

which the activity of a creator is assumed, but not expressly proved, and in the course of it he deals with some of the obvious objections to the theory. It is objected that God, having no unsatisfied desires, cannot possess the necessary impetus to action, to which the reply is that he acts for the benefit of other selves, which is a sufficient if not a selfish motive. The further objection that in that case he should create pleasure alone in the world is met by the retort that in his action God is moved by the necessity of conforming to the tendencies of beings conditioned by their former actions, and that pain is no unmixed evil since it leads beings to realize the vanity of mundane existence. Nor is it a disproof of his independent divinity that in creation he should award beings lots according to their deserts, which is the due mode for a master to treat his servants. The minor objection to creation that the knowledge of words would be impossible is incidentally refuted by the quaint argument that it is the pain of birth which causes ordinary beings to lose their memory while the mindborn sons of Brahman suffer no such pain, and from their past memory are able to revive at once the conventions of language.

More serious is the argument that the syllogism adduced does not prove the result. A jar is certainly produced by the potter, but in addition to the knowledge of his material, his desire, and action he must have a body in order to bring about the result, and therefore God must have a body, which is contrary to our observation. The answer to this is that mere possession of a body cannot be the real point in question, for else a man while in sleep would be an agent; it must rather be the character of being an operator of instruments sufficient to bring about a result, and an unembodied being can possess this power, as in the case of the soul which moves by its volition the body. True the body exists and belongs to the soul, but it is the soul which impels, and God has the atoms to impel in lieu of the body which the soul has as its object. Nor is there any real difficulty in understanding how he can possess intelligence, desire, and volition as eternal, whence his power of creation may be derived. On the other hand, it is urged that the souls and the atoms together can account for the whole of creation. To this Çrīdhara replies that this cannot be, since, until creation has operated, the souls are not united with sense organs through which alone they can possess cognitions. If it is replied that the soul has an inherent intelligence which is all-pervading, the answer is that this is contrary to experience which shows that the soul on birth in a body finds all things new and that therefore it does not continuously function, so that we are compelled to resort to illegitimate hypotheses if we depart from the sound view that a soul needs sense organs to be conscious. It follows, therefore, that creation requires the operation of an active intelligence which is that of God. The unity of God follows from the fact that there is no ground to accept a multiplicity of equally omniscient beings to perform the work of creation, and further such a multiplicity would by interference rather hinder than further the result.

The qualities [1] of God follow from his complete knowledge; he cannot be ignorant, nor have attachment or aversion from objects; hence he cannot have any activity, or acquire merit or demerit, or their consequences pleasure and pain. Nor can he have impressions, since all his knowledge is immediate and eternal. This enumeration, however, leaves one obvious difficulty;

[1] NK., p. 58; SSS. vi. 14. He is all pervading, and has individuality, conjunction and disjunction.

where shall we class the desire and activity which are manifested in creation? The point was evaded by some authorities who denied desire and activity, asserting that his pure and unimpeded intelligence constituted his creative power, thus reducing to intelligence the only special quality of God. But the modern Nyāya[1] on the other hand ascribe to God the possession of eternal happiness, thus bringing themselves into harmony with scripture and doubtless with popular belief. The same period is responsible for a determined effort to ascribe to God a body for the purpose of creation despite the refusal of Çrīdhara and Udayana to countenance this folly.[2] On one theory our merit may endow God with such a body as in an incarnation, just as a man's merit provides a body for his wife; another view makes the atoms, or the ether to be the body of God, the former being a natural development of Çrīdhara's parallel between the body and the atoms, though Çrīdhara does not press the parallel; yet another conceives the creator to be formed of two bodies in creation, himself and the object to be created, while yet another holds that God obtains a body for himself in the same way as does a demon by possessing some human medium.[3] To such idle follies was popular theology reduced.

The obvious objections to the proofs of the existence of God were urged by rival schools.[4] The assumption

[1] So also NSāra, p. 40; Raghunātha (PTN., pp. 1–8) ascribes time and space to God, and (pp. 15–22) denies him extension.

[2] Cf. SSS. vi. 13.

[3] Athalye, TS., pp. 141, 142.

[4] Cf. the Jain attacks, ṢDST., pp. 117 ff.; *Syādvādamañjarī*, pp. 49 ff.; Çañkara, BS. ii. 2. 37–41; Vaibhāṣika views, SSS. iv. 4. 23–38; SS. i. 92–9; the Mīmāṅsā agrees in denying God and creation or destruction; PSPM., pp. 85–8; ÇV., pp. 356 ff.; see also KKK. ii. 45 ff., and for a modern restatement of the issues Pringle Pattison, *The Idea of God*, pp. 298–321. See also Arist. *Met.* xii. 6 ff.

that the universe is a product can be assailed; we can adduce only individual cases of products; to assert that the whole of which they are parts must be a product is a paralogism. Nor indeed can we prove that every thing is produced, even among ordinary things, for our sphere of knowledge is severely limited. Again the atoms, ether, time and space, souls and minds are admittedly eternal and uncreated; therefore the argument that the universe must have a creator is inconsistent and illogical. Nor indeed is it legitimate to call the world a product and argue thence to the cause, unless the cause can be proved independently. Moreover, God as possessing will must have desire and pleasure and pain, and so is no more than glorified man. In truth it is plain that a creator who is only powerful to create and destroy at intervals in strict accordance with merit and demerit and who exercises no influence at all on the fates of mankind is a strange anomaly.

But, whatever the difficulties in the theory, it is plain that it was impossible for the schools to remain without it, for they could not otherwise conceive the beginning and end of the world in which they believed as an established traditional doctrine, and which, it must be remembered, was especially connected with Çiva as the destroyer and the Brahmanical deity *par excellence*. Moreover, even had they been willing to ignore this dogma, they would have been in no better case, for, on their theory of eternal independent substances, there is no ground of connexion between self and body, and an intermediary must be found. The Jain view of self-moving atoms is more simple in one sense, but it is less philosophical, reflecting as it does nothing but a primitive animism. The intervention of God as the first origin of motion was thus natural, and it obviously adapted itself well to the traditional cosmogony. But, even so, one difficulty remains obvious; how comes it that all the souls lose their activity at the time of dissolution, and regain it at the coming into being of the world? Such a preconceived harmony is inexplicable unless a direct intervention of God is imagined, consisting at least in postponing, while not diverting, the fruition of action—as in deep sleep, but, curiously enough Çrīdhara shrinks from drawing this obvious, and indeed necessary conclusion. While the Vedānta suppresses the reality of the individual in the absolute, and the Sāṁkhya insists on the existence only of mutually unconnected individuals, in both cases denying any possibility of system in the universe, the Nyāya-Vaiçeṣika produces, but in a mechanical and external form, a certain measure of unity. All three, however, agree in denying any real value to human experience and endeavour, and stand in fundamental contrast with the tendency of recent thought, whether theistic[1] or atheistic,[2] to view the process of the universe as real and to insist on the fact, not of the independence and self-sufficiency of the individual, but of the necessity of the communion of selves as the basis of their reality.[3]

On a lower plane of popular thought stands the conception of the *Nyāyasāra*,[4] reflected in the *Sarvasiddhāntasaṁgraha*,[5] in which Çiva appears as the omniscient creator by whose grace, the reward of devotion,

[1] e. g. G. H. Howison, *The Limits of Evolution*, pp. 325 ff.; Hastings Rashdall, *Theory of Good and Evil*, ii. 289 ff.

[2] e. g. J. E. McTaggart, *Studies in Hegelian Cosmology*, pp. 37 ff.

[3] Contrast Pringle Pattison, *Hegelianism and Personality*, pp. 225 ff., and *The Idea of God*, pp. 385 ff. In B. Bosanquet's *Value and Destiny of the Individual*, as in F. H. Bradley's *Appearance and Reality*, the individual is overwhelmed in the absolute as in Çañkara.

[4] pp. 38, 40, 41.

[5] v. 10, 31–5 (Vaiçeṣika); vi. 10–21, 40–4 (Nyāya).

the worshipper obtains release in the form of eternal pleasurable consciousness. This in the Nyāya and Vaiçeṣika we find, as in the Vedānta of Rāmānuja, an effort to adapt philosophy to meet the cravings of popular theology.

ENGLISH INDEX

SANSKRIT INDEX